Motivation Ethics

ALSO AVAILABLE FROM BLOOMSBURY

Citizen Killings, Dean-Peter Baker
Public War, Private Conscience, Andrew Fiala
The Ethics of Nonviolence, Robert L. Holmes
Trust, Ethics and Human Reason, Olli Lagerspetz
Value Theory, Francesco Orsi
Luck Egalitarianism, Kasper Lippert-Rasmussen

Motivation Ethics

MATHEW COAKLEY

Bloomsbury Academic
An imprint of Bloomsbury Publishing Plc

BLOOMSBURY
LONDON · OXFORD · NEW YORK · NEW DELHI · SYDNEY

Bloomsbury Academic
An imprint of Bloomsbury Publishing Plc

50 Bedford Square	1385 Broadway
London	New York
WC1B 3DP	NY 10018
UK	USA

www.bloomsbury.com

BLOOMSBURY and the Diana logo are trademarks of Bloomsbury Publishing Plc

First published 2017

© Mathew Coakley, 2017

Mathew Coakley has asserted his right under the Copyright, Designs and Patents Act, 1988, to be identified as Author of this work.

All rights reserved. No part of this publication may be reproduced or transmitted in any form or by any means, electronic or mechanical, including photocopying, recording, or any information storage or retrieval system, without prior permission in writing from the publishers.

No responsibility for loss caused to any individual or organization acting on or refraining from action as a result of the material in this publication can be accepted by Bloomsbury or the author.

British Library Cataloguing-in-Publication Data
A catalogue record for this book is available from the British Library.

ISBN: HB: 9781350004580
PB: 9781350004597
ePDF: 9781350004573
ePub: 9781350004603

Library of Congress Cataloging-in-Publication Data
A catalog record for this book is available from the Library of Congress.

Typeset by Fakenham Prepress Solutions, Fakenham, Norfolk NR21 8NN

CONTENTS

Acknowledgements vi

   Introduction and overview 1
1 Consequentialism and the moral agent question 17
2 Motivation ethics 59
3 Deontology and the moral agent question 91
4 Moral demandingness and two concepts of evaluation 113
5 The problem of special relationships 133
6 Global duties and the state 149
7 Political legitimacy and the good 161
8 Interpersonal comparisons of the good 181
9 Conclusions 207
   Epilogue: On the scope of reason 215

Notes 235
Bibliography 253
Index 257

ACKNOWLEDGEMENTS

My debts for this book are vast and span several institutions – most notably King's College Cambridge, New York University and the London School of Economics and Political Science. My intellectual debts to Russell Hardin are enormous, but so too are the personal ones for his continued advice and encouragement. Bernard Manin's support has been truly exceptional, far more than I deserve, and proved invaluable at multiple junctures. Dimitri Landa's help and advice (and injunctions to get writing) helped enormously, and the book furthermore owes much to Ryan Pevnick's extensive comments. While finishing it the support of Chandran Kukathas and Christian List was crucial.

I was lucky enough to have colleagues at the LSE who voluntarily gave up their free time to read and discuss each chapter, a process that as well as providing much substantive feedback also provided invaluable insight into what was clear, and notably into what was not. I'm extremely grateful as such to Carlo Argenton, Simon Beard, Ed Hall, Pietro Maffetone, Christoph Schickhardt, Kai Spiekermann, Luke Ulas and Rikke Wagner.

I also owe enormous gratitude to the range of people who were kind enough to offer detailed comments on chapters, often several, not least among them Nicholas Almendares, Matthew Clayton, Jonathan Cottrell, Ronald Dworkin, Sean Ingham, Dale Jamieson, Janos Kis, Diana Marian, Yascha Mounk, Thomas Nagel, Paul Ngomo, Peter Northrup, Pasquale Pasquino, Andrea Pozas-Loyo, Michael Rosen, Samuel Scheffler, Lucas Stranczyk and Liam Von-Thien.

The process of working with my Editor – Liza Thompson – has been ideal: professional and extremely pleasant. I'm very grateful to her and also to Frankie Mace for their advice and work. And my partner Cam has been wonderful, as always, tolerating a home permanently strewn with open books and annotated print-outs.

Finally, most doctoral students and early career researchers soon find out that (understandably) almost no one will prioritize reading their work, even if they'd like to, given less tasks and more time. I instead got doubly lucky – my advisors bucked this trend, and one of my colleagues, Michael Kates, would read, comment, discuss and argue about any of my ideas that sounded even vaguely interesting. Any arguments in this book that are bad, mis-premised, poorly expressed or contain hidden problems are entirely due to me. That there are not many more of them is due to Mike.

Introduction and overview

Lives can go better, or worse. Exactly what in principle determines this is disputed – is it, for instance, that people experience better mental states via more happiness or wellbeing? Is it that their desires are met or things they value occur? Is it that some things that are objectively good for them obtain? Or perhaps some combination of these?[1] Whichever is correct, we can think of these as comprising an individual's 'good', or more crudely their 'interests'. And since many are affected differently by different scenarios, we can think of the good of all affected as the 'overall good'. This, in a sense, is the moral evaluation of what happens to morally valuable beings.

But we can also think of the moral evaluation of what is done, of actions. Is killing someone morally right if it will save the lives of others? Is giving most of one's developed-world income to charity a moral duty or morally heroic? Are actions benefitting one's own children at the expense of others morally wrong?

As beings that think about what we and others have done, and might do, we can think about how to evaluate our choices, and disputes about the moral evaluation of actions are disputes about 'the right'. (The term covers a range of possible different ways of describing positive and negative or better and worse moral action evaluations: right and wrong, a duty, impermissible, morally required, good, bad, exceptional, depraved and so on.)

Finally, actions are not simply things that happen: they are undertaken by agents with a range of aims and intentions and for a range of reasons. Evaluating agents is commonly referred to as that of moral worth or that of the moral agent.

Overall, therefore, we can potentially evaluate what happens to people (the 'good'), actions (the 'right') and agents ('moral worth'). But how should we relate these sites of evaluation?

Perhaps the most obvious way is to focus on actions and the good of those affected by different actions. We might as such link the evaluation of actions to the good of the agent (egoism), to the good of to whom we act (a harm-based deontology), or to the good of all affected (consequentialism).

To get a sense of the differences, consider a somewhat stylized situation where someone faces a choice between killing one innocent person to save the lives of three others. For the consequentialist it is *the good of all* that in principle matters – thus assuming their lives are relevantly similar, the morally right thing to do would be to save the three people and kill the one.[2] For the harm-based deontologist it is the good of *to whom we act* that matters – harming them by killing them is impermissible – thus, even if it would bring about more good overall, killing the one would be wrong. For the egoist it is the good of the agent that matters – they should do what will best promote *their own personal good* (thus if killing the one will lead to better outcomes for them personally they should do it; if not, not).

All three structures have obvious merits. Consequentialism, in linking right actions to the good of all, seems to treat everyone's interests as equally worthy of moral concern.[3] A harm-based deontology seems in a range of cases to better cohere with common intuitions,[4] and also to reflect the idea that it is what we do to people, not merely what occurs, that matters to the moral evaluation of actions.[5] The egoist can hold that their theory alone can answer the question 'Why is it in my interest to do what is right?' because for them doing so is by definition in one's interest.[6]

Relatedly, each of the rival theories has well-known critiques of and counter-responses to the others. What these theories share however is the focus on actions – they look at various features of the actions and base evaluations on these. That is, they follow Rawls' characterization that 'The two main concepts of ethics are those of the right and the good; the concept of a morally worthy person is, I believe, derived from them.'[7] This is the 'action morality' approach, and the early part of this book argues that the task of determining precisely *how* an action morality should derive moral worth is surprisingly problematic. Action moralities, it turns out on careful examination, struggle to respond compellingly to the demand for agent evaluations.

Before sketching the overall problem, it is worth noting the alternative approach: instead of determining moral evaluations by focusing on features of actions we might focus instead on features of agents. As such we might adopt at least one of three options.

Firstly, we could hold there are certain agential features – 'the virtues' – that are constitutive of the good agent and that the possession of which enables the agent to lead a good life (a virtue ethics view).

Secondly, we might hold that there is a particular good will, which would motivate an agent possessing it to avoid certain actions and to undertake others (a will-based deontology).

Or thirdly (the positive suggestion of this book), we might evaluate agents by how motivated they are to promote the overall good (of all) – what is here referred to as 'motivation ethics'.

That is, we can think of different structures of moral theories as representing the alternative answers to two distinct choices.

Firstly, we need to choose the primary object of moral evaluation – is it actions or agents? Specifically, do we start by specifying that morally good actions have certain features (for 'action moralities') or that morally good agents do (for 'agent moralities')?

Secondly, we need to decide *whose* good to base moral evaluations upon – is it all affected, to whom actions are done, or the agent themselves? These choices correspond to six possibilities:

		Primary object of evaluation	
		Actions	Agents
Determinant of evaluation	own good	egoism	virtue ethics
	good of to whom done	harm-based deontology	will-based deontology
	good of all	consequentialism	motivation ethics

None of the book's substantive arguments hang on acceptance of this schema. It does however help highlight the scope of the arguments – why for instance the problems consequentialism faces (see Chapter 1) will also apply to a harm-based deontology (see Chapter 3) but not to motivation ethics (see Chapter 2) or a will-based deontology (see Chapter 3).

Content wise, there are a few things about the above schema that perhaps need clarifying. Firstly, that consequentialism's primary object of evaluation is actions – after all there is rule, virtue and motive-consequentialism, and these evaluate agential features (rules can be internalized). This is true, but what makes consequentialism a paradigmatic action morality is that the evaluation of the agential features is entirely contingent on the actions they produce. There is not, for instance, a motive that for motive consequentialists is intrinsically morally good; rather it is whatever motive produces the overall set of actions that bring about the actual or expected best consequences. Ultimately what matters for consequentialists is what any psychological feature causes an agent to do, and we morally evaluate the set of actions they actually or in expectation undertake (compared to alternatives – different versions of the theory disagree on how to group the alternative actions).

Secondly, as noted, 'to whom done' covers the key deontological insight that we don't simply bring about outcomes but when we act we do things to people, and there might be some categories of harm to the good of those we act upon that should be impermissible (this is usefully often described as a side-constraint[8]). That is, it may be impermissible to kill someone even if it will best promote the overall good. Here it is the good of the person that the agent might act upon – i.e. directly kill – that determines the evaluation, not the good of all affected. The formulation 'to whom done' leaves open, however, the question of precisely how a deontological theory will identify who is acted upon (so long as it is not everyone affected or the agent alone). Prominent suggestions for harm-based theories, for instance, are (i) in contrast to what one allows – the 'Doctrine of Doing and Allowing' – or (ii) based on what one intends or foresees, such as with the 'Doctrine of Double Effect'.[9]

And thirdly, the six possibilities in the schema obviously do not exhaust all possible moral theories, but also do not exhaust all the possible claims of the cited moral theories. A virtue ethics theory could hold that not only will fully virtuous individuals promote their own good – that they flourish, experience eudaimonia or live the fully good life – but that they may also aid others; a will-based deontological theory could maintain that a person with a 'good will' will not only treat those to whom actions are done as an end, but they may also lead themselves a life that best promotes their personal rational good. A harm-based deontological theory might hold that there are some duties based on promoting the good of all – just that this goal cannot be pursued when it requires inflicting certain harms. *What the schema tries to capture however is what type of theory the logical possibility corresponds with and what feature is primary.* A theory that holds the good of the agent is promoted by possessing a certain set of agential features is a virtue ethics theory; a theory that stipulates a 'good will' that would cause the agent possessing it to avoid doing certain things to people is a will-based deontological theory. Such theories may sometimes make further claims, but at a minimum the possibilities carved out above correspond to recognizable structures, and we can usefully scrutinize them.

The moral agent question

This book is ultimately an argument in favour of motivation ethics – that the moral evaluation of agents should be based on how motivated they are to promote the good (of all). The overall argument will be that the primary object of evaluation should be agents not actions due to the 'moral agent question', and that the good of all is the justified determinant of moral evaluations.

Thus early chapters explore how theories that initially supply evaluations to actions – the left-hand side of the previous table – can evaluate agents, that is: once we have related the right and the good, how should we determine moral worth?[10] The overall argument is that this 'moral agent question' is surprisingly hard for such theories to answer in a compelling manner (this part is thus implicitly also an argument for a will-based deontology and for virtue ethics as well as for motivation ethics).

To get a sense of the difficulties, consider an action morality that divides some actions into those that are right and wrong (or required or impermissible – the precise terminology will not matter here for now) based on some of their features, such as their consequences, their harm, their effect on the agent's interests etc. Now how should we evaluate agents? Well one suggestion, that of 'evaluative coherence', is that we do so on the basis of the actions agents undertake (typically, roughly, generally and so on). This seems to reflect the normal way we deploy moral language: to accuse someone of repeatedly acting morally wrongly does imply a negative moral evaluation of them. But, if so, then the evaluation of the agent will not be determined by their features and is thus potentially arbitrary. Why?

Consider a hypothetical set of life choices and a particular agent. For some choices she would act rightly according to the action morality – call these R choices. For some she would act wrongly – call these W choices. We can sketch this as follows:

[figure showing a rectangle with W and R letters scattered throughout]

Now, if the evaluation of the agent is going to be based on whether she tends to act rightly or wrongly, this is going to depend on what set of choices she happens to actually face. Imagine two identical agents who face different life choices sets – A and B:

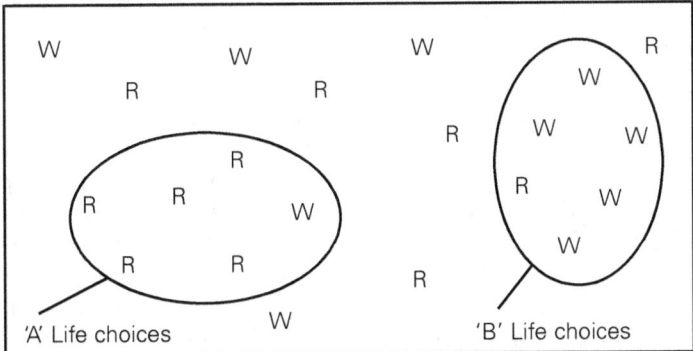

The agent who faces the A choices tends consistently to act morally rightly and thus is morally good. The agent who faces the B choices tends to act morally wrongly and thus is morally bad. But of course by stipulation these agents are identical. Thus their contradictory evaluations appear arbitrary (in that they are not determined by their features).

To briefly illustrate, consider act consequentialism – where the right act is that which will bring about the best consequences – and take two identical egoists who always do what is in their own self-interest. The first faces situations where her egoism consistently causes her to produce the best consequences. The second faces situations where her egoism consistently causes her not to produce the best consequences. Assuming rough evaluative coherence, since the first consistently acts morally rightly and the second consistently acts morally wrongly, for act consequentialism the first is a morally good agent, and the second a morally bad agent (or, at least, the first is a morally better agent). They, however, have identical features, so their evaluations seem arbitrary and incorrect as such.

Now, there seem to be many, many ways around this problem – rejecting evaluative coherence or the need for agent evaluations, basing agent evaluations on something other than the evaluation of what agents do, denying this will tend to happen in the long term and so on. None of these responses proves to be without serious problems. These are just a few of the challenges in responding to the 'moral agent question' that action moralities face.

Since motivation ethics shares with consequentialism the determinant of evaluation – it is the good of all that underpins evaluations – and since consequentialism is perhaps the most clearly articulated action morality, Chapter 1 discusses consequentialism's difficulty with agent evaluations.

At one stage I considered calling this chapter 'Why I am not a consequentialist?', but rejected this title mainly because frankly who cares about my personal philosophical journey, and partly because such a title might encourage substance-free ad hominem (or, worse, some pat-psychology, 'the scorn of the apostate' etc.). But a slow and steady shift away from acceptance of the theory is in fact what happened. Some years ago I believed consequentialism to clearly have the best arguments in its favour – notably, that it's the overall consequences of what we do that matter morally – and that the standard criticisms of the theory were too contingent on our intuitive responses, or too contingent on somewhat unlikely or unrealistic causal claims. I then started worrying about the agent evaluation problems.

Quite a few years of thinking through these issues personally produced various stages of denial (of course these problems apply only to some consequentialist theories surely?), of dismissiveness (let's just not worry about agent evaluations), of ideology (only consequences matter dammit!) and finally of deference (consequentialists are super smart, they know the moral luck literature too – surely they've got some good responses I just haven't thought of or been able to find).

What finally caused a serious re-appraisal was the experience of discussing the problem with fellow consequentialism sympathisers, for their responses would repeatedly shift – often through the stages I had personally been through – and then shift back to one of the responses or to disengagement. If you ask a relatively simple question of a position, repeatedly, and always get very problematic – but confidently asserted – answers, then it's time to take a deep breath and consider that there might not be a good answer period, that the position should be rejected.

I still believe consequentialism to be an utterly brilliant theory, one of breath-taking scope and power. It's just that when you start thinking through the possibilities of agent evaluation it's hard to resist the conclusion that the theory is incorrect, and for a deep structural reason not because we are focusing on the wrong variant, and not because of our (potentially unreliable) intuitions. The first chapter of this book tries to set out – as clearly as possible – how and why this is the case.

Chapter 2 then outlines motivation ethics, how it overcomes the difficulties, and how it doesn't create analogous problems with regard to actions. This chapter in effect demonstrates how the problems are not a generic feature of moral luck that all theories would face, and how the difficulties are not created by basing moral evaluations on the interests of all. It is a particular feature of consequentialism that is problematic: determining moral evaluations by the goodness of the consequences. We can reject that but still hold that everyone's interests count equally, and still hold that agent and action evaluations are possible. Motivation ethics demonstrates how.

Chapter 3 then discusses how the agent evaluation problems may accrue to harm-based deontological theories and why a will-based deontology might overcome them and be preferable to a deontological version of motivation ethics. The core problem of the first three chapters thus concerns how in principle we should morally evaluate actions and agents and the difficulties of action moralities.

If the arguments of the first three chapters succeed, or more generally if we are to make qualitative agent evaluations, then we can think of two ways these might be determined. One option is 'comparativism', where a qualitative label implicitly references a comparison to some distribution of agents. To illustrate, consider what makes the statement that 'Bob is tall' potentially correct. Well, it is not that Bob is a particular height simpliciter. Rather it is that Bob is a particular height compared to some – implicit or explicit – distribution. For this reason it can be true that Bob is tall in the context of contemporary people in general but also that Bob is not tall in the context of basketball players.

The alternative way of determining qualitative labels is 'absolutism', where the correctness of the label is based on some absolute properties. One example would be if we said that Bob is right handed. Whether this is true or not does not depend on whether we are speaking of Bob in the context of people in general, ambidextrous basketball players or whomever.

But which – comparativism or absolutism – is correct for qualitative moral agent evaluations ('morally good', 'morally heroic' etc.)? Chapter 4 outlines this choice via the problem of moral demandingness. That is, it argues that the complaint that some moral theories are 'too demanding' is in fact a valid worry *if* qualitative moral agent evaluations should be comparativist: if, in other words, when evaluating someone as morally good or bad or heroic we should be comparing them to an implicit sense of human variance and possibility. The version of motivation ethics defended in this book is explicitly comparativist, unlike perhaps all current prominent competitor moral theories, and having set out this choice the chapter argues in favour of comparativism and against absolutism.

When does the different approach of motivation ethics make a concrete difference?

The proposal of motivation ethics is not only a different moral theory both to normal action moralities and to the ideal agents of Kant and virtue ethics theories, but it also represents, along with the general action/agent morality divide, a different way of thinking about a range of practical moral problems. Moral demandingness is one such issue. What others are there?

Well, by basing evaluations on a particular motivation, motivation ethics would be expected to supply markedly different moral evaluations to a more standard action-based theory in two broad cases in particular: (i) where the agent has in play significant motivations to promote the good of specific others; and (ii) where most humans would be expected to have in play significant self-regarding motivations. Chapters 5 and 6 therefore discuss the theory respectively as regards to special relationships (such as with family and friends) and global duties and state coercion.

Special relationships

Consider, for instance, the apparent conflict between moral concern being universal and the partiality of parents significantly motivated to promote the interests of their children. Is this motivation, or the set of actions that will likely ensue, morally right? The difficulty here for an action-based theory is that such concern seems likely to cause an agent to act wrongly – such actions seem to be biased yet morality is supposedly unbiased – but for a variety of reasons we may not be justified in evaluating an agent showing concern for their children as morally bad. Many theories thus aim to show that the act of favouring one's children can somehow be justified by an equal concern.

Motivation ethics, in contrast, holds that while one's motivation to promote the good of all others comprises one's moral evaluation, *it is possible to have other motivations*. Thus, under motivation ethics, a parent's significant concern for their children is likely to lead them to act well as a parent. Whether or not they act well morally will additionally depend on how motivated they are to promote the good of all others. In principle they may have both motivations, however, and there is no prima facie conflict between living morally and possessing a significant concern for one's children.

The apparent conflict arises from the observation that, if we evaluate actions by their impact on all impartially considered, then concern for particular individuals is prima facie morally suspect. But if instead we morally evaluate agents by how motivated they are to promote the good of all this still leaves room for other motivations – both those focused on concern for particular individuals, or on the agent's own projects. It is the evaluative primacy of actions that produces the problems, not the principle that moral concern is impartial concern for all, and the underlying argument of this chapter is thus that the problem of special relationships is a predictable symptom of the moral agent problems discussed in earlier chapters.

Duties and states

A second important category where motivation ethics radically diverges from a more traditional good-based action-morality arises when the presence of certain institutions radically alters the ease or difficulty of a range of other-affecting acts. For example, consider our duties to those outside our borders. Currently, the citizens of all developed democracies provide significant amounts of domestic public goods, and trivial amounts of such goods aimed externally, especially welfarist goods such as education or healthcare. Yet if moral concern is equal concern for all humans, then such goods should either not be provided at all (for right-cosmopolitans) or should be provided to those outside of the state's borders (for left-cosmopolitans). The apparent consequence either way is that a moral duty to provide, say, high-quality free primary education to all of one's co-nationals may not be justifiable – it is either not a duty, or required to all who might benefit, and most of such resources should thus be spent abroad.

Political associationists – rejecting such a conclusion – have therefore tried to show that our apparent favouring of co-nationals can be justified by some common feature, such as being part of a people, having associational duties similar to that of family and friendship, engaging in reciprocity, being subject to common coercion and law-authorship and so on, but then face difficulties showing these cleanly stop at the border and really do still represent equal moral concern for all.

Motivation ethics starts however with the question of what would we expect of highly, slightly or not-at-all morally motivated individuals. That is, even in a democratic country where the citizens were moderately or highly motivated to promote the good of all others, including those outside their borders, we would still plausibly expect a greater provision of domestically focused public goods due to non-moral concern for one's own children, family or broader economic future. What would be different is that our aid and trade policies would plausibly be more responsive to their impact on the world's poor.

If we simply look at actions we obscure the fact that many actions are motivationally multi-determined (someone can pay taxes for purely selfish reasons assuming effective compliance threats) and heterogeneous in their demandingness (paying 10 per cent of income in sales tax to support co-nationals is hard to avoid; donating 10 per cent to support the global poor takes significant commitment). For motivation ethics, what crucially distinguishes moral actions from non-moral ones is that moral actions require a degree of motivation to promote the good of others. Hence, in evaluating how we respond to global disparities, it is the actions that reveal our level of concern for others that reveal and constitute how morally well we act, not apparent disparities between external and internal provision.

Underlying the analysis of our duties to those outside and within our borders is the premise that our basic duties are things we would expect a morally good agent to undertake, and that to assess these duties we therefore need a conception of such an agent else we run into the moral agent problems of Chapter 1. Thus although Chapters 5 and 6 take up two 'applied' topics (special relationships, and duties and global justice) the central argument is that key problems – that of a conflict between partial familial concern and the equal concern of morality and of a conflict between acts that benefit one's co-nationals and the moral irrelevance of borders – are both predicated on the assumption of action primacy, and in particular both derivative of that approach's moral agent problems. The difficulties are created by the action morality assumption that the primary object of moral evaluation should be actions. This – according to these chapters – is what we should reject.

Legitimacy and the good

One way of evaluating institutions is by their impact on the relevant good – i.e. interests – of all affected (different accounts of justice disagree on either what the relevant good should be, or on how clashes between different goods should be resolved – should for instance liberties be given priority, or certain rights be afforded, or the interests of the worst-off have some sort of priority, or people be compensated for bad luck?). These are debates about the justice of institutions. Motivation ethics holds that moral agents should be motivated to promote the overall good, namely the interests that justice promotes. Institutions are better as such the better they promote the good.

Yet a rival approach is to hold that it is also the way decisions are arrived at or by whom they are undertaken that matters, in that what we should seek are legitimate institutions. Democracy, to take the current dominant example, is thus not desirable purely for its outcomes but because it is legitimate, in that only democratically elected governments have a right to rule and are generally owed obedience.

Chapter 7 argues that this approach to institutional evaluation is remarkably hard to motivate in that the duties and justifications that are normally held to establish the value of legitimacy are *prima facie* morally undesirable. The underlying argument is that, as with motivation ethics, once we concede that the good matters to moral evaluation – that it matters what happens to people – then creating a new normative category of legitimacy risks sanctioning harm with no out-weighing benefit. As such, to accept motivation ethics is to reject most common conceptions of political legitimacy, and vice versa.

To illustrate: assume we have a general duty to obey the law if passed by a legitimate state and consider a range of possible laws. There will be some such laws that on their merits we should obey no matter what state passes them, e.g. 'do not murder'. And there will be some laws that on their merits we should disobey, no matter who passes them, e.g. 'do not serve Jewish people'. In both cases the duty to obey is redundant. Thus it only appears to make a difference overall in cases where, on the merits, we should disobey the law as it harms the relevant good of those affected, but we are required to obey if commanded by a legitimate state. But why is this desirable? Why would we want a duty whose sole effect is to require us morally to obey laws that on their merits should be disobeyed? Or to put this another way: if we have a duty to obey just laws in any state, then which are the unjust laws that we should obey in a democracy because it is legitimate? The implication is that legitimacy is morally undesirable.

For many contemporary theorists this is self-evidently wrong. Thus a range of potential solutions or responses are explored, among them that legitimacy is needed due to reasonable disagreement, that it accrues to epistemically superior institutions, that it is necessary due to pre-political rights, that is supplies pre-emptive duties, or that it applies to morally optional acts. None of them are without problems of their own.

The underlying argument of this chapter is that there is a fundamental tension within political morality between good-based normativity (that of how people's interests are affected) and legitimacy-based normativity (that of how or by whom decisions are arrived at), and that we should consider either rejecting or seriously rethinking the latter. It is truly hard to establish why legitimacy is morally desirable. This conclusion is decidedly radical: it contradicts most of our contemporary assumptions about democracy and its justification, and even undercuts the assumption that there is a meaningful unitary normative concept of 'democracy'. The reader must judge if indeed it is correct.

Is the overall good possible?

Finally, the previously outlined chapters have all assumed it is possible to think of the 'overall good' as the combination of the good of individuals (what is often called social welfare or overall utility), even when some people benefit and some lose from an action, as is often the case. But how can we add up the benefits and losses to different individuals? How, in other words, can we make interpersonal comparisons of the good? If we cannot, then the proposed version of motivation ethics is not a viable general moral theory.

Now, almost no one fully endorses this line of thought: almost no one holds for instance that we cannot meaningfully compare the badness of one individual's itchy finger to that of another individual's broken and bleeding leg. But seemingly crazy thoughts have been right in the past, so it matters that we have a principled account of why this is so and why possible problems can be addressed.

The general worry that sceptics of interpersonal comparisons have raised is based on what we can and cannot know about individuals. Sceptics argue that we can know for an individual that one situation has more or less or the same welfare than another: that is we can know for individuals how situations are ranked in terms of welfare. However, since we cannot 'get into' people's heads and know more than this – such as precisely *how much* welfare each individual has in each situation – then we cannot 'add' these numbers up. A further type of scepticism then denies that such numbers could even be meaningful.

Chapter 8 argues, however, that we should treat the task of making interpersonal comparisons as an epistemic problem – as a problem of how to justifiably relate evidence of individual amounts to beliefs about overall amounts – and that if we do so then prominent sceptical critiques can be addressed.

To see how, consider, by analogy, that we ask a group of students in a room to write down their birth city, species of first pet and favourite author's surname and also individually to rank these by word length. Cambridge, Dog, Melville, for example, would thus be ranked: City > Author > Pet.

Now imagine we want to know, of all the students in the room, which has the most letters overall combined – the cities, pet species or authors? But imagine too, as the welfare sceptic argues, that all we can know is how individuals personally rank these, not the absolute values (we cannot simply ask each student in turn how long their city words are for instance). Must we abandon the task of forming justified beliefs about the city, author and pet words overall?

Well no. As we begin to learn the individual rankings – such as City > Author > Pet – we can use these to form a justified belief about the overall amounts. In doing so we would have formed beliefs about the overall amount of something merely given evidence of the rankings of individuals. But such a task is exactly what the welfare sceptic holds impossible. Expanding upon and refining this insight, Chapter 8 shows that in the good/welfare cases *if we simply require beliefs that are unbiased and coherent* then we can use a range of well-established epistemic principles to form overall beliefs and implicitly make interpersonal comparisons.

Most interesting of all, perhaps, the chapter explores how even if we deny that there is anything meaningful about absolute welfare levels – it is only meaningful as such to think of someone's welfare in situation A *in comparison* to in situation B – then we can still form interpersonal comparisons using the epistemic approach, and the more we learn about individuals the more robust will be our conclusions about overall welfare and the overall good.

*

Methodology

In a straightforward sense, this book is a series of arguments for a particular set of conclusions in moral and political philosophy, and against prominent existing alternatives. However, like all such works, it is also simultaneously an implicit argument in moral methodology: it offers certain types of considerations in favour of claims and not others, and asks certain types of questions. In this regard, it makes two big and fairly consequential methodological moves, and these are perhaps both worth explicitly flagging here at the start.

The first methodological move is to ask a particular type of question, namely: how would theories that evaluate one type of object evaluate other types of objects (or deny the need)? This 'multi-object approach' begins with the observation that there are distinct potential objects of normative evaluation: actions, agents, interests ('the good') and institutions. Theories, and their rivals, often take one or two as their focus and provide competing evaluations based on these. Debate is then structured as such.

So two competing theories within ethics might disagree as to whether a particular type of action is morally permissible, and the debate will presumably focus on their rival justifications and the cases where they give conflicting answers. Or two theories of institutional evaluation might disagree as to whether legitimacy flows from consent or from a fair procedure, and each will appeal to rival considerations and discuss potential situations where they would produce divergent answers.

But we can also step back and ask: is the theory in principle compatible with an acceptable account of the evaluation of the *other* potential sites of evaluation? This is the core question that each critical chapter of this book adopts. Hence, for instance, it asks how theories that directly morally evaluate actions might evaluate agents. Or how theories that directly evaluate institutions via their legitimacy might evaluate their actions or impact on interests. Or how a theory of our duties can evaluate agents living under different institutional arrangements.

While a compelling theory of legitimacy or of institutional justice, for example, does not *need* to provide an account of individual level duties or of the evaluation of agents it does need to be compatible with one, and one that itself is compelling. Similarly, action-focused theories do not need to explicitly provide agent evaluations, but they do need to be able to acceptably do so (or deny this as a requirement).

Finding a normative theory that satisfactorily covers all the possible objects of evaluation is obviously very ambitious. The argument of this book, however, is that simply demanding this of prominent theories can help us critically compare them, and choose between them. Rival theories of actions, or of agents, or of institutions will often be making shared assumptions that seem innocuous in the context in which they are being deployed. But by asking how they could evaluate other objects we may make these explicit and question them. This is to ask how theories could evaluate multiple objects, even if they don't currently.

The second big methodological move concerns the criteria we should use to choose between moral theories, and is both critical and constructive.

It's critical in that it questions whether it is even possible that intuitions about cases could be a justified partial guide to correct normative beliefs. This is set out explicitly towards the end of Chapter 3 with the 'Intuition Regress Problem', a claimed demonstration that there could be no non-circular non-arbitrary justification for giving intuitive-status any role as a guide to correctness. If true, then showing a theory has intuitive implications for various cases is ruled out as a consideration in favour of that theory.

Thus, although there are illustrative examples throughout, this book attempts to advance the core critical arguments of Chapters 1 to 8 *without relying upon* case-based intuitions at all. There are lots of examples and the implications for cases are well discussed. It's just that the argument for the substantive positions never depends on one's intuitions – or that at least is the aim.

As a methodological constraint this is very demanding: no doubt there are such judgements implicitly dotted throughout; the key claim, however, is that none of the arguments depend upon them. The reader must judge the extent to which the book succeeds in meeting this very restrictive condition. Whether it is necessary will depend on the force of the 'Intuition Regress Problem' with which Chapter 3 concludes.

But if the book rejects any role for case-based intuitions, then how on earth can it choose between moral theories? Internal coherence is obviously not enough. The constructive methodological move here is to instead impose a condition of non-arbitrariness on normative beliefs for them to be correct and to see – once they are making multi-object evaluations – if particular theories can meet it. This is very different to using our intuitions concerning conclusions: non-arbitrariness is a property of how the justifications of beliefs relate, not a property of how we psychologically react to specific implications.

Throughout the book the main condition used is a very minimal one: that if it is correct to evaluate an object as P and is not correct to evaluate it as not-P then this should be determined by features of the object. However, Chapter 8 uses a seemingly different version, that of being 'unbiased' when using individual-level welfare information to form overall beliefs, in effect not making overall welfare conditional on 'arbitrary factors'. This raises the question of whether non-arbitrariness is simply a label for a set of diverse principles – with the justificatory worry of 'why those ones?' – or something more fundamental. The Epilogue as such responds by discussing what a generalized condition of non-arbitrariness might look like, what it could apply to, and how and why it might be justified.

Criticizing a theory for supplying arbitrary evaluations represents a very different type of argument to criticizing a theory for having implications that seem counter-intuitive, odd or bizarre. Because although you can always reject someone's intuitions – by having alternative ones – generally rejecting non-arbitrariness is much harder: once you do so, in a sense, then 'anything goes'. This criterion thus compliments the worries raised about using intuitions, and responds to the claim that if you reject intuitions then analytic moral philosophy simply entails getting one's beliefs coherent. Not so, according to the Epilogue, for non-arbitrariness may help us to reject many sets of beliefs, even if perfectly coherent. This is a large topic, and one that the final chapter will not do justice to, but it hopefully highlights the potential and challenges of non-arbitrariness as a condition on beliefs, and provides a more explicit justification for the use of it at key argumentative junctures in the book.

A final brief note on persuasion

Much moral philosophizing takes place using a commitment to reflective equilibrium – examining our principles and our intuitions about particular cases and trying to find some balance or coherent fit between these. One admirable feature of this approach is that those engaged in it are typically open to persuasion and to theory-revision (if someone can raise a suitably intuitive example that withstands scrutiny for instance). As such, a book examining general principles and their fit with thought-experiment cases can justifiably hope to persuade a reasonable portion of moral and political philosophers to modify their positions.

Yet, as noted, this book eschews such a method due to the Intuition Regress Problem set out in Chapter 3. All of the arguments here, in contrast, are about principles, and typically about what follows from being committed to non-arbitrariness and coherence in one's normative beliefs. Isn't it naive to think such a style of argument would convince? If you entirely reject 'psychological appeal to established theorists' as a partial criterion then you seem much more likely to end up with conclusions lacking psychological appeal to established theorists.

This is obviously a worry about semi-intuition-based approaches versus pure principle-based ones. It's also a worry though about the status quo versus alternatives that reject rather than modify it. This came up recently when I gave a version of the argument of Chapter 8 – on how to make interpersonal comparisons of welfare/the good – to a group of academics and PhD students predominantly from the Government Department at Harvard. The questions were thoughtful and above all content-based and thus wonderful. Towards the end, however, one of the senior academics asked if I really honestly thought the arguments would persuade life-long overall-welfare sceptics (who as a group currently dominate within economics and social choice theory).

His implied conclusion – that they would not be persuaded – was probably accurate, at least for most such sceptics. But the unstated premise, that they were the real target audience, was off the mark. Since he was quite a bit older than me, the politest way of responding I could think of was to be oblique, and thus to simply note that 'there are cohort effects'.

The point, however, generalizes. Both consequentialism and overall-welfare-scepticism will have long-standing adherents for whom no argument could dislodge them from the position, for any argument that conflicts with it must, ipso facto, be wrong, any troubling implication be a bullet that should be bitten. (There is some irony that of the positions argued against in this book, perhaps the two most entrenched – consequentialism and scepticism about interpersonal comparisons – are typically in direct contradiction with each other.) Implicit in such an attitude is a requirement that any new proposal must meet a test of 'show me how it agrees with most of my existing settled judgements'. Clearly, a critique of the core principles underlying such judgements will not meet this.

Similarly, if someone has spent twenty or more years engaged in scrutinizing and systemizing their ethical intuitions, then scepticism about such a method of moral theorizing is likely to receive short shrift, or provoke a strong desire to catch the sceptic in some consistency slip: 'Ah ha! The author does use intuitions in footnote 107!'

Yet offering non-intuition-based abstract arguments against deeply held positions is not necessarily futile. Though obviously it gets harder the longer someone has accepted and promoted a theory, many people do still retain a truly open and enquiring mind. All of us involved in academia will have had colleagues who, despite holding remarkably consistent positions during careers spanning many decades, were nonetheless continually interested in the merits of new arguments and new angles on old ones, who strove to see the pros and cons of a position, not just identify where they disagree with the conclusion and why they are therefore right, yet again. Despite holding long-standing beliefs, many minds remain admirably open.

And even when not, principle-based argument is not futile because the longer-term battle truly lies elsewhere. Every year people come anew to moral and political philosophy, every year those with not-yet-settled positions journey further into this wonderful, wonderful subject. Arguing against entrenched positions is not futile. There are cohort effects.

CHAPTER ONE

Consequentialism and the moral agent question

1.1 The problem in outline

Consequentialism, in its simplest form, is the theory that the moral rightness and wrongness of actions should be determined by the goodness of their consequences. Such a theory is an 'action morality' in that it primarily evaluates actions. How might it evaluate agents? This is the 'moral agent question': what, for an action morality, makes someone morally good (or bad)?

This chapter will argue that this is actually a very difficult question for consequentialism to address adequately, one for which there is no clear good answer and indeed not even an answer without very serious problems.

Now, this seems absurd. It seems superficially that exactly the opposite would hold, for two reasons. First of all, that there are logically just many, many potential ways to answer the moral agent question. Perhaps under consequentialism morally good (or bad) agents are those that undertake, or are expected to undertake, morally good (or bad) actions: that is they tend to act rightly or wrongly. Or perhaps agent evaluations are meaningless or cannot correctly be made. Or perhaps it is not the evaluation of what agents do, but of something else, that should determine their evaluation. Or perhaps the question of agent evaluations doesn't matter – it is knowing what is right and wrong that is important. Since consequentialism, strictly speaking, doesn't logically entail any particular answer, it seems ridiculous to maintain that all of the possible answers will be irredeemably problematic.

Secondly, it is not that there is only one type of consequentialism. There is the historically influential act consequentialism,[1] but also rule-consequentialism,[2] and virtue-consequentialism,[3] and motive-consequentialism[4] and global consequentialism.[5] There are direct theories, and correspondingly for these an indirect variant. There are subjective theories and objective theories. There are numerous accounts of what precisely makes consequences good. And this does not even exhaust the list at all. So it seems truly absurd to maintain that none of these is compatible with a satisfactory answer to the question of what makes someone morally good or bad.

And yet that is what this chapter will try to establish. The larger point, one taken up in subsequent chapters, is that this is in fact a structural feature of consequentialism: it cannot acceptably respond to the moral agent question because of the way it links the evaluation of actions and of agents to the overall good.

To see the initial difficulty consider direct consequentialism, that is where the right act (or rule, or motive, or virtue, or combination thereof[6]) is that which will bring about the most good, impartially judged. As such it has a clear and remarkably compelling rationale: faced with a choice of what to do we should bring about the best consequences, and the actions or set of actions that do so are right. It thus morally evaluates actions based on their consequences. What relationship should hold with the evaluation of agents?

The most intuitive and obvious relationship is that of rough 'evaluative coherence', namely that the moral evaluation of agents and the actions they perform should broadly cohere: morally good agents are those who generally act rightly; morally bad agents those who generally act wrongly; morally better agents are those who generally do morally better actions.[7] This is certainly how moral evaluations feel: being accused of acting morally wrongly feels like a negative moral evaluation of oneself. Additional deeper problems with rejecting evaluative coherence are subsequently discussed, but for now let us assume this is roughly correct. If so, then we face the problem that the correct evaluation of an agent will not be determined by features of the agent. The reason this is true for consequentialism is that whether an agent consistently acts rightly or wrongly – and thus, with broad evaluative coherence, is a morally good or bad agent – depends not on their features, but rather on the external situations they encounter, over which indeed they may have no control.

An agent who has constitutive features P (or Q) may act rightly (or wrongly) facing life situations X, and wrongly (or rightly) facing life situations Y. Thus being P or Q may mean he is morally good or that he is morally bad; an agent who is P might be morally better than one who is Q, or the complete opposite.

Or to put this schematically: consider an agent and a range of hypothetical choices they might face. For some of those choices – 'R-choices' – they would act rightly. For some – 'W-choices' – they would act wrongly. Now if there is coherence between the evaluation of an agent and the actual actions they generally take then their evaluation will be entirely contingent on whether they mostly face R or W choices, something not dependent on their features. As noted in the introduction, we can represent this visually:

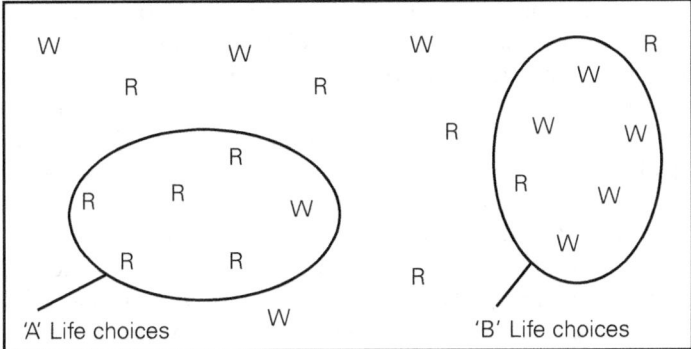

That is, if the agent faces the 'A' life choices they will as a result – according to consequentialism – be a morally good agent overall. If they face the 'B' life choices they will as a result – according to consequentialism – be a morally bad agent overall. But of course their features are by stipulation the same in both alternate life-scenarios, and the worry therefore is that the evaluations are arbitrary and as such incorrect.

In the abstract this sounds an obscure complaint, but it can perhaps be best illustrated concretely via two derivative instantiations, the first of which is the identical agent problem: namely, that agents with identical constitutive features may be consistently evaluated in completely contradictory ways.[8] Here for instance is a simple example applying to almost any consequentialist theory.

Consequentialism and the egoist

Consider an egoist who acts selfishly in all that she does. She follows selfish rules, cultivates selfish virtues, has selfish motivations. She does not care at all for others; indeed, if she thought it to her advantage, she would cause immense suffering and harm to them. Given certain life choices she may always act rightly under consequentialism and be overall a morally good agent: if she is poor, it might be that her selfishness is consequentially optimal (indeed it may have significant positive externalities for others). Given other life choices, she could always act wrongly and be overall a morally bad agent: if she is rich and others very poor, then her selfishness may produce very bad consequences compared to other behaviour. She could be identical in both cases and yet morally evaluated in utterly contradictory ways.

There seems something at least *prima facie* problematic about two absolutely identical agents – with identical beliefs, identical emotions, identical motivations, identical characters – being morally evaluated overall by a theory in directly contradictory ways despite the fact that they would do exactly the same things faced with the same situations.[9]

To be very clear: the core problem this chapter will focus upon is not that these cases produce counter-intuitive conclusions. This, of course, may still be true as, with evaluative coherence, consequentialism can deliver agent evaluations that seem perverse. The type of features we normally regard as morally abhorrent, for instance, can be those of a morally ideal agent: the pathological racist nationalist if fighting in a long, just war – one where victory will bring about markedly better consequences than defeat – may act rightly when all others fail to do so, they lacking his fervour, passion and intensity in combating the enemy and risking his own life to fight his foes, who after all he regards as inferior and with virulent hatred.[10]

The fact that consequentialism can have counter-intuitive implications has long been well debated; adding a set of counter-intuitive agent evaluations to the list would be to simply augment well-trodden ground. The problem this chapter is going to subsequently explore instead is that the agent evaluations appear arbitrary, and incorrect as such.

As noted, one way of illustrating this problem is via identical agents who are overall evaluated contradictorily. Another way is by considering comparative agent evaluations. Here is an example.

Consequentialism, the fundamentalist and the agnostic

Fundamentalist Sally gives half her income to charity to appease her vengeful God, she cares nothing for those she helps, and indeed she looks forward to their eternal torment. Agnostic Bob gives a quarter of what he similarly earns out of a desire to relieve the suffering of others. Their lives are otherwise similar. For almost any consequentialist theory Sally undertakes morally better actions: she has consequentially better motivations, follows a better rule (give half of income to charity), does better acts and so on. Sally, for the consequentialist, is a morally better person than Bob.

Whilst Sally does consequentially better actions, this isn't because she is at all concerned with producing the best consequences overall or even somewhat concerned with other people; she merely has fundamentalist beliefs that happen to cause her self-interest to lie in producing good outcomes. Hence why her being a morally better agent than Bob seems perverse: the good of all, the principle that underpins the evaluation of actions, is something utterly unimportant to her, yet because she happens to promote it she is evaluated as morally better than someone who does actually demonstrate a sincere and significant concern for others. Again, something seems amiss here. And as previously, what centrally matters for present purposes is not the intuitive disquiet, but the fact that it is easy to think of different sets of life choices where these evaluations would be reversed. The evaluation does not seem compelling as it is not consistent, specifically as it does not depend on the agents' features (and thus could have been reversed while the agents remain unchanged).

To forestall one misreading of the issue: a distinction between on the one hand moral agent evaluations and on the other hand notions of moral praise and blameworthiness seems superficially that it might be able to help with these worries – someone could always act wrongly but be praiseworthy, someone else always act rightly but be blameworthy – but the appearance is deceptive, for the critique can be repeated scrutinizing the relationship between praise/blameworthiness and the action evaluations. If these cohere the problems of the moral agent problem accrue. If they do not cohere then there is the related worry about evaluative coherence: should one live a morally praiseworthy life, or should one act rightly? The term 'agent-evaluations' is meant to potentially include a wide range of different formulations: moral worth, being a moral agent, praiseworthiness and blameworthiness and so on

Furthermore, it is important at the outset to note that the overall problem being posed – how should consequentialism evaluate agents? – is distinct to the most prominent worries raised about consequentialism's criterion of rightness, such as that it does not respect deontological side-constraints[11] (see also Chapter 3), that it unacceptably threatens an agent's integrity or is too demanding[12] (see also Chapter 4), or that it yields too strongly counter-intuitive judgements in a range of cases. And it is distinct to the question of whether we should adopt a pluralistic set of virtues rather than a single criterion of rightness.[13]

That is, for the sake of argument, let us assume that all of these critiques fail – that there should be no side-constraints on bringing about the best consequences, that consequentialism does not necessarily threaten one's integrity and is not inappropriately demanding,[14] that intuitions suggesting otherwise are not a problem[15] and that there should be a single measure of morality not a pluralist set of virtues. In other words let us assume consequentialism has the correct account of the rightness of actions. We still face a further question: how should it evaluate agents? This chapter will suggest that the theory's difficulties in addressing this question should cause us pause in accepting it, even for those un-persuaded by the classic deontological, intuitionist or virtue-based critiques.

The moral agent problem is as such distinct to these long-standing worries. The initial difficulty illustrated above arises from the combination of these four premises:

Moral agent evaluations: Human agents can be morally evaluated.

Rough evaluative coherence: The moral evaluation of an agent and her actual or expected actions should roughly cohere.

Agential non-arbitrariness: The correct moral evaluation of an agent should be determined by features of the agent.

Direct consequentialism: The right act (or motive, or virtue, or rule, or combination) is that which will lead to the best actual or expected consequences.

The problem, as the previous examples illustrated, is that these appear to be incompatible. As such we have to either reject one of the premises, suitably modify one, deny they are incompatible, or deny that even if so there is a problem.

Here are seven options. Firstly, of course, we might reject agent evaluations altogether. Secondly, we could reject broad evaluative coherence between an agent and her actions. Thirdly, we might change the set of consequentialist theories being considered, by either (i) emphasizing that it is an agent's long-term actions that should determine her evaluation, not those in isolated cases; (ii) appealing to the distinction between objective and subjective evaluations; or (iii) rejecting direct-consequentialism and adopting an indirect variant. Fourthly, we could retain but modify evaluative coherence and hold that the set of choices that should matter are not the actual or expected ones an agent faces but certain hypothetical ones. Fifthly, we might appeal to an ideal agent who always acts rightly no matter what the choices. Sixthly, we could simply deny there is a problem here: it's fine to morally evaluate identical agents in contradictory ways and to more broadly reject 'agential non-arbitrariness'. Or, seventhly, we could admit there is an agent evaluation problem, but deny its seriousness: consequentialism remains a compelling theory 'all things considered'. None of these will prove to be without serious difficulties of their own.

Since the critique being advanced is a variant of 'argument by iteration' – we take a possible solution, show it is problematic, and then move on to another – the consequentialist could still wonder if the discussion has simply omitted some problem-free alternative. This is liable to prove a false hope, however, as the options are logically exhaustive, as the end of section two sets out. One of them must be accepted, with the attendant problems, or consequentialism itself must be rejected.

That a potential problem exists does not, of course, dictate how we should respond or the extent to which we should worry about it. Section 3 therefore discusses several combination or meta-responses that appear to either acceptably reframe the issues or downplay their difficulty. Namely, (i) that consequentialism's agent evaluations are simply instrumental, and that's just fine; (ii) that this is all just a reflection of what consequentialism is; (iii) that consequentialists are aware of these problems and won't be persuaded or worried; (iv) that some sort of hybrid theory could overcome the problems and still be recognizably consequentialist.

Finally, even if she admits all the alternatives are problematic, and that there is no option omitted, then one last response from the consequentialist might be to claim that since the initial worry is related to a particular concept of moral luck – what Nagel has called 'circumstantial luck'[16] – that the overall difficulties might potentially apply to moral theories *in general* and thus to any potential credible alternative.

Now, strictly speaking, this is not quite right: consequentialism's difficulties responding to the moral agent question are not necessarily those of moral luck as several of the possible answers do not create any moral luck problems at all, such as for instance those rejecting evaluative coherence, citing ideal agents or basing evaluations on hypothetical choice sets.

Furthermore, credit where credit is due, recognition of the overall problem in fact predates the entire modern moral luck literature, as it can be found, somewhat disguised, in Mandeville.[17] For while a range of Scottish Enlightenment thinkers observed that individuals acting selfishly can bring about great social good, perhaps most famously Adam Smith, it was Mandeville who had arguably previously drawn the deeper moral insight from this fact: that the correct normative evaluation of agents cannot simply reflect the consequences of what such agents do, as given certain circumstances an individual living a life of vice may produce more social good than an individual living a life of virtue, yet our judgement of vice and virtue remain correct even if not publicly celebrated.

This, it should be noted, is a non-standard reading of Mandeville as foretelling a deep problem for the coming utilitarianism. The alternative reading, that subsequently became dominant, is that he is simply ridiculing common ideas of virtue and vice and thus implicitly laying the ground for utilitarianism. I personally think this latter interpretation underestimates how truly subversive his work is. Whichever is correct, however, at a minimum he still brilliantly hints at the logical tension between non-arbitrary agent evaluations, evaluative coherence and consequence-based action evaluations.

Thus while the overall problem need not be one of moral luck, the thought that these are generic difficulties seems plausible. One could argue that it is not consequentialism per se, but rather simply either the making of moral action evaluations or the basing of evaluations on the overall good that produces these worries. The next chapter therefore outlines why this is not necessarily the case, in particular how we can overcome the problem *by reversing the order in which the right and moral worth relate to the good*, in other words by adopting as the two main concepts of ethics the moral (agent) and the good, with the right derived from them. I call this 'motivation ethics' – that the moral evaluation of agents should be based on how motivated they are to promote the good of others (highly moral agents are highly motivated to do so, morally depraved agents are not even slightly motivated to do so and so on) – the subject of Chapter 2.

1.2 Possible responses to the problem

1. Rejecting the possibility of moral agent evaluations

One way to respond to the moral agent question is to deny one of its enabling premises, namely that moral agent evaluations can be correctly or meaningfully made: perhaps we can morally evaluate actions, but never agents. Consequentialism would thus tell us what a morally right or wrong action is, but simply supply no moral agent evaluations and deny they could be correct. To talk of morally good and bad agents would be meaningless. This would address the moral agent question by rejecting the potential correctness of key concepts upon which it depends.

Note also that the option being discussed here is not agnosticism – which would be roughly 'I'm not sure how the theory should make agent evaluations' – it is the rejection of the very possibility of such evaluations.

To claim the moral evaluation of agents is not meaningful, or cannot in principle be made, is, however, to leave oneself vulnerable to a variant of amoralism. If by 'J is a morally bad person' we must mean nothing, then the amoralist can accept consequentialism entirely and agree that, yes, doing X rather than Y does produce more suffering / less utility etc. But if they were to do X that would not represent any negative moral judgement *of them*. It would have been better, on this view, had mass-murderer Timothy McVeigh not killed so many people, but this isn't a criticism *of him*: it is merely a fact about the world. Many find amoralism an unattractive position, but it is not clear if one holds that moral agent-evaluations are meaningless and can never be correctly made that the amoralist is open to valid criticism: their actions are, but they are not. If incompatibility with amoralism is a basic requirement of any compelling moral theory then this option should be rejected.

2. Rejecting rough evaluative coherence

What if, however, we reject rough evaluative coherence? An action-focused morality could allow that the moral evaluation of agents simply involves different considerations to the moral evaluation of actions: thus a moral agent is not one who generally acts rightly, and an agent who consistently acts morally wrongly may be morally better than one who consistently acts rightly. We have a theory of right action, and a theory of the moral evaluation of agents, and neither is derivative or systematically integrated with the other.

Having rough evaluative coherence is not at all the same as having an evaluative identity: one can have evaluative coherence but still hold that acting wrongly does not always entail a negative evaluation of the agent, nor acting rightly a positive one, so long as there is a general, typical or expected connection. Rejecting broad evaluative coherence requires more than this if it is to overcome the moral agent problems however, it requires in effect that in many situations being a morally good or bad agent *not be systematically related* to acting rightly or wrongly respectively.

If this is possible, then one can still retain the claim that action evaluations are determined by features of the action (such as the consequences), agent evaluations are merely different things and based on other features (intentions, beliefs, emotions, attachments and so on).

Now, as noted earlier, there is something deeply phenomenologically jarring about this suggestion: acting morally wrongly, disregarding one's moral duties, or doing what is morally forbidden does seem to provide a clear presumptive negative moral evaluation of the person who does so.

Additionally though, rejecting broad evaluative coherence may also leave us with widespread prescriptive ambiguity. For a theory that lacks broad evaluative coherence it could be that 'one ought to do X and not do Y, but a moral agent would do Y'. Now, if ought implies 'what a moral agent would do', then we face a contradiction. If ought merely implies 'the action that is morally preferable', or some similar purely behavioural description, then there is a conflict between living as a moral person would live, and acting rightly. If one thus seeks to live as a moral agent would, which is not identified by virtue of the action evaluations (for consequentialists by virtue of the consequences of those actions), then such a theory loses its pragmatic import: the theory tells one what a right action is, but such a recommendation does not tell an agent what they should do or be like if they seek to be moral.

That is, without evaluative coherence, to do what is morally good (what is expected of a morally good agent) will often be to do what is morally wrong. In which case it is not obvious what the prescriptive status of 'morally wrong' is here: it does not – without evaluative coherence – identify what one should avoid doing to live a morally good life and to be a morally good agent; in fact it often conflicts with it.

The degree of evaluative coherence will trade off against the initial agent evaluation difficulties, specifically the worry that the agent evaluations are arbitrary as they are not determined by features of the agent. The closer the agent evaluations track the action evaluations the more evaluative coherence, but at the same time the more pressing and stark will be the agential difficulties: our agent evaluations will be dependent on more and more external contingencies. Conversely, the more compelling our theory of agent evaluations – by including more and more intrinsic agent-based considerations – the less evaluative coherence, and the more widespread and stark will be the prescriptive ambiguity and the disconnect with our normal broad association of the evaluation of an agent and their actions.

What rough evaluative coherence requires

It's very easy to reject some 'straw-man' version of evaluative coherence by noting the many ways action and agent evaluations may come apart, thus it's worth being super clear why this observation does not address the substantive issue.

Firstly, 'rough evaluative coherence' does not need to assert that the expected or typical coherence must hold *both* between doing what is right and being a morally good agent and between doing what is wrong and being a morally bad agent. We could have such coherence while still maintaining for example that those who aren't morally good often nonetheless do what is morally right.

Secondly, 'rough evaluative coherence' does not require coherence between different belief holders: someone might be justified in believing something is the morally wrong thing to do, and someone else justified in believing that it is what a morally good agent would do – this difference being down, for instance, to different empirical beliefs. It's commonplace to observe that two consequentialists who disagree about the consequences of an action may disagree about the rightness of the action and thus perhaps one will think something the morally wrong thing to do, the other think it is what a morally good agent would do. They might still both have internal evaluative coherence if they think that the morally right thing to do is that which a truly moral agent would do (when not making mistakes, having false beliefs etc. etc.).

All evaluative coherence requires is that the agent evaluations cohere in some systematic way with the action evaluations from some unified epistemic perspective. To put this in error-free terms: can we expect morally good agents to mostly do the morally right thing assuming they have fully correct empirical beliefs and make no execution errors? If so, there is rough evaluative coherence, even if we interpret 'expect' fairly loosely such that for various reasons in particular cases this might not hold.

This is why the term 'rough' is included: because the relationship of evaluative coherence between agent and action evaluations might be specified in a range of ways, and the question of which of these is precisely the right conception doesn't matter for the problems of this chapter. 'Rough evaluative coherence' is meant therefore to be reasonably permissive of the precise content of actual evaluative coherence. For instance, it might be coherence between the agent evaluations and what the agent would have been justified in believing was the right thing (given various cognitive, informational or other epistemic constraints). It might exclude execution errors where the agent tried to do something but failed due to a range of unforeseeable contingencies. It might want to aggregate actions in a range of ways, so that the agent evaluations depend on a certain amount of action consistency or are based on the importance of the moral interests at stake in the actions and so on.

For present purposes, 'rough evaluative coherence' is intended to allow for a range of views as to the precise correct form of coherence, only that there should be some expected or systematic coherence between the moral action and moral agent evaluations (there is a specific account of evaluative coherence in Chapter 2, but for now rival accounts are potentially included).

Further worries with the rejection of evaluative coherence

For these reasons, simply asserting that people can make mistakes or do the wrong thing for the right reasons or do what they were justified in believing was the right thing but in fact wasn't – these are 'straw man' rejections of evaluative coherence. A real test is: imagine an agent who has correct empirical beliefs, doesn't make execution errors, and reasons perfectly. If she correctly regards herself as someone who deliberately, consistently and knowingly does what is morally wrong is it fine for her also to correctly regard herself as a truly morally good agent. If so, we have potentially rejected rough evaluative coherence.

To reject evaluative coherence – while still supplying agent evaluations – is thus to hold that there should be an account of agent evaluations that doesn't ultimately cohere with or track the account of action evaluations. It's not that we take the action evaluations and then add a series of considerations that might modify the agent evaluations in certain situations: we have a separate theory of agent evaluations. Moral agents are going to do certain things (perhaps often the morally wrong thing), and when we label actions as morally right we aren't also implicitly labelling them as 'what a moral agent would normally/typically/in expectation do' – they're just morally right simpliciter. It is this division that produces the following choice: should you morally do what you are justified and correct in believing is morally good – what a moral agent would do – if you are also justified and correct in believing it to be morally wrong? This is the problem of prescriptive ambiguity.

A separate but perhaps more theoretically corrosive difficulty with rejecting evaluative coherence is that without it the qualitative moral action evaluations seem to have to be determined solely by stipulation, as nothing substantive hangs on their correctness. This creates two problems: (i) that the line between rightness and wrongness is arbitrarily determined; and (ii) that there will be a rival superior mirror theory that has evaluative coherence.

The reason is that the making of justified action evaluations requires answers to two logically separate questions. Firstly, what determines whether actions are morally better or worse? Secondly, how should we correctly qualitatively morally evaluate those actions once we have an account of moral betterness/worseness? Now if we have evaluative coherence, we in principle have a means of justifying the specific evaluations – the positive ones are what we would expect of morally good agents and the negative ones what we would only expect of morally bad agents (under certain circumstances, such is in general, or in the long term, or typically, or ignoring execution errors, or ignoring false empirical beliefs, or from the perspective from a particular agent etc. etc.).

If we don't have some sort of evaluative coherence, however, then designating some actions as morally right and some as morally wrong seems to have to rely upon arbitrary stipulation: in so doing we can't appeal to the agent evaluations, and we can't appeal to the morally relevant features of the action evaluations because these are captured by the betterness and worseness relation (assuming that isn't necessarily a binary relation – and when it comes to the goodness of the consequences it isn't).

To see this in practice, take the following two theories (for simplicity assuming act consequentialism, though the point generalizes):

Bestness-consequentialism
The morally right thing to do is an action which will bring about the best consequences, actions that do not do so are morally wrong.

Worstness-consequentialism
The morally wrong thing to do is an action which will bring about the worst consequences, actions that do not do so are morally right.

Now imagine there is a choice of four mutually exclusive actions, A1, A2, A3, A4, where if we were to rank them by the goodness of the consequences then A1 will lead to the best consequences, followed by A2, followed by A3, with A4 producing the worst consequences. If we ask of our two theories how to morally evaluate these actions as morally better or worse then they will agree: A1 is morally better than A2, which is morally better than A3, which is morally better than A4. That is:

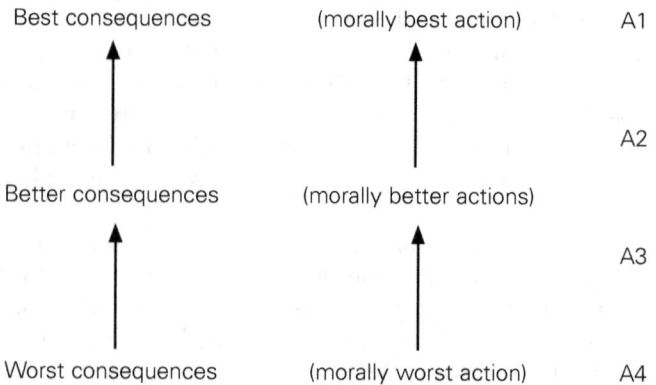

Now take our two versions of consequentialism and how they would morally *qualitatively* evaluate the actions:

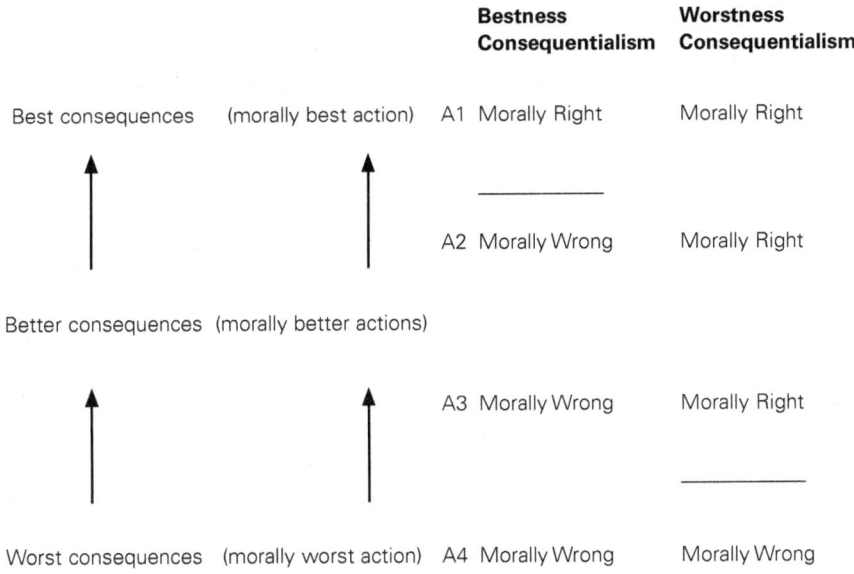

The theories disagree on the 'line' between moral rightness and moral wrongness (whether it's the line between A1 and A2, or the line between A3 and A4). But what stops them both being right?

Well, if there's rough evaluative coherence, then there is a substantive dispute here: there's a dispute about what a morally good agent would do when faced with the choice between actions A1–4, and because of this *both theories cannot be correct*. Hence, with rough evaluative coherence, bestness consequentialism provides an expected moral criticism and allied moral evaluation of agents who simply avoid doing the consequentially worse thing – that is do A3, for instance. The agents should be morally evaluated negatively because all they did was avoid the very worst action, but properly moral agents would do more than this: they would act rightly. This is something, again with evaluative coherence, that advocates of worstness consequentialism must reject. The two positions – with evaluative coherence – are arguing about something substantive, namely what a morally good agent would do or avoid doing.

It's possible, alternatively, to have an apparent disagreement and this be non-substantive, in that one or more of the terms has simply been asserted but whereby nothing really hangs on its correctness. Imagine, for instance, we're arguing about whether the moon is predominantly made of cheese. I'm arguing it is, and you're arguing it isn't. This seems to be a substantive empirical dispute. But imagine I define a 'lunar-cheese' as 'anything consisting of that thing of which the moon is predominantly made'. Now clearly, accepting my stipulated definition, the moon is predominantly made of cheese. This isn't, however, a substantive empirical disagreement anymore: all I've done is to stipulate an answer. It's now merely a debate about labelling where nothing depends upon it. It only appears to be a substantive debate because our normal language usage holds that cheese has a very definite set of empirical properties in terms of its physical content, and this background assumption makes it look like a substantive disagreement. To see that this isn't the case, however, imagine we replace the term 'lunar cheese' with 'blahblah'. We can all agree that the moon is made of 'blahblah'. Nothing hangs on this.

Without evaluative coherence, the same holds, for instance, for the disagreement between bestness and worstness consequentialism, even though they appear to be engaged in substantive disagreement. Take someone arguing for the correctness of bestness consequentialism. Since there's no evaluative coherence, their bestness-consequentialist agent-evaluation theory could be accepted by someone who accepted worstness consequentialism, so they clearly aren't having a disagreement about agent evaluations. And obviously both theorists agree entirely on what makes actions morally better or worse – they have identical rankings of the actions in terms of moral betterness and do so for the same reasons (the consequences) – so they aren't disagreeing about this.

So for bestness consequentialism to be justified and worstness consequentialism to not be justified it needs to be the case that there is something substantive that hangs on this, where this isn't circular or just stipulatory. There doesn't seem to be any ground, however, for doing this, as the two theories agree on all the properties that morally rank actions, and agree on all the properties that morally rank agents (or determine agent evaluations). Of course, we can simply stipulate an answer – we might say for instance that actions are morally right only if they are morally best, that is solely that action that there is most reason to do. But this is just assertion. Worstness consequentialists can say that actions are morally wrong only if they are morally worst, that is solely that action that there is most reason to avoid. Without evaluative coherence there's no obvious reason why bestness consequentialism and worstness consequentialism can't both be correct – by 'morally right' they just mean different things.

By contrast, a theory of moral rightness and moral wrongness is normally taken to not just identify which actions are morally better or worse. Instead it draws a line between some actions and others, with some being morally right and some being morally wrong, and with where the line is drawn having potential implications for how moral agents should or would act. Disagreement as to where to draw this line should be a substantive disagreement between rival theories, and with some sort of evaluative coherence it is: it's disagreement about what a moral agent would do (or avoid, or what a morally bad agent would do), both theories can't be correct and for moral agents, or those aspiring to be, which is correct and why is going to highly informative. But without evaluative coherence it's hard to see when anyone should care: replace the term 'morally right' for the bestness consequentialist with the term 'blahblah', where an action is 'blahblah' if it produces the best consequences. Since 'blahblah' actions aren't what we'd expect of moral agents, and since failing to do the 'blahblah' actions doesn't represent any negative moral evaluation of agents, then it's very unclear why this labelling matters.

The fundamental point is that for there to be a substantive dispute between two positions there has to be a premise that we're justified in accepting, whereby this entails that the two positions *can't both be right*, but that the premise itself does not settle the matter (such as if for instance it is logically incompatible with one of the positions). So if the dispute is over whether the moon is predominantly made of cheese, then if we accept that cheese has certain specific necessary and sufficient empirical properties – such as that it is mainly made of the type of proteins and fats that are found in milk – it follows that the answer can't both be 'yes' and 'no' and furthermore that our definition of cheese doesn't settle it either way. Hence it's a substantive dispute (unlike in the lunar-cheese case).

Similarly, if we accept evaluative coherence, then a dispute between two rival theories of moral rightness and wrongness is a substantive dispute *as they both can't be correct, and this isn't due to arbitrary stipulation: evaluative coherence itself doesn't settle which is correct*. Take, for instance, an account of evaluative coherence whereby under certain specified conditions 'Morally good agents would do what is morally right and not do what is morally wrong'. As such, if two theories disagree under such conditions as to what is morally right and what is morally wrong, then they cannot both be correct: it cannot be that a morally good agent would do P and not do Q, and also simultaneously they would do Q and not do P, where P and Q are mutually exclusive actions such that it is impossible to do them both.

If we reject evaluative coherence, then bestness consequentialism needs to provide an account of why worstness consequentialism cannot *also* be correct, and this account needs to not assume or require simply asserting the falsity of worstness consequentialism.

If we simply say that the right thing is only that which we have most reason to do, then obviously we've ruled out a rival theory that says wrongness is solely that thing that we have most reason to avoid – but this is just lunar-cheese-like stipulation, as is clear is we replace bestness-rightness with 'R-Blah' and worstness rightness with 'Wa-Blah'. Why not hold that often actions are 'Wa-Blah' but not 'R-Blah'? Without evaluative coherence, it's just labelling: they both can be correct.

Thus to reject evaluative coherence a theory needs to supply an alternative premise that indicates why disputes about the right are substantive disputes, not definitional or stipulatory ones even when two theories agree on the agent evaluations, and agree on what makes actions morally better or worse. It's decidedly unobvious what this might be, and since the two theories agree on the morally relevant empirical features of actions and agents it's hard to see even in principle how this would not ultimately require arbitrary stipulation. This is 'the problem of justifying the line' (between rightness and wrongness).

But this is not even all rejectors of evaluative coherence need to do. They need to also establish that evaluative coherence is positively a bad thing. This is because there will always be a rival theory that can substantively agree on the agent evaluations *and* have evaluative coherence.

For any action morality 'X' that denies rough evaluative coherence, but does accept the meaningfulness of agent evaluations, then there is going to be a correct theory of those agent evaluations 'Y' that does not cohere with the action evaluations. This simply follows from the rejection of EC. But as such, there is going to be a rival moral theory that accepts *this* theory of agent evaluations, i.e. that accepts Y, but then asserts evaluative coherence – so it supplies action evaluations whereby actions are morally better or worse as to whether we would usually expect them of morally better or worse agents, and of actions being morally right if we would expect them of morally good agents (under certain idealized situations, such as the agents are not making any large errors of fact and so on). This is 'the mirror theory' problem.

For an action morality to reject any sort of rough evaluative coherence is not only to depart from the way most people use moral terms and potentially mislead. It is to create prescriptive ambiguity as doing what is morally wrong will often be what moral agents would do; it is to render the theory's qualitative action evaluations lacking in any obvious justification aside from definition via arbitrary stipulation; and it is to leave the theory with a seemingly superior rival 'mirror' version that shares the agent evaluations but also has such coherence. There are good reasons why declaring something 'morally wrong' is usually taken to indicate that it is something that morally good agents would not do: this isn't just an unjustified quirk of language usage.

3. Broadening the theory under consideration

There are three obvious ways we might broaden the consequentialist theory under consideration. We could appeal to long-term actions not those in isolated cases. We could draw a distinction between objective evaluations – what is right given correct beliefs – and subjective ones – what is right given the agent's beliefs. Or we could reject direct consequentialism and adopt an indirect variant.

(i) Long-term actions

The earlier examples were of situations where identical agents were evaluated contradictorily, such as with the egoists, or where two agents were not comparatively evaluated compellingly, such as with fundamentalist Sally and agnostic Bob, as the evaluations did not necessarily reflect their features. But what if the correct evaluation of an agent should cohere with her actions, but those actions are evaluated over the long term, or in expectation of the long term?[18] A fundamentalist might be expected to produce bad long-term consequences after all, and egoists might over their lives tend normally to act wrongly.

The first problem with this response is it leaves too much to empirical contingencies. For there is nothing in consequentialism per se that will guarantee over the long term it is impossible of two identical agents that one consistently acts wrongly and one rightly – indeed, if whether or not egoists act wrongly or rightly tends to depend on whether they are relatively wealthy or poor, then this might be expected to be often extremely consistent in the long term, and in expectation. The moral agent problems remain.

And secondly, this response misdiagnoses the source of the problem. The difficulties of agent evaluation arise due to the very basic action-based structure of consequentialism, and they potentially accrue to such evaluations not only in specific situations *but in general*, both in the long term and in expectation. The critique is structural and the examples illustrative: hoping that given certain empirical contingencies the examples may not hold is to fail to address the basic worry. It is taking the right and good to be primary and the moral (agent) derivative that creates difficulties in supplying moral agent evaluations.

For similar reasons, appealing to 'systematic' consequences is not going to address the worry. For instance, as noted by Smith,[19] at a range of levels of economic development egoism may have systematically socially beneficial consequences. But obviously, once there is a large above-subsistence surplus of transferable consumption goods and huge inequality, those who are wealthier being egoistically motivated may have systematically bad consequences. And indeed *this is what we should expect*. Many of our motivations have really quite significant externalities, externalities removed from why we possess or retain the motivations, and externalities contingent on circumstances also orthogonal to why we possess the character features producing them. If we are evaluated by the overall consequences then our evaluation is going to be dependent on such contingencies, things that may be long-term and systematic. Hoping this may not occur is empirically unsupported and, more fundamentally, does not address what should obtain when it does occur.

(ii) Subjective vs objective evaluations

Consequentialism was said earlier to evaluate actions based on their consequences. But what if instead acting rightly involves doing what the agent is justified in believing will bring about the best consequences, even if sometimes this will not bring about the actual best consequences. We could thus have evaluative coherence between the agent evaluations and *subjective* action evaluations.

The subjective/objective rightness distinction may have important implications for a range of problems to do with the evaluation of actions. It does not, however, have any special resources to address the moral agent question, as exactly the same agent-evaluation problems apply whether we base evaluations on actual or intended or expected consequences. The identical agent problem and the comparative agent problem, for instance, can arise for agents acting objectively *or* subjectively rightly/wrongly. In the egoist case, for instance, the two individuals act both objectively and subjectively wrongly or rightly as the case may be, yet their evaluation is contradictory. Sally brings about *both* objectively and subjectively better consequences than Bob. Whatever the uses of distinguishing the subjective and objective rightness of actions, it does not address the worry that inferring agent-evaluations from either of these entails that such evaluations will not be determined by the agent's features.

(iii) Can indirect consequentialism help?

The initial problem was outlined using direct consequentialism, where the right act (or rule, or motive, or virtue, or combination thereof) was that which brought about the actual or expected best consequences. But perhaps the correct response to the problems is to adopt an indirect variant where the right rule, motive or virtue is that which would bring about the best consequences if others adopted that rule, motive or virtue.[20]

*

(*A very brief aside on terminology.*)

Some people refer to 'direct consequentialism' as that which evaluates acts only, and to 'indirect consequentialism' as that which evaluates rules, motives or virtues directly, and thus acts indirectly. Alternatively, others use direct consequentialism to refer to the direct evaluation of acts, rules, motives, virtues or all four, and indirect consequentialism to refer to the evaluation of a rule, motive or virtue were all, or almost all, to adopt it. This book does the latter because if you do the former you seem unable to separate out the following two theories (amongst others):

M1: The right motives are those which would cause the agent to produce the best consequences.

M2: The right motives are those which would produce the best consequences were all (or almost all) agents to possess them.

If both are 'indirect consequentialism' then we have lost a useful distinction (we can classify the second as 'acceptance motive consequentialism' or similar if we wish motive consequentialism to be 'indirect' and act 'direct', but since it's obvious that 'act-consequentialism' is not 'motive consequentialism' why bother?). For that reason, this book calls M1 a type of direct motive consequentialism and M2 a type of indirect motive consequentialism (the same holds for virtue consequentialism and rule consequentialism).

This does not mean the first view – that only act consequentialism can be 'direct consequentialism' is incorrect – there is no correct and incorrect here, we are just seeking clarity, to reasonably hew to convention, and to be able to cleanly capture the differences between views. What matters is the content.

*

So can indirect consequentialism overcome the problems? Unfortunately, it is not at all obvious that it can. Consider, for instance, indirect rule consequentialism where the rules are morally better the better consequences they would bring about were all or most to adopt them, and right if they would bring about the best consequences were all or most to adopt them. With evaluative coherence morally good agents are those that follow such rules or act in conformity with them, morally bad agents those who do not (typically, or in expectation, or generally etc.). The problem, however, is that doing so may be over-determined, in that one does so for a range of reasons, and radically empirically contingent, in that which rule is hypothetically optimal may depend on contingencies outside the scope of the agent's control or concern. That is, it might well be that Sally follows the optimal rule (give half of one's income to charity) and is morally good while Bob does not and is morally bad, even though 'following a rule whose general adoption would hypothetically lead to the best consequences' is irrelevant to them both: she seeks eternal life; he wants there to be less suffering.

Or take an indirect motive consequentialism and someone who has a dominant motivation to care for those closest to him – family and neighbours perhaps. For the theory, is such a person morally good? Well, if he lives in a poor village-based society then quite possibly: if such a motivation were universal we might get near-optimal outcomes.[21] But in a society sufficiently wealthy where the giving of aid to those non-near but in great need was consequentially optimal then an identical agent would be morally bad for the indirect motive consequentialist. The problem remains.

And indeed this is what we should expect. To see why, consider again the graphic used previously. That is, take a particular agent and act or rule consequentialism. Call 'R' choices those that if she faces them she will act rightly according to the theory. And call 'W choices those that if she faces them she will act wrongly according to the theory. (Or for motive or virtue variants call R choices those choices where she would act as an agent with the right motives or virtues, W choices those where she would not.) The problem, as noted, is that the choices she actually faces could mostly include R choices or mostly include W choices and thus, with evaluative coherence, she could be consistently evaluated as morally good, or morally bad, while still having the same features:

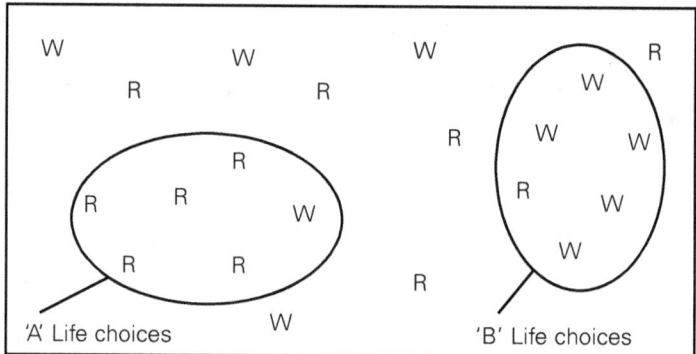

With this in mind, it's possible to see why all of the suggested changes to direct consequentialism will not succeed in addressing the problems. Looking at long-term actions we may include in her choice-set more choices – in circle A and B more Ws and Rs – but nothing guarantees that different possible sets of life choices will not contain very different ratios of Rs to Ws. Furthermore, what subjective and indirect theories do is to change the evaluation of many choices – for a given agent some of the Rs become W's and vice versa. Yet again this does nothing to prevent the distribution of Rs vs Ws within hypothetical life-choice sets being very different.

Considering the problem schematically thus reaffirms what was perhaps already obvious: if direct consequentialism suffers from the problem then so too will indirect and subjective variants, and appealing to long-term consequences won't remove the difficulties.

Indirect variants are perhaps least easy to illustrate because their evaluations are harder to ascertain as they require a difficult to justifiably determine hypothetical (such as that the rule that is right is that which leads to the best consequences if all or almost all others adopted it, but which others – what justifies the boundaries? Nation, time, geography, social situation, age?). Yet the overall structural problem is still here no matter what the determination. Agents typically follow rules or have motivations due to some of the consequences they will actually bring about, others of the consequences are in a sense externalities. Few of us do so because of the hypothetical net consequences they would bring about were all others to adopt the rule or cultivate the motivation, and thus if we evaluate actual agents based on whether they do so or not this is likely to be radically contingent on whether what they actually do coheres with what the theory tells us would be hypothetically optimal. It is basing action evaluations on the consequences – actual, expected or, as with indirect variants, hypothetical – that creates the difficulties for agent evaluation, and thus if we want to continue to do so we have to address the problem directly.

Since consequentialism is described throughout this book as an action morality (because it evaluates the rightness and wrongness of actions either singularly or as a set arising from a rule, motive, virtue or combination) a quick reading might suggest that the view being criticized is just act consequentialism. Thus, to be super, super clear: here are some of the views included all of which suffer from the same type of agent-evaluation problems:

Direct objective act consequentialism: The right act is that which will lead to the best consequences.

Direct subjective act consequentialism: The right act is that which the agent is justified in believing will lead to the best consequences.

Direct objective rule consequentialism: The right rule is that which if followed by the agent will lead to the best consequences.

Direct subjective rule consequentialism: The right rule is that which the agent is justified in believing if followed will lead to the best consequences.

Indirect rule consequentialism: The right rule is that which, if all or most agents followed it, would lead to the best consequences.

Direct objective motive consequentialism: The right motive is that which if possessed by the agent will lead to the best consequences.

Direct subjective motive consequentialism: The right motive is that which the agent is justified in believing if possessed will lead to the best consequences.

Indirect motive consequentialism: The right motive is that which, if all or most agents possessed it, would lead to the best consequences.

Direct objective virtue consequentialism: The right virtues are those which if cultivated by the agent will lead to the best consequences.

Direct subjective virtue consequentialism: The right virtues are those which the agent is justified in believing if cultivated will lead to the best consequences.

Indirect virtue consequentialism: The right virtues are those which, if all or most agents possessed them, would lead to the best consequences.

Direct objective global consequentialism: The right set of acts, rules, motives and virtues is that which for the agent will lead to the best consequences.

Direct subjective global consequentialism: The right set of acts, rules, motives and virtues is that which the agent is justified in believing if adopted will lead to the actual best consequences.

There are furthermore some extra variants of these – virtue consequentialism, for instance, can have either virtue cultivation or simply virtue possession as the key (and, if the former, needs to distinguish it from an act consequentialism that considers acts affecting one's future character subject to direct evaluation). Motive consequentialists can hold it is a particular motive or more generally an agent's whole motivation set that counts, and thus have variants of the theory.

In short, the list is not exhaustive of every consequentialist view ever proposed (how could it be?), but it does capture a very, very wide set of theories. All of them suffer from the same agent evaluation problems to the extent act-consequentialism does, because they share with act consequentialism the feature that moral rightness and wrongness is determined by the consequences of the act / rule / motive / virtue or combination thereof. If act consequentialism can overcome the difficulties then so can the other variants. If not, we have good reason to think that they will not either. The same will hold for any alternate version of the theory as long as moral rightness and wrongness is determined by the actual or expected consequences of what we do (or of the rules we follow, virtues we cultivate, motives we possess, dispositions we acquire, habits we form, or any of these in combination).

4. Appealing to hypothetical choices

Consequentialism's difficulty with agent evaluation arose because the agent evaluations were based on the evaluation of the actions the agent actually or in expectation undertook, but this depended on which choices they faced. Hence whether they faced the 'A' or 'B' set of choices radically changed their evaluation, but their features were constant.

But what if we stipulate that the set of choices agents should be evaluated upon is not the particular set of choices they face or we expect them to face in the future, but some super 'hypothetical set'? So, rather than evaluating someone who faced the A choices based on how she acted, she should be evaluated based on how she would have acted had she faced some different set.

There are at least two difficulties with this response: potential prescriptive failure and the justification of the super-set.

One feature of this 'hypothetical set' response is that someone could always do what is morally wrong and yet be a morally good agent, someone always do what is morally right and yet be a morally bad agent (this *has* to be a feature of the response, otherwise it cannot address the problem). The difficulty here, however, is the rejection of evaluative coherence between the agent and her actual actions and the ensuing prescriptive failure.

An agent thinking about what it is to be a morally good agent and to lead a morally good life – if based on hypothetical choices – doesn't need to think about the choices she actually faces but rather how she would act given hypothetical choices. This potentially abandons one extremely desirable feature of consequentialism: that it evaluates the choices we actually face and, with evaluative coherence, gives us guidance about what we should do as morally good agents. Whether it does abandon this will depend on how closely the hypothetical set tracks our actual set of choices (in principle though the bigger the set the less important become the choices we do face, so opting for 'all possible choices' even if possible is going to have severe difficulties with the prescriptive force of morality). The more closely the hypothetical set tracks the actual choices, the more salient to the agent evaluation becomes the empirical contingencies that produced those choices.

For instance, imagine we purely morally evaluate agents based on whether they would tend to produce the best consequences living on the Starship Enterprise: a no private-money economy, strong humanitarian group norms etc. As such we may well evaluate as morally good someone who typically acts wrongly in the situations he actually faces, such as the fickle money seeker who yearns for social approval. This is a problem if moral agent evaluations should have some prescriptive force in the here and now, in those situations agents actually do face (obviously, the fickle money seeker may consistently act wrongly now, but what makes him – under this suggestion – a morally good agent is that he would have acted rightly had he faced the hypothetical choices, i.e. lived aboard the Starship Enterprise). A moral theory without, or with muted, prescriptive force in the situations we actually face is problematic.

Secondly, there is the separate additional difficulty of how this hypothetical set is to be selected and justified compared to alternatives. Imagine an agent and two sets. One – the 'R-set' – contains an infinite number of hypothetical choices where the agent would act rightly. The other – the 'W-set' – contains an infinite number of hypothetical choices where the agent would act wrongly. We are, according to the 'hypothetical set' response, to morally evaluate the agent based on some part-combination of the 'R-set' and 'W-set'. If we mostly pick from the R-set the agent will be morally good. If we mostly pick from the W-set the agent will be morally bad.

The prescriptive worry arose if the hypothetical set was not based around the actual choices an agent faces (if it is, the overall worry arises). The justificatory worry is slightly different: it is that since there are multiple, in fact infinite, hypothetical sets, we can either determine the set that 'counts' based on (i) agential features, or (ii) something else. If it is based on agential features, then what we have done is to implicitly assert that there are morally good agents with features X, and morally bad agents with features Y.

So, for example, someone who thinks that having the Aristotelian virtues makes one morally good could construct a hypothetical set of choices where having such virtues leads one to produce the best consequences impartially judged and say that we should evaluate agents as consequentialists based on whether the agent would produce the best consequences given this set (that is, whether they have the Aristotelian virtues or not). This is in principle fine *if we then also abandon consequentialist action evaluations*, but obviously it is unclear if we do abandon consequentialism's theory of the right and wrongness of actions what is left of the theory. However, if we don't abandon the consequentialist action evaluations, then acting rightly and acting wrongly in the world we live in need not broadly cohere with being morally good or bad, and we potentially have a widespread prescriptive failure.

Alternatively, we could not implicitly base the 'hypothetical set' on agential features, yet if we take this route then the choice of set is going to potentially yield arbitrary agent evaluations, as the evaluations will depend on something other than the agent's features (when justifying the set choice).

For example, imagine that some agent – Bernard – would tend, under consequentialism, to act morally wrongly if an eighteenth-century pirate, act morally rightly if living on modest means in Switzerland in the 1990s, and act morally wrongly if living with a significant income in the UK in the 2000s. Bernard in fact lives on modest means in Switzerland in the 1990s and consistently acts rightly. Now, imagine our hypothetical set is the choices an eighteenth-century pirate would typically face, and it is not that some agential features are inherently good or bad (it is not, for instance, that concern for others is inherently good). Bernard is now correctly evaluated, under this suggestion, as morally bad. But any justification of this risks being arbitrary as the selection of the set of choices to evaluate Bernard upon – that of being an eighteenth-century pirate – isn't justified by reference to any particular character traits, thus evaluating his character traits based on it is problematic.

Thus overall the hypothetical set approach, though seemingly attractive, must encounter one of the earlier problems, with exactly which problem depending on how the set is determined. And this is exactly what we should expect. The problems arise from seeking evaluative coherence and non-arbitrary agent evaluations while retaining consequentialist action evaluations. But one must be rejected; a hypothetical set simply reframes the trilemma. If the set fails to resemble the actual choices the agent faces, we undercut evaluative coherence and face prescriptive worries. If it does resemble the actual choices because they are the actual choices then it produces arbitrary agent evaluations. In of itself the hypothetical set response lacks the resources to address the problem if some other response cannot.

5. What about ideal agents?

One thing, however, necessary for the problem to arise is that there are hypothetical choices where an agent would act rightly and some where they would act wrongly. But perhaps we can reject this for some 'ideal agent': that is, stipulate that there is some possible agent who would always act rightly, and thus be morally good, *no matter what the choices*. One worry, of course, is that such an agent could not even be human, but if for the sake of argument we leave that empirical issue to one side, does this answer the overall problem?

In one sense it may do, but it is a 'non-answer'. It addresses the problem in that we now have a non-arbitrary evaluation of that particular agent (and we can imagine perhaps an agent who would always act wrongly no matter what the choices, and have similarly a non-arbitrary evaluation of that particular agent). The difficulty, however, is that this would be a useful general answer *if it allowed us to infer evaluations about agents in general*. But this is exactly what it cannot do. The difficulty for agents in general is that, under consequentialism, there are situations they might face where they would act wrongly, and situations they might face where they would act rightly. Basing their evaluation on how they act in the situations they do actually face is thus not going to be determined by their features. Noting that there could be an ideal agent where this wasn't the case tells us nothing however about what should happen when this is the case. By its very premise, the ideal-agent answer cannot provide any guidance for the non-ideal agent cases, which plausibly cover almost every human agent that has existed and will do in the near future. This is what makes it a 'non-answer'. We still need a general response to the problem.

6. Denying there is an agent evaluation problem: So what if the evaluation of an agent is not determined by any of her features?

Consequentialists could simply bite the bullet: it just really is that the evaluation of agents does not depend upon their features per se but the situations they happen to face. If a selfish individual in life faces situations X, Y, Z, then she will do what is right and be morally good. If she faces situations P, Q, R, then she will do what is wrong and be morally bad. Whether she is morally bad or good just depends on what situations she faces, even if she has no control over them or even preference between them.

This, I think, without abandoning mainstream variants, is potentially the best response to the moral agent question available to consequentialism. But the central difficulty with it is that it seems to violate a very basic principle of normative evaluation, namely that a correct exclusionary evaluation of X should be determined by properties of X (by 'exclusionary' is meant that if you evaluate something overall as P it should not be also evaluated as not-P; obviously, if no matter what they do everyone is always a morally good agent and also a morally bad agent then we don't face an arbitrariness worry but rather one over evaluative coherence).

Consider the following three claims:

1. Aristotle was a great ethicist if today it is raining and a terrible ethicist if it is sunny.
2. *A Theory of Justice* is a brilliant work of political theory if it is Monday, but an awful work of theory if it is Tuesday.
3. *Moby Dick* is one of the best novels ever when the English football team is winning, but one of the worst whenever they are losing.

What appears awry with these claims is that the evaluations (a great/terrible ethicist, among the best/worst novels, a brilliant/awful work of theory) do not seem to be an evaluation of the object (Aristotle, *A Theory of Justice*, *Moby Dick*) as they do not depend upon features of the object: Aristotle has the same constitutive features if today it is raining or sunny, *A Theory of Justice* is identical on Mondays and Tuesdays, and no matter how England's valiant footballers play not a single word of *Moby Dick* is changed. Someone making the above statements seems to just misunderstand what is being referred to.

What specifically is going wrong in these examples is a failure of the descriptor to appropriately supervene on properties of the object. So too with consequentialism. If an egoist is a morally good agent given X, a morally bad agent given Y, and X and Y are not, nor do they affect, any properties of the agent, then the evaluations – morally good / bad – seem erroneous.

When we evaluate object X either in absolute terms, or in comparison to Y, for this evaluation to be *non-arbitrary*, and therefore to be compellingly *of* X then it has to be *about* X in that it is based on properties of X, on things that we think make this X what it is. It being Monday not Tuesday is not a feature of *A Theory of Justice*, hence why the evaluation of the book being contingent on the day of the week seems awry. Consequentialism's implied agent-evaluations are similarly problematic because they are not appropriately determined by features of the agent. This, as we saw with both the identical agent problem and comparative agent problem, then underpins unease about such evaluations.

The core problem does not therefore rest on the previous examples – that of the egoists, or of Sally and Bob – and the moral agent question is not addressed by simply asserting different intuitive judgements about the illustrative cases. To address it one has to show why the apparent arbitrariness of consequentialism's agent evaluations was either not true or, if true, does not undermine the correctness of the evaluations.

Now, although there is a specific concept of non-arbitrariness being used here – that exclusionary object evaluations should be determined by features of the object – as discussed in the Epilogue, this is potentially justified by a much broader account of arbitrariness in general, one applying to justified ethical and empirical beliefs.

As such, simply providing some doubts about the specific version of 'Agential non-arbitrariness' included earlier is not enough: the premise is sufficient to create the difficulties for consequentialism but not necessary, one could use any principle that entails – for instance – that identical agents should not be morally evaluated overall in directly contradictory ways.

Thus one option would be for consequentialism to supply a different rival general account of arbitrariness, one presumably that entailed that the contradictory exclusionary evaluation of identical objects was not arbitrary. Ideally this would not only give us an account of the possibility of such a position, but of its justification. I don't personally think there is such an account that can be general and yet not undermine its own adoption. But even if so, we'd need a further set of arguments then showing why that account supported consequentialism not rivals (as in adopting non-arbitrariness as a fundamental guide to correctness we have presumably put to one side the traditional justifications of consequentialism).

Coming up with, and justifying, a new general theory of non-arbitrariness specifically in order to defend consequentialism is obviously a huge task (and one I don't personally believe is possible). However, a different more straightforward way of rejecting the force of 'agential non-arbitrariness' is to argue that as a principle it is simply intuitively supported, and thus that it should be just one consideration among many, sometimes outweighed.

'Your reliance on non-arbitrary agent evaluations is intuitively determined'

Critiquing the account of non-arbitrariness for being ultimately just intuitively supported seems particularly effective in the context of this book because Chapter 3 concludes (with the 'Intuition Regress Problem') by setting out why there could be no non-circular non-arbitrary justification for using intuitions as a guide to the correctness of moral theories. So if this current chapter's insistence on non-arbitrariness in agent evaluations is intuitively determined, consequentialists can either reject this if intuitions are necessarily unreliable, or hold it not a major consideration if it's merely one intuition among many (that acting rightly involves doing what is best for everyone is, after all, pretty intuitively compelling).

I'm personally not sure if non-arbitrariness really is that intuitive – it seems too abstract a principle to evoke the usual sort of reactions – but, either way, it being intuitive isn't the argument for it: it's that you cannot hold justified moral beliefs without accepting non-arbitrariness. While this idea is taken up in the Epilogue it's worth explicitly discussing here why 'your-agent-evaluation-criteria-are-just-intuitively-justified' misconceives and underestimates the nature of the problems.

Assume, for argument's sake, that simple act consequentialism is the best form of consequentialism (you can re-run the discussion with any variant, nothing hangs on illustrating with act consequentialism). If we are justified in accepting act consequentialism then we need to be justified in accepting it over Not-Thursday Act-Consequentialism:

Act-Consequentialism: The morally right act is that which will lead to the best consequences.

Not-Thursday Act-Consequentialism: The morally right act is that which will lead to the best consequences unless it's a Thursday, in which case this does not hold.

Now the obvious option for the consequentialist here is to say that Not-Thursday Act-Consequentialism contains an arbitrary premise. In other words that evaluations should not depend on it being Thursday when the content of the evaluations – the act and its consequences – can be identical on Thursdays and Wednesdays. For instance, Not-Thursday Act-Consequentialism entails the following:

P1: If saving a drowning child on a Wednesday will lead to the best consequences it is the morally right thing to do.

P2: If saving a drowning child on a Thursday will lead to the best consequences it is not the morally right thing to do.

This is arbitrary as the evaluation – morally right/morally wrong – is not determined by some features of the object of the evaluation: the saving of the child and bringing about the best consequences. Thus the consequentialist can explicitly reject Not-Thursday Act-Consequentialism simply by adopting the general principle that arbitrariness in moral evaluations indicates non-correctness and tying this to features of the object. But, if she does so, then the claim that non-arbitrariness in agent evaluations is 'simply' or 'purely' intuitively determined, and by implication rejectable via alternative intuitions, is not open to her.

Perhaps, however, rejecting Not-Thursday Act-Consequentialism need not be done via non-arbitrariness directly, but rather via reflective equilibrium or intuitive status. Not-Thursday Act-Consequentialism is, after all, a bizarre-seeming view. Thus a consequentialist could hold the following three premises correct:

Cons1: Intuitive status is a guide to correctness.

Cons2: Non-arbitrariness is not a guide to correctness.

Cons3: Consequentialism's act evaluations are intuitive; 'agential non-arbitrariness' is not intuitive (and thus not worrying).

We seem at last to have arrived at a position whereby consequentialism can be justified and the agent evaluations can be non-problematically arbitrary in the sense previously discussed.

The difficulty, however, is that non-arbitrariness is so very hard to reject as a foundational and necessary condition of justification. For consider the following rival premises:

Int1
Intuitive status is currently a guide to correctness.

Int2
Intuitive status is a guide to correctness unless it is before the year 2050.

To justify the previous Cons1 we need to be justified in rejecting Int2 in favour of Int1 (waiting until 2050 isn't an option either, because there's always a possible Int3 with a later date ...).

The problem is that you can't reject Int2 on grounds of it being counter-intuitive, because that's entirely circular reasoning. If we assume Int1 then obviously we can reject Int2 in favour of Int1 as Int2 is counter-intuitive. But to do so we need to assume Int1, that is we need to assume the very thing we are trying to justify.

The difficulty here, in a sense, is that once you admit arbitrariness as an acceptable feature in one part of your theory-structure it will potentially undermine every part and every background justification you appeal to: for how can you defeat the arbitrary view that that type of justification doesn't hold in this particular case? The very act of seeking justified beliefs commits one to non-arbitrariness as a foundational commitment. This justificatory criterion is not based on intuitions at all, and the ultimate worry about consequentialism's agent evaluations is not based on intuitions: it's based on the foundational commitment that correct evaluations are non-arbitrary evaluations (or perhaps: correct beliefs about evaluations are non-arbitrary beliefs about evaluations). This topic is taken up in the Epilogue. The point for now is simply that consequentialism's previously discussed problems can't be dismissed with the claim it's intuitions all the way down.

7. Ignoring the problem, or giving it marginal weight

There is a sense in which consequentialism takes the moral evaluation of actions (either singularly or as sets arising from rules, motives or virtues) to be the primary task of a moral theory. This then causes difficulties in deriving agent evaluations. But perhaps consequentialism could accept this: yes, the agent evaluations may be problematic, but ultimately it is the action evaluations that we care about, for it is actions that have consequences, and we want there to be better rather than worse consequences. On this view, choosing between moral theories should be done on a range of criteria, and action evaluations should carry more weight than those of agents. Consequentialism, after all, has an impressive argument for its action evaluations – we want there to be more good and less bad in the world – and this, so the argument would go, should trump any concerns about the evaluation of agents. As Rawls argues, 'All theories are presumably mistaken in places. The real question at any given time is which of the views already proposed is the best approximation overall.'[22]

This seems plausible so put, but it may understate the overall problem. For the action evaluations and agent evaluations are potentially not *independently* correct of each other. If a correct moral theory should have evaluative coherence then correct action evaluations will cohere with correct agent evaluations, or we will need an account of how to relate them if not via general coherence. The criticisms of consequentialism's agent evaluations are thus simultaneously criticisms of its action evaluations: the two potentially stand or fall together. If the agent evaluations are not correct then this suggests the action evaluations are not correct either: consequentialism is incorrect in what it labels as morally right and wrong. The difficulties as such are hard to ring-fence.

The overall problem has been this: if the rightness of individual actions (or those as part of a set arising from a motive, rule or virtue) is determined by the expected or actual consequences, and if the rightness of actions broadly determines the goodness of agents, then an agent's evaluation will not be determined by any of her features. Denying the meaningfulness of agent evaluations leaves the theory vulnerable to amoralism. Appealing to long term consequences or those expected fails to respond to the possibility that the problem occurs in expectation and in the long-term, as in fact seems likely. Denying the general link between the rightness of actions and the goodness of agents creates prescriptive ambiguity. Holding that agent evaluations should not be determined by any agential features raises the worry that these evaluations are arbitrary and therefore incorrect. And citing the over-riding importance of the action-evaluations ignores that if the agent evaluations are incorrect that may entail the action evaluations are incorrect too. How might consequentialism evaluate agents, if at all? This is the moral agent question, and there is no problem-free answer.

Surely though that last claim is too strong: what the above discussion has done is to take some options and discuss their difficulties. Perhaps however there is some further option that has simply been left out?

This hope for the consequentialist is not well founded, as the previously discussed options are exhaustive. To see how, we can break them down into a set of premises which between them logically exhaust the possibilities.

Here, for instance, is one way to carve up the choices:

1. Agent evaluations cannot be correctly made.
2. Rough Evaluative Coherence is correct (i.e. agent evaluations should be determined by an agent's actual or expected actions), but consequentialism will not provide arbitrary agent evaluations because:
    a act-consequentialism will not provide arbitrary agent evaluations;
    b some other variant of consequentialism will not provide arbitrary agent evaluations.
3. Rough Evaluative Coherence is not correct, in that:
    a hypothetical actions should determine agent evaluations;
    b something apart from an agent's actual, expected or hypothetical actions should determine agent evaluations.
4. Rough Evaluative Coherence is correct and consequentialism will provide arbitrary agent evaluations but:
    a arbitrary agent evaluations can be correct evaluations; or
    b if two correct ethical premises (such as Rough Evaluative Coherence and Consequentialism) logically entail an incorrect ethical conclusion then the premises can still be correct.
5. The evaluations of all varieties of consequentialism are not correct.

These are logically exhaustive. One can furthermore summarize the above formally.

Let AE be 'Moral agent evaluations can be correct'. Let CON be 'Consequentialism is correct', let ACT-C be 'Act-consequentialism is correct' and let 'OTHER-C' be 'Some type of consequentialism other than act-consequentialism is correct' (such that CON↔ACT-C v OTHER-C). Let EC be 'Evaluative Coherence is correct'. Let 'ARB-Agent' be 'Arbitrary Agent evaluations', and let 'CORR(X)' represent 'X is correct'. The options above can therefore be rewritten as:

1 ¬AE
2 (a) It is not that AE ∧ EC ∧ ACT-C → ARB-Agent
   (b) It is not that AE ∧ EC ∧ OTHER-C → ARB-Agent
3 ¬EC
4 AE ∧ EC ∧ CON → ARB-Agent; and either:
   a CORR(ARB-Agent) or
   b CORR(X) ∧ (X→Y) ∧ ¬CORR(Y) is not a logical contradiction
5 ¬CON

These are logically exhaustive:

$$1 \lor 2a \lor 2b \lor 3 \lor 4a \lor 4b \lor 5 \leftrightarrow (P \lor \neg P)$$

The task for consequentialists – if they wish to avoid accepting 5 and abandoning the theory – is to decide which of the other options is least bad and whether the problems previously discussed can somehow be overcome. The fact that the difficulties were explored as argument-by-alternative does not mean hoping for some un-discussed possibility is wise.

2.3 Combination and meta-responses

All of the individually exhaustive alternatives have problems. But it's possible to construct a plausible-seeming response to the moral agent question that elides several of them or, alternatively, to 'go meta', such as by stating what this might all mean, or citing people's likely reactions or beliefs. Here are some such claims that appear promising and why, on examination, they fail to avoid or overcome the difficulties.

'Consequentialism's agent evaluations are instrumental'

The claim simply that consequentialism's agent evaluations should be instrumental and that this is not problematic appears attractive perhaps for at least two reasons. Firstly, since all forms of consequentialism supply some instrumental evaluations, extending these to agents in general is a natural move. Act consequentialism, for instance, already evaluates acts instrumentally – by their consequences – thus doing so too with agents is a natural fit for the theory, with similar possible moves for rule, motive, virtue and global variants.

Secondly, it seems also to be the case that we make instrumental evaluations of everyday objects all the time, and these appear non-arbitrary. We can readily understand the idea of a good hammer, for instance, where by 'good' we are implicitly referring to it being instrumentally useful at a range of tasks, such as pushing a nail into wood. Consequentialism, so the analogy would suggest, can simply provide similar instrumental agent evaluations.

On the surface instrumentalism therefore has a lot going for it. To make the suggestion concrete we need, however, to specify 'instrumental when?' That is, take the following eight possible situations and the premise that consequentialism's agent evaluations should be instrumentally determined by the consequences.

Agent-instrumentalist consequentialism: 'An agent is morally better than another if they would bring about better consequences were they to face situations represented by ...'[23]

1. The life choices faced by middle-aged women in late twentieth-century rural Britain if they have several children and are relatively poor.
2. Those situations where someone possessing the Kantian good will would bring about the best consequences.
3. The life choices faced by early twenty-first-century recipients of large inherited wealth who have extensive dependent extended families and reside in a middle-income country.
4. The life choices of an arable worker in the developing world who is part of the ethnically dominant majority in a country with significant inter-community turmoil and where her family has reasonable political sway.
5. Those situations where someone possessing the Aristotelian virtues would bring about the best consequences.
6. Those situations where a pure egoist would bring about the best consequences.
7. Those situations that an agent happens to actually face.
8. ...

Now obviously this list can go on and on, so if instrumentalism is correct we need to decide which of these should determine the moral agent evaluation. Here are four alternatives: (i) do it the way we do it for everyday objects; (ii) let any situation determine the evaluation; (iii) have some specific situation determine the evaluation; (iv) have only the actual situations the agent faces determines the evaluation.

Instrumentalism (i): Conventionalism

Imagine we think that part of what makes a good hammer instrumentally 'good' is that it is good at pushing a nail into wood. Now, obviously, other things could also be good at this: an elephant could lean against the nail and push it into the wood. So what makes the first 'correct', assuming we wouldn't describe the elephant as a good hammer? Well, presumably, amongst language users we simply use the term in particular ways, that is we have some conventions about what a good hammer is and which tasks count. Among different language or usage communities and in different contexts one might therefore employ the term with some variance: builders in cold climates might insist a good hammer has a non-metal grip to prevent it icing up, for casual DIY enthusiasts a good hammer might be also easily storable, for the very elderly it would be relatively light. For any such account, however, we can presumably give a rough description of the type of tasks and respective situations the evaluation is dependent upon and therefore the type of features a good hammer has. Everyday-object instrumentalism is as such conventional.

And this is an option for consequentialism if it wants to make instrumental agent evaluations. One issue is that this probably isn't the way most people typically employ such evaluations; they probably refer partly to intentions and character more explicitly than the bringing about of the best consequences when faced with certain situations. However, it's possible to imagine a community where the common agent evaluations were functionally consequentialist, perhaps where a morally good agent was seen as someone who would bring about the best consequences for his family and near-neighbours (i.e. face situations where no one else apart from these were impacted).

Why then isn't this a persuasive option for consequentialism? Well, straightforwardly, because making consequentialism's moral evaluations conventional undercuts any prescriptive edge to the theory – whether someone is a morally good agent will just depend on what the language norms are in a particular community. If, for instance, those situations where you might aid poor people or non-human animals aren't the ones the community typically considers salient to being a good agent then they won't count. But of course, there might be some sub community where they do count. With conventionalism, when this happens one option is to assert the superiority of the majority or mainstream judgement, but this will merely render consequentialism a very conservative reflection of current norms and yet lacking any obvious justification. It's not even that one could assert here that the majority or dominant elite is more likely to be right – under conventionalism the majority or dominant elite are by definition right.

While it's true that we do make everyday instrumental evaluations of common objects, the boundaries between these evaluations, such as what separates a good hammer from a good mallet, and therefore their correctness criteria, seem to be typically conventionally determined. To use this as a model for how consequentialism should make moral agent evaluations is to strip the theory of its normativity – it no longer offers justified guidance on how we should live as a moral agent, it simply reports on how the term is used.

Instrumentalism (ii): Laissez-faire instrumentalism

If it simply defers to how the majority or socially powerful use the term 'a good agent' (or how they think about the type of situations where bringing about the best consequences would be done by a good agent), consequentialism faces the obvious problem of establishing why its moral evaluations still retain any prescriptive moral force. The alternative, however, is to hold that agent evaluations can be meaningful with regard to any relatively well-defined situation.

Under laissez-faire instrumentalism we would side-step, for instance, debates about whether an elephant leaning against a nail made the elephant a good-hammer and allow us to use the term 'good hammer' to refer to achieving the goal in any situation.

Perhaps this is fine in non-moral contexts, but for a normative theory like consequentialism it comes with large costs because it permits the rejection of any evaluative coherence between an agent's evaluation and acting rightly (or wrongly). Under laissez-faire instrumentalism someone who consistently acts morally wrongly would be correct in maintaining that he is nonetheless a morally good agent under consequentialism because he is using the term 'morally good' to refer to those sets of situations where he would bring about the best consequences. Of course, he didn't actually face those situations, and those situations might be fairly wacky. But since under laissez-faire instrumentalism any set of situations can count, everyone can be a morally good agent under consequentialism, even if always acting morally wrongly.

By rejecting evaluative coherence with the situations the agent actually faces consequentialism undercuts its action evaluations in those situations: acting morally wrongly doesn't make one a morally bad agent; whatever one does one can correctly hold that it is some other hypothetical set of situations that determines the agent evaluations.

If this is to be rejected we need to stipulate that certain situations (instrumentally) determine the moral agent evaluations and that others therefore do not. One way is to hold that particular specified situations are the ones that count, the other is to hold that it is the situations the agent actually faces that count.

Instrumentalism (iii): Specific-situation instrumentalism

Rather than relying on convention or alternatively holding that any instrumental evaluation can be correct we instead could hold that one particular set of situations determines consequentialism's moral agent evaluations. For instance, we could pick one of (1) to (7) from above. If we chose (1) say, then the theory would hold that 'agents are morally better the better consequences they would bring about were they hypothetically to face the situations represented by the life choices faced by middle-aged women in late-twentieth century rural Britain if they have several children and are relatively poor'. This would immediately provide us with consistent agent evaluations: two egoists, for instance, would be both evaluated the same, as comparatively would any two agents. So what is the problem?

Well, it is two-fold. Firstly, that we require some justification of why this situation or set of situations is the one that counts, because obviously changing the situation to another would potentially reverse the agent evaluations. The worry here is that any such justification is arbitrary if it does not implicitly or explicitly reference agential features (in which case we have abandoned instrumentalism and are in fact providing an account of intrinsically better or worse agential features).

The second problem is that we have also rejected any sort of evaluative coherence, so that to be a morally good agent is not to generally act morally rightly, and to be morally bad is not to generally act morally wrongly. In fact it's perfectly possible that the reverse will hold: a morally good agent will consistently act morally wrongly; a morally bad agent will consistently act morally rightly. This undercutting of consequentialism's action evaluations arises because the situations 'that count' so to speak are not the situations the agent actually faces but some hypothetical choices. In other words, the idea that we should make instrumental agent evaluations by reference to some specified situation(s) is structurally the same as the earlier discussed 'hypothetical set' response: either the justification of the set is going to be arbitrary, or we are going to lack evaluative coherence, or indeed both.

Instrumentalism (iv): It's the actual situations that count

Finally, consequentialism could hold that agent evaluations are purely instrumentally determined and that it's the actual situations that agents face that count. This has the obvious advantage of linking being a morally good agent to generally or typically acting morally rightly.

The problem, however, is this does nothing to address the worry that such agent evaluations are therefore going to be straightforwardly arbitrary. Two identical agents could be morally evaluated overall in directly contradictory ways; two agents could have had their comparative moral evaluation reversed had they faced different situations while changing none of their features.

To hold that agent evaluations are instrumentally determined by the situations agents actually face is simply to adopt direct act consequentialism and to reintroduce the earlier problem. It is one way of verbally reframing it; it provides no new account of how it might be addressed.

Non-stated agent evaluations

The previous discussion took the idea that consequentialism's agent evaluations should be instrumentally determined and asked: determined by the consequences of the agent facing which situations? How we in principle selected the situations that count (or held all such situations count) entailed which of the earlier problems the suggestion ran into.

Part of the appeal of gesturing towards instrumentalism as the obvious solution is that it is a familiar type of evaluation. Yet the analogy doesn't work because the evaluations of everyday objects and those of a moral theory are not of the same type. You may instrumentally evaluate a hammer as 'a good hammer' with reference to certain tasks, and I may instrumentally evaluate a hammer as 'a good hammer' with reference to different tasks. In a sense, however, nothing really hangs on this: we can both be right. Instrumental evaluations – within some conventional linguistic bounds – are as such normally permissive, not exclusionary: as long as we are clear on the situations or tasks being referenced then they can all be correct. This, however, is problematic for a moral theory as moral evaluations are normally taken to be exclusionary: to describe something as morally wrong implies that it is not correct that it is also morally right.

Aside from the false everyday object analogy, claiming that consequentialism should simply supply instrumentalist agent evaluations seems an overall plausible answer to the moral agent question because the answer is general enough to be unclear as to which problems it will run into when made specific. As soon as we make it clear, however, the plausibility vanishes.

This is true more widely. It's very easy to provide a somewhat persuasive response to the moral agent question *so long as that response is sufficiently vague and leaves enough ambiguity as to which of the problems it faces*. 'Agent evaluations are instrumental', 'they're extrinsic', 'they're relational', 'they're based on the consequences', 'they're contingent on the agent', 'they're determined by green pixies based on a spin of a standard Vegas roulette wheel' – all bar one of these are plausible, but that's because all bar one of these are not clearly enough spelled out to assess: (i) whether there is evaluative coherence; (ii) whether the agent evaluations are determined by features of the agent; (iii) which of the canvassed problems the suggestion runs into. (The pixie-gamblers suggestion lacks evaluative coherence and provides arbitrary agent evaluations, as such it runs into all of the difficulties except those of the hypothetical-set response). Consequentialism can have a theory of moral agent evaluations that is plausible so long as that theory is sufficiently vague or, better still, not even stated. Or it can have a theory of moral agent evaluations that is explicit and clear but, if so, it will also be deeply problematic. The former would be ok if the latter was not true, but it is.

As such, the dispute is not over whether there exists an under-specified or ambiguous answer to the moral agent question that is superficially plausible. Of course there is; there are plenty, in fact. The dispute is over whether there exists a clear and well-specified answer that can actually address the problems. That is where the action is. The very openness of the moral agent question, and the wide range of possible responses, no doubt obscures this fact.

It is here – in preventing the 'ambiguity trick' of providing a vague general answer to the moral agent question – that the illustrative examples of the two egoists and of fundamentalist Sally and agnostic Bob are so useful. If an answer is minimally clear it should allow us to know how to morally evaluate the agents in these cases, or indicate what else we would need to know. How should consequentialism morally evaluate agents? It's not a particularly complicated question.

'What consequentialism is' responses

Here are a few variants of the same sort of idea:

C1: 'Consequentialism is a criterion of rightness.'

C2: 'Consequentialism is a theory about the evaluation of actions, not agents.'

C3: 'Consequentialism evaluates agents instrumentally – by their consequences – and thus obviously does not evaluate agents intrinsically.'

C4: 'Consequentialism *just is* the theory that the consequences determine the moral evaluation. Consequentialism treats agents exactly like everything else – like actions, like motives, like institutions, like policies – they should be evaluated by the consequences.'

One might or might not hold all or some combination of these. Importantly, however, none of them are justifications of how the theory overcomes the problems. The dispute, after all, is not about what consequentialism is – I will happily defer to the consequentialist's preferred definition – the dispute is about what the theory's criterion of rightness entails for the possibility of making moral agent evaluations. The worry is that the theory cannot make non-arbitrary agent evaluations without rejecting evaluative coherence. We are not arguing about what the theory is (unless there is some non-discussed variant which can make non-arbitrary agent evaluations with evaluative coherence, in which case this is an excellent place to start).

'What consequentialists believe/feel' responses

Relatedly, consider the following:

C5: 'Consequentialists don't care about the evaluation of agents; they care about the consequences of what we do.'

C6: 'Consequentialists won't be worried by these problems because they are well aware that there are moral luck difficulties.'

C7: 'Consequentialists share a core intuition – that the goodness of consequences matters – things that conflict with this are ipso facto rejected.'

These might all be true. But again, none of them are justifications of the theory or of how it overcomes the problems. They are simply reports of the psychological states or attitudes of consequentialists. Fine. A critic can accept C5, C6 and C7 easily, just as an atheist can accept 'Most theists aren't worried by the problem of evil because they believe in a loving god' without viewing this as an argument for why the existence of suffering is reconcilable with a caring deity.

Similarly, 'Flat-earthers won't be persuaded by evidence of a ship sailing around the world' is not an argument for a disc-shaped planet. C6 is perhaps the least convincing as it represents not even an assertion of authority but an appeal to indirect authority. It's a bit like saying 'No, the Emperor definitely has clothes on because after all his courtiers are well aware of the rumours that he's naked.'

Simply stating what consequentialists believe, or that they are not worried, or that they are unlikely to be convinced, or that they are aware of the problems, this is not an argument, it's the reporting of the content of the psychological states of those that accept a theory. It's not uninteresting, and it's potentially the beginning of a fruitful discussion. But it's not an argument.

Why not a hybrid theory?

But why not a hybrid theory? Surely it would be possible to evaluate actions in terms of rightness based on their overall consequences, and agents in terms of their having a good motivation (say).

The difficulty is that what this suggestion does is to re-introduce the earlier surveyed worries over rejecting evaluative coherence, that, for instance, we are going to face a potentially large set of situations where doing what is morally good, what we would expect of a morally good agent, is to act morally wrongly. In which case it is hard to see what the status of moral wrongness is here.

That is, if agents are morally good based on a motivation X, but actions are right or wrong based on the overall good of their consequences, then there is nothing to stop morally good agents from consistently acting wrongly, and morally bad agents from consistently acting rightly due to the set of situations they systematically face. Now, one way to mute the force of the problem would be to hold that what 'matters' is the agent evaluations, but as such what we have done is to in effect ignore the consequentialist theory of rightness and to reject the common assumption that when consequentialism identifies what is morally right (and wrong) the theory is identifying what we should (and should not) do as moral agents. To abandon this is, as discussed in 1.2 (2), to abandon the prescriptive force of morality, to raise worries over the arbitrary stipulation of the line between rightness and wrongness, and to leave the theory vulnerable to a superior mirror version with evaluative coherence.

An alternative version of a hybrid theory might hold that *both* the consequences and the presence of a particular motive determine the action evaluations.[24] [This is part-consequentialism, part-motivation ethics – the theory discussed in Chapter 2. As discussed subsequently, because of the consequentialist part it still suffers from all the problems.]

So imagine, for instance, that the moral action evaluations are determined partly by how good the consequences are and partly by whether the agent undertaking them had a good motive, and assume for argument's sake that the theory has some justification for the relative weighting. The theory has rough evaluative coherence (morally good agents tend to act rightly; morally bad agents tend to act morally wrongly). Does this type of theory overcome consequentialism's difficulties? Well, no, because the evaluations *still depend on the consequences*. Take, for instance, two identical partial egoists who also have the required moral motivation. The first consistently faces situations where her motivational set will cause her to produce the best consequences, the second consistently faces situations where her motivational set will cause her to not produce the best consequences. Since the consequences of how they act partly determine the agent evaluations, the first will be evaluated as a much more moral agent than the second, even though they share the same features. (And one can see too how analogously all the comparative agent problems will apply).

Ultimately, if we determine moral agent evaluations entirely, or even partly, by the goodness of the consequences of what agents do then the evaluation of agents will be dependent on the situations they face and not determined by their agential features. Holding there is an intrinsically good motivation potentially reduces the scale of this problem, but if the consequences still matter it does not remove it.

Isn't this a generic moral luck problem or one outweighed by the importance of the overall good?

Even if we do acknowledge the agent evaluation difficulties, however, there are two additional arguments that seem open to the consequentialist in addressing the moral agent question: (i) that the theory incorporates a universal conception of the good – everyone's interests count in assessing the overall good, and count equally – and thus represents the correct way of respecting the equal moral worth of all, a consideration that should over-ride any agent-evaluation worries; or (ii) that the initial problem appears on the surface to be a generic feature of moral luck that would potentially apply to all theories that supply moral evaluations to actions and agents.

Now, strictly speaking, the problems of moral luck are not, in fact, conflate-able to those of the moral agent question as moral luck is only a challenge to certain possible responses (and, furthermore, is typically framed as a difficulty of intuitive-fit, which the problems of this chapter do not depend upon). The claim that these were all generic problems though would potentially represent a strong response, if it were correct.

The argument of the next chapter, however, is that the problems are not endemic but rather created by a particular structure of moral theory, and thus that we can overcome them, supply moral evaluations to actions and agents, and that we can do so while still retaining the good of all as the determinant of evaluation: it is not *this* that produces the difficulties. We can reverse the order in which the right and moral agent relate to the good by evaluating agents by their strength of motivation to promote the good and then determining action evaluations derivatively. This is the motivation ethics approach, and the subject of Chapter 2.

CHAPTER TWO

Motivation ethics

2.1 The theory in outline

Chapter 1 discussed the difficulties consequentialism faced with agent evaluation. If it derived such evaluations from the evaluation of the agent's actions, then the agent evaluations were not determined by features of the agents. Basing agent evaluations not on the evaluation of what agents do left the theory with prescriptive ambiguity – living as a morally good agent and acting rightly were not systematically related. Denying that agent evaluations could be made left the theory vulnerable to amoralism. Holding that agent evaluations not based on features of the agent were unproblematic failed to respond to the worry that such evaluations were arbitrary and as such incorrect. And citing the over-riding importance of action evaluations failed to recognize that criticisms of consequentialism's agent evaluations were simultaneously criticisms of its action evaluations.

Why do these problems arise? The ultimate cause is consequentialism's action-morality structure, in that it evaluates actions based on their features (such as the good of their overall consequences) rather than evaluating agents based on their features and then deriving action evaluations from these. Overcoming the problems thus requires abandoning the action-morality framework.

Here again was the basic structure of standard consequentialism:

Consequentialism
The right is that which best promotes the good.[1]

That is, it holds the right and the good primary and moral agent evaluations derivative. I am going to propose in this chapter that we consider instead reversing the order in which the right (action) and the moral (agent) relate to the good.

Motivation ethics
Agents are morally better the more motivated they are to promote the good.

So that, for instance, a highly moral agent is highly motivated to promote the good of others, a morally depraved agent is un-motivated to promote the good of others and so on. The main difference is in whether we make actions or agents primary: consequentialism holds that actions are morally better if they better promote the good of all, and right if they best do so. Motivation ethics holds that agents are morally better the more motivated they are to promote the good.

The difference between the two theory-structures – that of consequentialism and of motivation ethics – is perhaps clearest if framed in terms of the role they give to that which is objectively valuable, as both agree that this should be central to moral evaluation, but disagree as to how:

Consequentialism
Morally better actions[2] are those better promoting what is objectively valuable.

Motivation ethics
Morally better agents are those more motivated to promote what is objectively valuable.

While they seem to have some similar components, these two structures of moral theory – if we assume some sort of evaluative coherence – are also logically contradictory (either, with evaluative coherence, entails the other is false).

This difference between them is fundamental and leaves the two theories with very different approaches to moral evaluations – witness for instance, as subsequently discussed, the stark differences between motive consequentialism and motivation ethics and their very different challenges and strengths, even as both are 'about' motivations and the overall good.

Considering it as a structure of theory, motivation ethics can therefore be thought of as two claims, with the first being the motivation ethics approach in general, and the second the moral theory version of motivation ethics that is defended in this book:

Motivation ethics (general)
Agents are better in terms of X-ness the more motivated they are that X obtains.

Motivation ethics (specific)
The objectively good goal (that is moral goal) – X – is that the overall good is promoted.

Thus one could accept the first, but alter the second (see, relatedly, Chapter 3 the discussion of why a deontological version of motivation ethics should be rejected). For the purposes of this chapter the moral goal will be taken to be that the overall good is promoted.

Any version of motivation ethics, however, will – by its very structure – entail at least three possible categories of evaluation, discussed here with regard to moral evaluations. Firstly, that of how motivated the agents are, that is their level of moral motivation. This is the moral goodness of agents and, derivatively, their actions.

Secondly, of what we might expect of agents *in general* with different levels of the moral motivation, such as whether there are things that are prima facie morally good or bad, even if in particular circumstances they might not be for a particular agent. This is an account of our general duties.

Thirdly, that of moral failure and moral progress: the ways we can live more or less moral lives. For example, there are multiple ways we can fail: by not having enough of the right motivation; by having the wrong motivation; or by being motivated by the moral goal but failing to actually successfully promote it (and, via their opposite, multiple ways we can live morally better lives).

These are the topics of the first part of this chapter. The second part discusses why an agent-centred prerogative is the wrong response to consequentialism's moral agent problems, and then why motivation ethics is not best thought of as a virtue ethics theory.

2.2 Individualized evaluations: Moral goodness

Motivation ethics holds that the degree of one's motivation to promote the good of others comprises one's moral evaluation, with 'the good of others' meant to refer to the good of all morally valuable others, minimally all human others.[3] As such particularistic motivations aimed at specific others – parental, friendship etc. – may often cohere but are not conceptually collapsible to moral evaluations, and may for some choices conflict, a topic explored in Chapter 5 on special relationships.

Thus for agent evaluations, a morally good (exemplary / heroic) agent is one significantly (highly / exceptionally) motivated to promote the good of others. A morally bad (or depraved) agent is one not even moderately (or even slightly) motivated to promote the good of others (and a morally heinous agent is one actively motivated to harm the good of others).

Action evaluations of moral goodness and badness are derived from the evaluations of agents. Thus, in the case of moral action evaluations, these are derived from what a (highly, significantly, moderately, slightly) moral agent would do, for instance:

For a particular agent:

- Doing P is *morally heroic* if a similar agent exceptionally motivated to promote the good of others would be expected to do P, but a less morally motivated agent might not.

- Doing P is *morally exemplary* if a similar agent highly motivated to promote the good of others would be expected to do P, but a less morally motivated agent might not.
- Doing P is *morally good* if a similar agent significantly motivated to promote the good of others would be expected to do P, but a less morally motivated agent might not.
- Doing P is *morally bad* if a similar agent moderately motivated to promote the good of others would be expected to avoid doing P, but a less morally motivated agent might do P.
- Doing P is *morally depraved* if a similar agent slightly motivated to promote the good of others would be expected to not do P, but a less morally motivated agent might do P.
- Doing P is *morally heinous* if a similar agent motivated to harm the good of others might do P, but an agent motivated to promote the good of others would not do P.

The term P could be an action or set of actions, and all the evaluations of course reference doing P relative to a particular choice set. The positive evaluations are also restrictive – to act morally well requires doing so partly with the right motives – whereas the negative ones are permissive: one can avoid acting badly out of non-moral motives. (As agent evaluations are primary this does not create worries over prescriptive ambiguity.)

To sum up, very roughly, an action is morally good (exemplary / heroic) if it requires being significantly (highly / exceptionally) motivated to promote the good of others. It is bad (depraved) if it requires not being moderately (or even slightly) motivated to promote the good of others.

Four things are perhaps initially of note. Firstly, 'similar' in what sense? Similar here refers to similar in terms of the agent's non-moral motivations and abilities. One very important implication is that something that is morally good for one individual might be morally heroic for another. Someone with a deep fear of water who still saves a drowning child might act morally heroically, whereas a water-loving swimmer might only act in a morally good manner (assuming what motivates them both is a concern for the child). While our duties – see 2.3 – are similar across agents, moral goodness is agent-specific and contingent on the ways the particular agent differs from agents in general.

Secondly, the term 'expected' in the formulations is included as there is sometimes an imperfect fit between what we are motivated to bring about and what ends up occurring. Even for such an agent-based account of moral goodness, 'resultant' moral luck will intrude as a feature of a more general gap between being motivated to bring about certain changes in the world and those changes occurring as a result.[4]

The potential falsity of our beliefs will also entail that an action can be subjectively morally good (or exemplary) yet may not be objectively so: the subjective evaluations reflect an interpretation of 'be expected' based on the agent's justified beliefs, the objective evaluations reflect an interpretation of 'be expected' based on true beliefs.

So, for example, imagine someone regularly gives money to a local beggar with the belief that this will improve the beggar's life. While this may be subjectively morally good, for it to be objectively morally good is has to be the case that it does actually improve their life, and not, for instance, have unintended negative consequences. What matters for objective moral evaluations is what actually obtains. The moral motivation, after all, is a motivation that the good of others is actually promoted, not that we *try* to promote it, do our duty, or can simply tell ourselves that we believed we were promoting it.

But have we not, with subjective and objective evaluations, reintroduced the worry here over a lack of evaluative coherence? For while a morally good agent will do what is subjectively good, she need not necessarily do what is objectively good (if, for reasons that she could not foresee, her action fails in some sense, or if she has false empirical beliefs). Consider for instance a case adapted from Williams.[5] Your friend Shahed is thirsty and so you pour him what you believe is a gin and tonic, something he loves. However, in fact someone has replaced your gin with petrol.

It's possible under motivation ethics that you are a morally good agent who here did what is subjectively good but is objectively bad. If so, we seem to lack evaluative coherence between the objective evaluation of an action, and the evaluation of an agent.[6] Why isn't this a problem of the same sort as when consequentialism lacked general evaluative coherence between an agent and her actions?

The key difference is that coherence in one's moral beliefs is desirable *from the perspective of a particular belief holder or agent* (and this is why the lack of it produced worries over prescriptive ambiguity: acting rightly and acting as a moral agent were potentially different even from the perspective of the person acting). Thus in the gin case, when you pour Shahed the drink, if you do what is subjectively good then it must be that you do what you could be justified in believing is objectively good. On the latter you can, however, be mistaken, but this is not a problem of the coherence of your beliefs, merely their fallibility. Thus the difference between subjective and objective evaluations poses no special problems for evaluative coherence so long as this goal is referenced to a particular belief-holder.

Thirdly, judgements of motivation levels are intended to be general judgements given what it is like to be a human: to be significantly motivated to further the good of others is to be significantly motivated for a human being. Now, in most cases our general sense of what it is like to be human may be sufficient to make such judgements – what level is high or exceptional for a human etc. Yet there remains an important issue as to the nature of this judgement. In other words, what, for a human being, is a reasonable, significant, high or exceptional level of a motivation to further the good of others? The default here is that this is best considered as an empirical judgement about psychological variation in humans, specifically about the variance, in contemporary and psychologically normal humans, of levels of the same rough type of non-egoistic motivations as the moral motivation. A reasonable level would thus be roughly that of most agents, a significant level of a sizeable minority who are less egoistic, a high level of the small minority with the least relative egoistic motivation levels and an exceptional level that of those very few individuals who manage to live with persistent and really dominant non-egoistic motivations.

Note that this is a judgement of the level of such type of non-egoistic motivations, not the content: it might be that while most people have large such motivations these are rarely directed at the correct good of all others, they might for example often include treating some humans as less than equal. That is, while it is true that one can act morally badly out of dominant egoistic motivations, one can also act morally badly by having non-egoistic motivations that are not focused on the real good of others (someone who thinks torturing people is in the interests of the tortured is going to act very badly indeed).

The content of the moral motivation represents a normative claim based on a theory of the good, even if motivation levels require themselves an empirical judgement of human nature, possibility and motivational variance. As the theory holds that it is agent evaluations that are fundamental, and comparative in nature, the qualitative labelling of motivational levels assumes secondary importance, as we can be clear in principle how agents could be, and live as, morally better or worse agents.

Yet our sense of human variance may still mask an important issue – namely whether it is right to for qualitative evaluations to be based on some distribution of others. This topic is taken up at length in Chapter 4, since it marks a significant departure from our common way of thinking about moral evaluations, and indeed even ideal-agent evaluations such as that of the Kantian or of the virtuous individual. For present purposes human variance is that implicitly being referred to.

Finally, why the good 'of others'? If motivation ethics morally evaluates agents based on their level of motivation to promote the good, why do the specific formulations refer to their level of motivation to promote the good 'of others'? This latter formulation is used for expositional clarity based on an implicit assumption that human individuals are much more strongly motivated to promote their own good than that of all affected, and thus that the two formulations, 'the good' and 'the good of others', will be functionally equivalent.

In those situations where this doesn't hold, however, then the correct formulation would be to base evaluations on an agent's motivation to promote 'the good'. The formulation 'the good of others' is merely employed to emphasize the expected centrality of a potential clash or tension between our own interests and that of others in many situations, and how this affects moral evaluations given our normally much greater motivation to promote our own interests.

How, though, does motivation ethics address the moral agent question or avoid analogous problems focusing on actions? The central way it does so is by deriving the moral evaluation of actions from the moral evaluation of agents *where the latter tracks specific features of the agents underpinning why they might or might not undertake the actions*, in this case how motivated they are to promote the good of others. In principle identical agents will not be evaluated differently, though in practice there is often much epistemic uncertainty over how we are truly motivated, for sometimes only when faced with certain situations do we find out much about ourselves. As the theory's primary focus is agents there is also no principled problem with comparative agent evaluation: morally better agents are those more motivated to further the good of others.

It is true that, with evaluative coherence, which the theory has, some superficially similar actions may be evaluated differently. If two people both help someone in distress, one for reward, the other out of concern for the other person, then the money-seeker merely managed to avoid acting morally badly, and the other acted in a morally good manner. That they superficially do the same actions which are then (if we know why they do so) morally evaluated differently is not problematic however as it fails to create the difficulties that accrued to similar agents being evaluated differently because the ultimate evaluation is of agents.

To illustrate, we can compare motivation ethics with motive consequentialism. For as both share the determinant of evaluation – it is the good of all that matters – they may superficially appear similar. Both seem to be focusing on motivations, and both conceive of promoting the overall good as central to moral evaluation. Yet they are operating within very different frameworks, and this difference matters greatly in overcoming the moral agent problems:

Motive consequentialism (or utilitarianism) holds that 'one pattern of motivation is morally better than another to the extent that the former has more utility than the latter'.[7]

Motivation ethics holds that an action is morally good (exemplary / heroic) if it would be expected of an agent only if they were significantly (highly / exceptionally) motivated to promote the good of others.

Now consider again from Chapter 1 fundamentalist Sally, who gives half her salary to charity to appease her vengeful God, but cares nothing for those she helps, and agnostic Bob, who gives a quarter of his salary out of a desire to relieve suffering.

For motive consequentialism Sally is a much better moral agent: her pattern of motivation is consequentially much better than Bob's (and incidentally if hers were widespread much better consequences might ensue than if Bob's were, thus this might hold for indirect motive consequentialists too). For motivation ethics, though she does what has good consequences, Sally is not a morally good agent, for she has no motivation to further the good of others: she is an egoist who happens to believe that her interests are best served by aiding others. Bob on the other hand is at least morally good and plausibly morally exemplary, for he demonstrates a level of motivation to further the good of others that is very high for a human being: most people with developed-world incomes, after all, fail to give a mere five per cent to charity. Even for an action morality focused on motivations – as with motive consequentialism – the structural difference with motivation ethics is significant.

Considering motive consequentialism also usefully highlights what the key source of difference is between motivation ethics and consequentialism. The dispute is not over whether we can meaningfully think of the overall good (a deontologist could easily accept this) – the difference is over the criterion of rightness. For motivation ethics, consequentialism is incorrect in how it determines what actions are morally right and wrong. Its theory of rightness – that the rightness of actions should be determined by the goodness of their consequences – is incorrect. Both theories use the overall good to morally evaluate actions, but the way they do so is very different. If consequentialism is correct then motivation ethics is not, and vice versa.

But aren't the action evaluations arbitrary?

The earlier argument was that consequentialism supplied arbitrary agent evaluations as these were not determined by features of the agents (or the theory had to deny the possibility of agent evaluations or rough evaluative coherence, with the attendant problems). But can we not flip this critique around and apply it to motivation ethics' action evaluations?

The reason this critique doesn't work is that there is a central dis-analogy: while the motives behind some actions are part of the undertaking of that action, the situations an agent faces are not part of the agent. They might influence the agent's future self, but this is a contingent feature – after all, they might not.

For similar reasons, any theory that supplies agent evaluations has ample grounds to identify what is wrong with the amoralist: in motivation ethics' case that she is potentially not motivated by the interests of others, in the case of virtue ethics that she lacks the virtues, for Kantians that she lacks the good will and so on. A theory that supplies action evaluations but cannot supply non-instrumental agent evaluations lacks such resources: if the amoralist consistently does what is morally wrong, this does not represent any valid criticism or evaluation of her, it is simply a feature of what she has done.

2.3 Generalized evaluations – duties

All the evaluations supplied above were 'individualized', that is, they provide a framework for thinking about how to evaluate the actions of an individual agent given a particular set of choices and facts about their psychology, commitments and beliefs. As noted, this means that it is possible that multiple individuals may undertake what appears to be the same action yet the moral evaluation of their actions in fact vary, such as the difference between saving a drowning child for money, doing so out of concern for the child, and doing so out of concern for the child while simultaneously overcoming a terror of water.

In addition, however, we may want to try to think through and discuss moral evaluations *in general*, such as whether there are things that we expect to be morally good or bad (or heinous or heroic) for agents in general even if in some cases this might be mitigated or amplified based on particular facts about the person in question. One of the main reasons for doing so is that this allows us to collectively think through a range of problems without having to know all the specifics of the particular individuals, and as such allows us to be able to better share the fruits of moral enquiry.

A rough analogy would be with the question of what is a 'good diet for health?' Well, at the time of writing, it is generally thought that five portions of fruit and vegetables a day, oily fish twice a week, and alcohol in moderation, is generally good for people. But not for some. Those allergic to fish, for instance, should definitely disregard part of this. While there might be a correct answer to the general question of what is a good diet for health, we should not expect this to be true of everyone. The individualized answer will be contingent on a host of particular facts – family history, exercise, known diseases, habits and so on. There are things that are true of people in general even if not true of everyone in particular.

Duties, if understood as things that morally good agents would generally in expectation undertake, or avoid with negative duties, as such follow the same logic. Thus the motivation ethics' account of duties follows fairly straightforwardly from its account of moral goodness (which is individually specific). So that:

- There is a basic negative duty to not do X if doing X would normally require being less than moderately motivated to promote the good of others.

- There is a basic positive duty to do Y if doing Y would normally require being significantly motivated to promote the good of others.

- There is a supererogatory duty to do Z if doing Z would normally require being exceptionally motivated to promote the good of others.

This does not, of course, guarantee that someone who fulfils a positive duty necessarily did what is morally good, or that someone who fails to fulfil a negative duty necessarily did what was morally bad: while there is general evaluative coherence between the moral goodness of an individual and their actions, there is only coherence between an individual's duties and their expected moral goodness, not knowing any of the particular ways he differs from agents in general. (In the same way, while eating a diet that 'generally' promotes health will be expected for most individuals to cohere with the diet that for them personally actually does so, there will always be exceptions assuming a certain level of human variance).

One thing also of note is that we may often have a positive or supererogatory duty to do one of a series of alternative actions. Giving 10 per cent of your developed world income specifically to Oxfam will not be a moral duty, but giving 10 per cent of your developed world income to charity to promote the good of others is, as is making a reasonable effort to work out what will best do this.

Now one worry here is that these duties have some 'grey area' at the margin. Does giving twenty per cent of one's income to charity require a significant level of moral motivation or an exceptional level?[8] The worry would be that this renders the account of duties 'too vague' given the goal of allowing us to discuss and collectively think through the range of common moral problems.

There is some truth to the premise of this critique – the boundaries are in principle not stark (see Chapter 4) – but not to the inferred critical conclusion. For even if the boundaries are rough, and actions near these difficult to judge, there are going to be a great many actions that fall quite some way away from the boundaries. Giving no money to charity is to disregard a basic duty. Inflicting pain on others (without their consent) is to violate a negative duty. Showing concern for future generations in how we live is a basic positive duty. Risking one's career and livelihood to challenge discriminatory office norms is to fulfil a supererogatory duty and, given the normal pattern of concern people have for their career, to act morally heroically. But if the person is instead seeking to be made redundant and indifferent to others he may have not acted in even a morally good manner, even though he fulfilled a supererogatory duty. Even if the border between India and Pakistan is disputed, we can still be confident on which side of it Mumbai is to be found.

2.4 Moral failure and moral progress

Built into the very idea of evaluating agents by their level of moral motivation is a tripartite account of moral progress and of failure in how we live and what we do with our lives. That is, if agents are more moral the more motivated they are that X obtains, then there are three main ways we might expect to live morally better lives (and via their converse three main ways we might fail morally and live morally worse lives). Firstly, we might become more morally motivated by increasing the relative strength of our moral motivation. Secondly, we might, through moral reasoning or external influence, improve on the content of the motivation, removing unjustified partiality or errors. And thirdly, we might improve our effectiveness at actually bringing about X, either by increasing our capacities and powers or improving our understanding of causal mechanisms and the relevant empirical facts.

Moral progress I: Becoming more morally motivated

Since agents are more moral the more motivated they are that X obtains (for the version of ME defended here, that the good is promoted), then one form of moral progress is obviously to become more motivated that X obtains.[9] But how might this work?

One way is to try to personally directly change how we are motivated, such as by (i) adopting as a goal various actions or activities that we think will aid others and that without adopting them explicitly as a goal we might fail to do, (ii) by seeking to reduce or enhance the potency of a range of motivations so that in the relevant expected situations they have more sway, or (iii) by shifting our beliefs, attention or framing of choices so that we will be more likely to do what will help others.

The extent to which this is possible will hinge on the empirical question of how plastic or malleable our motivational sets are, and how much influence we can have either via our desire to change the way we would otherwise live or via the belief that we should do so. To see why, we can imagine two fictional quasi-humans at different ends of a hypothetical scale.

Firstly, there is Malleable Mike. Mike's evaluation of his motivational set is perfectly causal. If he decides he'd like to love opera or never care about his own interests or always care about his own interests or desires to be a diligent chess player or never feel the urge to sleep then he instantly does so. Rather than the complex, sticky and messy patterning of human motivations, Mike's motivational set is like very, very malleable putty. He decides he'd like to be motivated like P and he is.

At the other end of the scale is the quasi-human Fixed Felicity. For Felicity, her evaluation of her motivational set is utterly irrelevant to the set's development or future content. She might want to try to become better friends with someone by spending more time with that person, she might want to acquire more diligent habits when it comes to work, she might seek to fall in love or to weaken her urge for snacking on smoked salmon. Yet all of this is irrelevant: her evaluative mental states cannot have any impact.

Specifically, underpinning the question of where on the scale between Mike and Felicity most humans fall, there are two different types of mental evaluative state that might alter our motivational set and as such allow us, via personal influence, to become morally better or worse and to live morally better or worse lives.

Firstly, there are our evaluative beliefs. These are causally inert, or causally potent, to the extent that were we to have different such beliefs we would come to have a different motivational set. For example, if someone believes that some desire she has is 'bad', then is she more likely to have that desire at at least the same strength than if she evaluated it as 'good' (or desirable, or the type of thing a person like her should have, and so on)? If yes, and if always yes, her evaluative beliefs are causally inert with regard to her motivational set. If she could always change her motivational set based on such beliefs then her beliefs are causally perfectly determinate as to her motivational set. My own opinion is that human psychology is such that the truth lies in between and will vary partly by content as well as a range of other factors that vary across individuals. Motivation ethics itself does not depend on this being one way or the other: what does depend on it is our potential for moral progress with regard to the relative strength of our motivations.

In addition to having evaluative beliefs, however, we might have second-order motivations. That is, we might be motivated to change how we are motivated. So, for instance, on a desire-based view, if we desire that some particular desire, P, is less strong, then our second-order desire is causally efficacious to the extent that it would change our level of P compared to alternative desires about P. So that, imagine we have a strong desire for sweets after dinner, but also desire that we didn't feel that way. Well if the second-order desire can effect how much we desire sweets after dinner then it is causally influential and the level of effect it has will speak to its level of influence. For Malleable Mike these might be perfectly influential. For Fixed Felicity exactly the opposite.

Whether these two types of evaluative state – evaluative beliefs and second-order motivations – are collapsible will depend on our psychological theory, and in principle motivation ethics is compatible with either (the question would be: can we have a second-order desire without having the evaluative belief that the first-order desire is good or in some respect positive or endorsed?). What the possibility of such beliefs and of such second-order motivations creates however is the possibility of personally instigated moral progress by improving how we are motivated: either by increasing the strength of the moral motivation or reducing the potency of those we expect to clash or be in tension with it.

Tracking this scale will be an assessment of our moral praise or blameworthiness for our character: the more effort it takes to live a more moral life, a life more motivated by the needs of others, the more praiseworthy we will be for managing to do so. This is not collapsible to evaluations of moral goodness: we can imagine for instance that Fixed Felicity could do nothing even with immense effort about how she in the future is motivated, and as such she would not be blameworthy even if she was only slightly motivated to promote the good of others, yet at the same time she would still not be a morally good agent. Blameworthiness and praiseworthiness speak to the question of how agents might otherwise have been, something conceptually distinct to the question of how to evaluate how agents actually are.

Finally, the above discussion has been with regard to motivational change from the agent's perspective, yet it is perfectly possible that external influences can change how we are motivated – either directly or via evaluative beliefs or second-order motivations. People growing up or living in an environment where concern for others is promoted and encouraged may end up showing more concern for others not because they are smarter than those in a less considerate society, nor anything due to genetics, but rather potentially – to the extent people really are motivated by a concern for others rather than simply to appear concerned – due to a combination of socialization, societal and economic change, political institutions and change in social norms. Moral progress, for motivation ethics, may come from various psychological features of the agent, but it may also come from various features of the agent's environment (and also thus, alas, moral failure may too).

In principle, however, whatever the causal origin, if a morally better life is normally a life lived more motivated that the good is promoted, then anything that increases the relative level of such a motivation can be a potential source of moral progress.

Moral progress II: Improving our moral understanding

In addition to changing our level of motivations it is possible we might change the content, specifically our normative beliefs. Imagine someone who comes to realize that animal suffering is objectively bad, or that the welfare of those who don't look like 'his people' is just as real. Such a person might not, in one sense, change his motivational set: he could still, for instance, be relatively altruistically motivated compared to egoistically. Yet his improved moral beliefs will likely lead him to act and live as a morally better agent. This is one extremely important source of moral progress.

In particular, even if one is somewhat sceptical that a range of egotistical impulses can be radically reigned in due to the relative implasticity of such human motivations, it will still be the case that people's beliefs might be capable of revision, and this will change what they do.

My personal opinion is that this has been the source of immense, though uneven, moral progress over the last hundred or so years. To crudely generalize: it was broadly the case that perhaps a majority of people in Britain at the start of the twentieth century thought that women were inferior to men, that white people were superior to other races, that animal suffering did not significantly matter, that gay people were morally depraved, that wealthy people morally deserve their wealth (rather than predominantly simply being lucky) and that the wellbeing of foreigners was of decisively less importance than that of our own people. At the moment there are still alas a large number of people who hold a range of these views, but the number is surely radically less. This is transformative moral progress.

It does not, strictly speaking, require that we change our assessment of the contours and patterning of human motivation: people who lived a century ago are extremely recognizably like us in their fear, and hope, and jealously and kindness. Yet, even those motivated to try to help others and leave the world a better place potentially have radically different beliefs about what this entails and in particular about whose interests are included in this and to what extent.

For motivation ethics we are morally better the more motivated we are that the good of all others is promoted. As such, the more our broadly altruistic motivations actually track the actual good of others the more moral lives we can expect to live. The content of our moral beliefs about the good, about what makes morally valuable beings' lives go better and whose lives are to be included, matters hugely. This is the second form of moral progress (of which ethical reflection, discussion and thought may well be a crucial contributor).

Moral progress III: Efficacy

The moral motivation is a motivation that X obtains. It is not a motivation that one *tries* to bring about X. It is not a motivation that one does one's duty or is seen to be a moral agent. What matters, for the version of motivation ethics defended here, is that the lives of others go well, that there is less suffering, less injustice, less oppression. As discussed, we can be more or less motivated that this occurs, and we can have better or worse views about what in principle this would mean: who is included and how. But we can also be better or worse at actually succeeding. This is the third type of potential moral progress in how we live: efficacy.

To see why, imagine someone who has broadly correct moral beliefs – his conception of the good is correct. And he is significantly motivated that this is promoted, that the lives of others go well. Yet he fails in this goal. He is, according to the theory, a morally good agent (assuming that he could not easily do something about his failure, so that his concern really is to promote the good of others not merely to try). Yet, he does not succeed in living an objectively morally good life. The reason for this can be at least two-fold: due to false empirical beliefs (the 'Leech bleeding problem') or execution errors (the 'Bertie Wooster problem').

For motivation ethics, an objectively morally good (or heroic) life is normally a life lived where we were significantly (or exceptionally) motivated to promote the good of others, where this made a major difference to how we would have lived otherwise,[10] and *where we succeeded in this goal*. But how might we fail?

Well, one way is by being mistaken about what will promote the good of others. That is, imagine a doctor living some time ago who believes that a range of diseases can be cured or ameliorated by having leeches suck the blood of the patient. It might well even be that, given the state of medical and scientific knowledge, that this is a justified – but false – belief.

Nonetheless, a doctor spending her career doing such bleeding will not live an objectively morally good life: she will harm others unnecessarily and avoidably. What is at fault here is not her motivations, but her empirical beliefs. She may well – assuming her motivation to help the others is sincere – lead a subjectively morally good life, but ultimately it will be, objectively at least, a life of significant moral failure. This flows, quite straightforwardly, from the fact that for motivation ethics the moral motivation is that X obtains, and as such whether X actually obtains – via our understanding of causal mechanisms – is central.

For this reason, morally motivated agents are agents motivated to try to improve their relevant causal understanding. It matters, for example, that we can find actual ways to better combat climate change and prevent the likely associated massive human welfare loss, not merely that we try. Succeeding matters, because what actually happens to others is what matters.

Secondly, and relatedly, we can think of an individual who is morally motivated, and who may well have a reasonable grasp of the relevant causal mechanisms, but who is just terrible at bringing about desirable outcomes due to repeated execution errors. This is the 'Bertie Wooster problem'[11] – no matter how sincerely Bertie sought to help various people, his blundering typically made things worse, at least in the short term. For motivation ethics, again, he will potentially fail to successfully lead a morally good or exceptional life, even if he is a morally good person. This need not entail Bertie is blameworthy; that will partly depend on what with effort he might otherwise have done. But it does mean that morally motivated individuals need to care about the ways in which they can fail to achieve goals, both in the short term and the long term, even if their motivation is sincere. What matters objectively is that we succeed.

As such, for motivation ethics what we often think of as virtues are instrumentally morally evaluated. Would becoming more courageous help me better promote the good? If so, cultivating this virtue might be moral, yet there is nothing necessarily moral about courage: if cultivated to serve the end of harming others it would immoral. If efficacy matters then clearly any traits we can develop that would aid this would morally matter too, but they would only do so contingently and instrumentally (the difference with virtue ethics is quite stark: see 2.7 too).

Overall, motivation ethics, both the version defended here and in general, entails a tripartite account of moral progress and failure. This corresponds straightforwardly to the fact that if it matters that X obtains, then as agents we can approach or depart from contributing to this: we can be more motivated that X obtains, we can have better beliefs about what X is, and we can more effectively bring about X via better empirical understanding or greater causal competency.

As such, the account of moral progress and failure is not, I think, an independent argument for motivation ethics (or against it) but simply a feature of the view. If agents are morally better the more motivated they are that X obtains, then we have an associated account of moral failure and progress. For intuitionists (see Chapter 3), this might bear on the correctness of the theory. But in principle it need not. It will simply speak to the question of, if motivation ethics is correct, how in practice, when thinking about what to do with our lives, we might come to live a morally better life, or fail.

Multiple evaluations, and on what matters

With the previous discussion in mind – of objective goodness, subjective goodness, duties, moral progress in motivation, in understanding, in efficiency and so on – why are there seemingly so many types of evaluation? These all stem from the core motivation ethics normative claim – that agents are morally better the more motivated they are that X obtains – *combined with a series of empirical observations about human beings.*

Subjective and objective evaluations of the moral goodness of actions stem, for example, from the core motivation ethics claim combined with the observation that an agent can have justified beliefs that are nonetheless false (thus subjective evaluations track justified beliefs, and objective ones track true beliefs).

Similarly, since there is empirical variation in the motivational sets of human agents, we can think of action evaluations specific to a particular agent (moral goodness) or generally true of agents (duties). The possibility of motivational change – in level or content, and of a change of causal potency – creates different possibilities for moral progress. And since we can personally potentially influence our future motivations, the question of how we do so and what level of effort we expend in doing so can result in evaluations of praise or blameworthiness for our character. All these simply stem from basing agent evaluations on the strength of a particular motivation (and deriving action evaluations from what such agents might and might not undertake) and combining this with certain prominent empirical features of human beings as agents.

To be clear: the case for motivation ethics, in competition to consequentialism say, does not at all rest on the judgement that agent evaluations are 'the most important' or 'what really matters', since it is entirely silent on this question. It merely draws upon the question of how and whether such evaluations should be made.

Yet that said, there is a natural focus for such a motivation based view on lifetime evaluations, on what we do with our lives and whether we manage to live morally good or even highly moral lives in that we have a real positive impact on the lives of others. My own opinion is that this is the 'most important' question. For motivation ethics the right way to think about this is to think about a hypothetical agent with the same abilities as yourself, the same potential and the same sort of choices, and to try to think of the type of impact on the overall good the hypothetical person could have if this were a moderate or even significant motivation in how he or she lives their lives and chooses what to do with their time, energies and abilities. This will potentially vary by individuals massively: some by background, genetics, opportunities, assets or all four end up with the capacity to have a much bigger impact on the overall good than others, and in their case living a morally decent or even exemplary life would involve having such a bigger impact.

It is this longer-term question that we should expect our dominant motivations to most clearly speak to and also to provide a framework for assessing how we live. For someone who is motivated that the overall good is promoted it is also this issue that ultimately matters: the type of impact you could have on the good in the long term, not merely in isolated situations. How important of a goal in your life would it have to be to achieve this? If you can impact the good positively with this only being one among many minor motivations then to do so is perhaps to avoid living a morally bad life but no more. If making a sizeable impact involves significant commitment then doing so is to live morally well.

This is invariably going to sometimes be a difficult question to think through: it involves a judgement of a range of psychological phenomena as well as general empirical mechanisms (would living like that really make such a difference? Would some goals end up de-motivating you in the long term? How much power and influence can you potentially wield, and will the process of acquiring this change what you will end up doing with it?).

Sometimes, however, it is going to be more straightforward: avoiding factory farmed meat is not that difficult, giving a proportion of your income to charity to reduce suffering can with practice become part of the way you live over time, and supporting political action in favour of institutions, policies and political actors liable to better promote the good is eminently feasible. Thus while the case for motivation ethics does not at all rest on the assertion that agent evaluations are 'most important', it does naturally lend itself to focusing on the levels of long-term motivational commitment it might take to impact the overall good when we choose what to do with our lives, and when we live as such.

We can therefore think of a range of hypothetical agents as a guide to the possibilities for our own lives. We can think of someone with the same abilities and opportunities as ourselves, but unconcerned for others: to live as they would is to fail to live a moral life at all. We can think of someone with a reasonable and consistent concern for others and think of the ways they might live, and how we might similarly live a morally decent life. And we can think too of someone like us yet very strongly motivated by the good of others, with this powerfully influencing their most important decisions. The closer we can approach this, the more moral will be what we do with our lives and how we use our potential as agents, as beings that can impact what happens in the world.

Is there a motive fetishism or self-defeatingness worry?

Since motivation ethics holds that moral agents are motivated to promote the good of others, what if best doing so would be to try to cultivate alternative motives? This may seem empirically unlikely but it is not impossible, and as such wouldn't a highly moral agent potentially want to become less moral because they are moral? The alleged dilemma would be that if we hold this isn't possible – in that moral agents should necessarily retain the moral motivation – then the theory would seem to be placing undue weight on motives compared to the good. We appear therefore to be faced with a choice either of holding 'what matters' is having the moral motive and motivation ethics being accused of motive-fetishism, or of having the moral motive possibly in some situations counsel trying to become less moral (where the worry then would be that the theory was self-defeating).

While the temptation here might be to dismiss these sort of concerns as empirically implausible, this would, I think, be unnecessarily defensive. It is true that, realistically, the best way for most of us to have a large positive impact on the lives of others will be to retain a strong concern for them, to try to buttress and entrench this in our motivational sets, to try to acquire the habits that allow this to lead to actual other-assisting acts, and to dampen and undermine those motivations that would conflict with this.

That said, this is an empirically contingent claim. One can think of situations where this would not hold, where for instance a morally heroic agent – one with an exceptionally strong motive to promote the good of others – came to realize that the best way of doing so in the very long term was to try to replace this motive with some other non-moral one. Imagine this occurred, and over time she did replace this motive with some other. What should motivation ethics say here?

Well, straightforwardly, that her decision to change her far-future self was morally heroic (assuming it really did require her being so other-concerned) and that the distant future self she created was less moral. *But so what?* Motivation ethics is not – at all – committed to the claim that the evaluation of agents should be the same over time if the agents' motivational features undergo radical change.

This would, of course, be a problem (of self-defeatingness) if the moral motive was a motive to be moral. But it isn't. It is a motive that the good is promoted, in other words that the lives of others go well. This is thus perfectly consistent with the idea that if we really can alter the motivations of our future selves then the moral motive might cause a highly moral agent to become a less moral agent. The empirics of this might be weird, but they are not impossible, and their possibility doesn't undermine the correctness of the theory's evaluations.

It is not, importantly, therefore that a highly moral agent would intrinsically want to become less moral because she is moral. She would want to become a better promoter of the good of others. That this might, in theory, entail her far-future self being a less moral agent is a side effect, not an intrinsically desired outcome.

One analogously can see this sort of dynamic in a more familiar worry about people running for elected office at a young age. It seems empirically all too plausible that while someone might start off in elective office (or in the long process of obtaining it) with a sincere and very strong concern for others, a concern that is much more potent than his own self-interested motivations, as time goes on the very experience of having one's own fate and that of others allegedly intertwined, and of surrounding oneself with those that agree, will cause the young politician to start to take it for granted that what is good for his career must ipso facto be good for the wider public. Every self-interested move, every act of ruthlessness towards others can be rationalized as, after all, once the individual personally gains power he will be able to make a huge positive difference, or so he tells himself.

This is a real and sometimes appreciated worry – it is why if you don't have a quite well-worked-through plan of what you want to do in politics (and a framework for evaluating new options) you will likely too easily adopt what is conventional and have little impact, or if your character is not fairly robust you will have it disfigured and warped to whatever structure of self-interested incentives you encounter.

All true, very true. But there is a perfectly coherent response from the young politician and that is to concede that he might become a much worse person by going into politics, but then to hold that nonetheless he might still have a more positive impact than alternatives. Even if he ends up with a lust for power some vestiges of his concern for others might still push him to have a better rather than worse impact.

This may be delusional optimism (and my own suspicion is that it normally is) but it is not incoherent: it is perfectly possible to correctly evaluate *the decision to become* a less moral agent as itself morally motivated. That motivation ethics entails that agents might – particularly if they are morally heroic – choose to put themselves in situations likely to make them less moral but more effective promoters of the good of others is a feature of the theory, yes. This is because while the theory does hold motivations central to moral evaluation, the theory does not hold possessing the moral motivation the central concern of moral agents.

To be highly or exceptionally moral is to be highly or exceptionally motivated that the lives of others go well, and it is possible this will cause an agent to acquire in the future a differently structured motivational set. One way we can impact the lives of others is by changing our future selves. While in practice this will almost always cohere with being more moral there are hypothetical empirical contingencies where it will not. So long as a theory does not hold that 'being moral' is the content of the moral motivation, however, there is no self-defeating conundrum here and no motive-fetishism.

The apparent problem comes from implicitly collapsing the evaluation of an agent at a particular time with the evaluation of their far-future self. But we need not do so. Consider, for instance, a seriously drug-addicted and sometimes violent father of an infant where the father, while estranged from the child's mother, still very much loves the child and feels the urge to be a big part of its life. He might well justifiably believe, however, that he will likely be a very destructive and overall harmful part of the child's life. It is perfectly possible that his love for the child might lead him to try to make his future self care for the child less (he might take a job a long way away for instance) and thus that child's life go significantly better. Imagine he does so. Is he a good father? There is nothing paradoxical about holding that his decision to remove himself from the child's life was that of a good father, it requiring a really quite significant concern for the child's interests, and yet also holding that the person he eventually becomes – someone who doesn't care about their child – is not a good father. This is even if we adopt a motivation-based view of being a good father (having, for instance, a real and significant motivation that the child's life goes well). The evaluation of an agent and his decisions at a particular juncture need not be the same as the evaluation of his future self even if shaping the future self was one of the goals of what the agent previously did.

Motivation ethics doesn't make a fetishism out of motives because, under the theory, moral agents don't make a fetishism out of motives: they care that the good of others is promoted. There is no problem unless we assume that the evaluation of agents at different times must be the same: yet if we evaluate agents based on their features and these features change then this justifies why the evaluation should change.

This, it should be noted, is a more general feature of any ethical theory that evaluates agents by a desire, inclination or motive that is not self-focused (not for instance focused on the desire to do one's duty or to personally obey the theory's commandments etc.).

Take for instance a quasi-Samaritan ethics where morally good agents are those actively helping people (not merely caring, but actively doing so). It is theoretically possible that a highly moral Samaritan agent would find themselves in a situation where actively helping others, perhaps saving the lives of several others, would entail it is very likely she will become paralysed. Imagine despite this she nonetheless actively helps the others – saving their lives – and does indeed become totally paralysed. Under the described quasi-Samaritan ethics she has now stopped being a moral agent as she is unable to actively help anyone. But her decision to become so was done because she was morally heroic. Her highly moral actions have caused her to become non-moral, under the theory.

But so what? Unless we think the moral evaluations of agents must be constant over time even if their features change (in this case their causal potency as an agent) there is no paradox or self-defeating feature. For most agent-moralities, there will often be extreme cases where doing something highly moral will predictably change one's far-future self possibly making her or him less moral. As long as 'being moral' or something similar is not the content of the moral motivation or desire then there is no problem here.

2.5 Why not an agent-centred prerogative?

Two important consequences of motivation ethics are that:

(i) When it is motivationally easy to promote the overall good, such as when the agent has no particularistic interests or commitments being harmed, then not doing so would be morally bad.

(ii) When it is motivationally very difficult to promote the overall good, such as when doing so comes at great personal cost, then not promoting the overall good can still be morally good (and promoting it is potentially morally exemplary or heroic).

These share some similarities with Scheffler's proposal of an agent-centred prerogative, whereby 'each agent would have the prerogative to devote energy and attention to his projects and commitments out of proportion to their weight in the impersonal calculus'.[12] That is, one can give a certain extra consideration to one's own interests (or projects) when weighing what to do, but still should give a weight to the interests of others, the extra weight for one's own interests being based on some factor M.[13] Since in situations (i) and (ii) motivation ethics and such a prerogative will provide roughly similar evaluations, how then are the two theories different, and would an agent-centred prerogative not be a potential response to the moral agent question?

The key difference in content arises because the motivational ease or difficulty of a range of actions will not necessarily track the relative weighting of our interests compared to the interests of others due both to various psychological and physiological human characteristics and perhaps most strikingly due to the alignment or conflict of interests. Sometimes doing what will best assist others is trivially easy. Sometimes it is incredibly demanding. This ease or difficulty is not solely determined by the pure weight of the agent's interests compared to that of others, but also by, and to the extent that, these are promoted by the same or different actions and one is motivated by the different interests.

With this difference in mind, we can see why such a prerogative lacks the resources to overcome the moral agent problems. For the central feature that created consequentialism's moral agent difficulties was that the evaluation of actions did not reflect both why an agent undertook the actions and how hard it was to do so, that is the agent's motivational set. Sometimes the prerogative reflects this, but it need not and often will not (as an agent's interests and the interests of others are not always in pure motivational tension).

To illustrate, consider a variant of the examples of Chapter 1. Egoist A consistently faces situations where promoting her own interests also best promotes the interests of others. Egoist B consistently faces situations where promoting her own interests also harms the interests of others, *and harms them beyond the weight permitted by the prerogative.* Given Scheffler's prerogative (and rough evaluative coherence), Egoist A is a morally good agent, Egoist B is a morally bad agent, but of course they may have identical constitutive features, raising the worries discussed in Chapter 1.

Similarly imagine that, even though giving 80 per cent of one's income to charity would be consequentially optimal, agents are allowed to give a certain weight to their own projects such that giving only 40 per cent is morally required. Even given such a prerogative, fundamentalist Sally who gives half her income to appease her vengeful god will be a morally good agent; agnostic Bob who gives a quarter to relieve suffering will be a morally bad agent. But of course given different scenarios their comparative evaluation could have been reversed. The problems remain.

Part of the appeal of the prerogative is probably that it begins to make moral action evaluations reflect the demandingness of a range of actions – and thus to help us make more plausible the implicit evaluations of agents that face such choices. But if the goal is to make compelling agent and action evaluations we need to begin, as with Chapter 1, with an account of what is wrong with the standard way of making action evaluations, *and thus what feature creates this and needs replacing.*

2.6 Is there a potential problem with a lack of calculation or practical reasoning?

For motivation ethics, evaluating hypothetical actions involves thinking through the different levels of moral motivation they would require. The conclusions of this process are a set of scalar evaluations: we can think of actions as highly, moderately, marginally moral, or morally bad or morally depraved and so on. Yet isn't there something phenomenologically wrong here? When we engage in moral deliberation surely there should be some sort of reasoning or calculation of factors that ends with the conclusion 'I should do X' or 'Y is morally permissible' or something like that. In principle deontological theories and consequentialist ones aim at this, or at least could under certain versions provide it. Isn't this then a real problem for motivation ethics?

The critique here cannot be simply that moral agents should use, or moral reflection should involve, reasoning in a broad sense, for motivation ethics requires this in significant amounts. Moral agents for instance have to think through difficult ethical questions – What is the nature of the good? How should the good of multiple persons be combined? – as well as empirical ones, such as how the world of causation works and what model of human psychology is best evidenced, and more generally what it is like to live as a human agent, how our emotions, desires and intentions interact, and how we may make moral progress and encounter moral failure.

The critique, to have bite, must in some sense be a claim about the type of reasoning a moral agent would engage in under a correct moral theory. Specifically, the claim would roughly be that moral reasoning should conclude in a belief of the type 'I should do X' or 'P is permissible.' Or perhaps to put it in the first person, the worry would be that for an agent thinking through 'What should I do?' there should be some sort of calculation of factors, or set of principles, that then produces some clear determinate recommendation. This is the calculation worry (or the worry concerning practical reason). There are, I think, three main responses open to the motivation ethicist in responding to it.

Firstly, to deny that this single-situation reasoning is really the best way to engage in moral deliberation. When we think of motivations at different levels what we typically are led towards are considerations of longer-term patterns of behaviour and considerations of certain interests. As such for motivation ethics the most useful focus is on how we live our lives in the long term and specifically on what type of impact we can have on the lives of others. Our judgements of human psychological patterning will inevitably shape the conclusions here except in the extreme cases.

Thus while murder is under motivation ethics going to be at least morally depraved and often morally heinous (and there is a very strong negative duty to not go around murdering others) the question of whether giving

10 or instead 15 per cent of one's income to charity is highly moral or extremely moral is going to involve psychological judgement of the relevant case, there is no 'Do X' that simply pops out of some reasoning process. As such, thinking about how we live our lives in the long term is likely to be a better form of moral reasoning, and the fact that this involves psychological judgement of the range of factors that impact our motivations is going to lead to these judgements being difficult at the margin, particularly if our cognitive frame is single-action cases. This type of reasoning is also going to deliver judgements concerning what would be involved in leading morally better (or worse) lives, as opposed to 'Do X' judgements.

The content of this response partly hangs on a psychological dispute about how our motivations impact our decision making, in particular how much short-term space and sway our deliberation has as compared with its role often being to provide a justificatory veneer for various ways of acting. But its underlying logic draws on the broader observation that if we are to evaluate agents by their features then this may well produce scalar agent evaluations – agential features typically come in degrees – and thus the accompanying action evaluations will be scalar too. As such this response rejects the premise of the critique: that moral action evaluations have to be intrinsically qualitative (a dispute that re-emerges in Chapter 4 on demandingness). To my mind, this is the best response.

A second response, however, is to meet the desire implicitly behind the critical premise – that is, to accept that some people apparently do want morality to just simply 'tell them what to do' – and therefore to convert motivation ethics to a formal rubric where we can do some sort of calculation which produces conclusions of the type 'Doing P is a positive duty' and 'Doing Q is morally very bad.'

That is, take a pair of possible but mutually exclusive actions, A and B. We can put these on a scale of motivational difficulty or ease based on how hard or easy their performance compared to the other would be for an egoist not motivated by the interests of others (either to promote or harm them). For convenience let this scale, 'D', range from -4 (extremely hard to avoid doing) to +4 (extremely hard to do), where 0 is that either action is trivially easy to undertake. So a moderately demanding action would be a +2 for example, something relatively difficult to avoid (compared to the other action) would be a -3 and so on. Thus taking the more demanding of the two actions (and assigning the other the same score but negative):

0 = motivationally indifferent
1 = moderately demanding
2 = fairly demanding to undertake
3 = very demanding to undertake
4 = extremely demanding to undertake

In addition to putting A and B on to a scale of motivational demandingness, we could also map A and B on to a scale of the impact of doing one action not the other in terms of the net interests of others – 'I'. By 'net interest' is meant the interests of others minus the interests of the agent:

0 = no other interests net involved
1 = minor other interests net promoted
2 = some important interests of others net promoted
3 = interests collectively significant in magnitude net promoted
4 = very important interests indeed net promoted

Thus if A has a significantly positive impact on others compared to B then A might get a score of 3 (and B as a result gets a score of -3).

We can then convert an action's scores to a numerical generic moral evaluation, that is for either action:

If $D \geq 0$ and $I > 0$ let $M = D(6+D)/(I+6)$
If $D > 0$ and $I \leq 0$ let $M = (6+D)I/4$
If $D \leq 0$ and $I \leq 0$ let $M = 3I/(1-D)$
If $D \leq 0$ and $I > 0$ let $M = 0$

If positive, the greater the action's score the more moral it is, where roughly:

0 to 1 indicates a moderately morally good action[14]
1 to 3 indicates a significantly moral action
More positive than 3 indicates a highly moral action

If negative, the lower the action's score, the morally worse it is, where roughly:

0 to -1 indicates a moderately morally bad action
-1 to -3 indicates a significantly morally bad action
More negative than -3 indicates an extremely morally bad action[15]

To prevent a serious misunderstanding: these scores are not the core motivation ethics theory. They are an attempt to simplify some of the theory's judgements into a formal framework. A very coherent motivation ethics position would be that the theory is correct – in that agents are morally better the more motivated they are that the good is promoted – and that several of these numerical functions are defective for not capturing various psychological factors of for simply having the values not quite right. Since it is very unlikely my personal empirical judgement is right on the shape of the functions this is the position I would in fact endorse.

Why these mathematical functions? They stem from a few rough *empirical judgements* concerning the patterning of human psychology, and the reader should readily replace them to the extent she disagrees with the empirics. The rough judgements are that (1) increased strength of moral motivation is non-linear and diminishing to the interests promoted (a motivation to help six people is not '50 per cent stronger' than one aimed at helping four people); (2) to be morally motivated is not usually to extinguish egoistic motivations but rather to merely dampen their force and potency; and (3) that the moral motivation is an increasing function of interests but at a lower rate than the fact of demandingness (for a moral agent to do a four-demanding rather than a three-demanding action takes a much greater moral motivation than the prioritization associated with a four-interest rather than three-interest act).

To illustrate, take the choice between giving 10 per cent of one's income to charity or giving nothing, and imagine, for simplicity, that these were the only two viable choices. Giving 10 per cent is moderately demanding (a score of roughly +2.5, thus giving nothing gets -2.5), and doing so, assuming a reasonably effective charity, would be expected to make a considerable positive difference to the lives of others (thus it receives a +2.5 and giving nothing a -2.5).

As such – given the illustrative figures – giving 10 per cent would get a score of roughly 2.5, making it significantly moral (what we would expect of a morally good agent) though in the middle of this range. Giving nothing would score roughly -2 making doing so clearly morally bad. However, as noted earlier, these are not the only two options. One could compare giving nothing with giving 50 per cent or 5 per cent. Thus although the framework above covers two-option pairs, one would need to expand the logic to multi-action cases (the obvious way is by sequential pair-wise comparison with the action that is motivationally the easiest).

Here, for illustrative purposes, are some other prima facie scores for various acts. The action of 'not killing a stranger' (easy to do, has a significant positive net effect, $D=-1.5$, $I=2.5$) would score 0, whereas 'killing a stranger' (hard to undertake, harms others, $D=1.5$, $I=-2.5$) would score roughly minus 4.5, making it extremely morally bad indeed.

The action of buying non-factory-farmed animal products rather than factory farmed ones is very slightly demanding for the non-poor ($D=1$) and has a potential fairly significant impact (say $I=1.75$) yielding a score of $M=0.9$ (doing so is on the border of being morally good), with not doing so scoring -2.6, making it morally bad.

To fill in the details on these examples one needs to make a series of judgements, which obviously can be rejected: maybe you think the supply chains on factory farming are too demand-insensitive so the impact of not buying such products would only be $I=+0.25$; if so, then the score will clearly change. What they do allow though is a response to the calculation critique: 'if $M<-1$ do not do that'; 'if $1<M<2$ then do this'; 'if $M>2$ then doing this is supererogatory'.

It is one though that I think does come with costs, for the scores are somewhat crude – as they strip out a lot of the individual level variance that goes into thinking through situations because they index on a generic egoist model – and because ultimately the evaluations are scalar and sometimes involve difficult psychological judgement: providing a formula is liable to mislead as to how confident we can be. But in principle, assuming the calculation critique could be well-motivated, then one can convert motivation ethics-style judgements into a formal rubric, which results in actions being put in the alleged-requisite categories.

The third response to the calculation critique (or that from practical reason) is to question the psychological assumptions about decision making that seem to underpin it.

For one thing that is striking about human decision making in most situations where potential decision criteria conflict is not how much reasoning is necessary to choose, but rather how little is involved, how efficient we are at letting our motivational set operate almost automatically. Reasoning as such plays a central role in strengthening the potency of certain motivations, and in directing our attention to particular features of choices, but much less in doing some sort of calculation or applying some formal rubric.

To take an everyday example, imagine that I am going to the sandwich shop. I am generally trying to eat more vegetables and fish. And I am trying to lose weight. Plus I am also very hungry after teaching. And there are a range of beliefs I have over which foods taste better or worse, which are good or bad for health in general and so on. Thinking of the different factors that must be weighed, this seems like it will involve a horrifically complicated exercise in practical reasoning or reason calculation. Do we weight these different considerations based on multiple criteria? And then perhaps weight these? Or rank them lexically?

Yet what is amazing is in fact how easy this decision is to make, and how almost effortlessly we make similar ones on a daily basis. Reasoning can play a central role here: it seems wise to think about which features of the choice should be salient, how I tend to choose in the long term, and what the factors involve (what for instance a healthy diet really is like). And it can prevent us from ignoring considerations that should be relevant, and help us try to change which motivations will be salient by making certain earlier choices (bringing a packed lunch, going to a healthier shop etc.). Yet is there some sort of calculation that goes on or even that I should engage in?

This is not to say that with very important decisions we should not reason. It is that we cannot assume that practical reasoning involves a determinate calculation ending with a 'Do P'. It might simply involve us taking our motivational set and possible behaviour and trying to evaluate it as better or worse on a metric or metrics. The 'conclusion' of this reasoning will be that certain future actions should be avoided if I want to live a moderately better life, and others should be undertaken if I want to live a significantly better life, and maybe some could be striven for if I want to live a remarkably better life.

What we can't do in the moral case however is to simply make some implicit variant of a moral-legal fallacy: that as laws often proscribe things we see as morally bad, that morality is therefore law-like. For the calculation critique (or that of practical reason) to have bite it needs to establish why moral evaluations should have a particular 'shape' and epistemic origin. One suggestion might be that we have strong intuition-based reasons for believing this correct (and as such see the discussion in 3.4); another would be that comparative evaluations – that of moral agents and their actions simply being better or worse – are somehow defective (see Chapter 4). Without these, we have some grounds for doubting how well justified is the desire for 'Do X' evaluations that pop out of a chain of reasoning; and motivation ethics can in any case be converted into a metric that meets the desire, albeit with an associated loss of richness and nuance.

2.7 Why isn't motivation ethics a virtue ethics theory?

Motivation ethics in general is the claim that agents are morally better the more motivated they are that X obtains, and the version defended here is that the right X is that the overall good is promoted. But the problem that led to the theory being suggested was illustrated with the difficulties of action moralities in general and consequentialism in particular. Why not then divide the theories up in a more standard way as the tripartite choice of consequentialism, deontology and virtue ethics, and place motivation ethics in the latter camp?

In a sense, it's fine to classify theories any way you want as long as you are clear about the content. Yet, one central argument of this book is that it is very useful to think of moral theories as having different structures based on their different justifications and goals, and this entails that motivation ethics and traditional virtue ethics theories are very different indeed.

A virtue ethics theory – as understood here – has two complimentary components:

(i) There are a series of character traits – 'the virtues' – that are constitutive of the virtuous individual.
(ii) An individual possessing the virtues will normally be expected to live a good life for them (or at least a better life than the non-virtuous individual).

The description of virtue ethics as identifying a virtuous individual who will lead a good life still leaves open the question of what this is, and how we might know (prominent suggestions are that the virtues allow their possessor to flourish, reach their potential or goal, or achieve eudaimonia[16]; that they allow access to a range of goods internal to a practice[17]; that they are appropriate to a specific social context or role[18]; some combination of all of these[19]; or some features of a trans-cultural paradigmatic character[20]).

Now, of course, one can classify virtue ethics differently – such as that virtue ethics theories are 'about character', and somehow then try to exclude motive consequentialism and a will-based deontology from this category. The advantage of the above classification is that it identifies why a virtue ethics theory is a structure of theory we should take seriously: such theories identify the good life and provide an answer to the question of why be just.

This question, however, usefully highlights why motivation ethics and virtue ethics are very different in their fundamental justifications. Virtue ethics theories typically aim to answer the famous question explored by Plato when Socrates confronts both Thrasymachus and Glaucon, namely why should we think that living justly is better for us than living unjustly?[21] (If living justly isn't just a creation of the strong, a convention, or something undertaken because getting away with injustice is tricky). This is the question of what is the good life. Thus although they differ remarkably on content, the most influential classical virtue ethics theories – notably that of Plato, of Aristotle, of the Epicureans and of the Stoics – all provide an answer to this question. Motivation ethics, importantly, does not. It is compatible with answers to this question, but does not supply one and, in contrast, it does not hold that agent evaluations should be determined by our answer to this question.

For motivation ethics there is a potential direct conflict between the good of the agent and the overall good, and morally better agents are those more motivated to promote the overall good. The morally heroic individual who devotes her life to reducing suffering by impoverishing herself through charitable giving, emotionally shuns the distractions of family and socializing, and who focuses her career merely on what can best help others and not on what would be also good for her – such an individual may well lead a very bad life for her and yet still, for motivation ethics, be morally heroic.

For motivation ethics the very enabling premise of Socrates' argument with Thrasymachus and Glaucon is false: acting justly (or morally better) need not be good for us. Interests can clash. But this does not entail that ethical evaluations are not meaningful, or must be based on what we have (enlightened self-interested) reason to do or be like.

Thus the difference between motivation ethics and virtue ethics, at least in its most historically influential forms, is really quite significant, and may for many people counsel in favour of virtue ethics. If you think that living a good life and living a virtuous or moral life should necessarily cohere, then virtue ethics, in constituting the virtuous individual as providing an answer to that first question, will enjoy advantages over motivation ethics.

Additionally, since the idea that living justly or virtuously is to personally live well is also very intuitively compelling, the more weight we give to our intuitive judgements then the more – arguably – we should prefer virtue ethics to motivation ethics (see Chapter 3, however, on whether intuitive pull can be justified).

To get a concrete sense of how motivation ethics is different to a virtue ethics theory, it's possible to compare motivation ethics with a virtue ethics view explicitly based on motivations, such as for instance Michael Slote's *Morals from Motives*.[22]

Slote has argued that a motivation agent-based view can underpin and make sense of a wide range of our reflected-upon moral judgements if we base evaluations on the presence of a motivation involving benevolence or caring about the wellbeing of others, along with a range of other motivations that, when held in the right 'balance', comprise the virtuous individual.

Now, methodologically, there is clearly a very large difference with this book, as it does not share Slote's methodological commitment to partly systemizing our considered intuitive judgements. However, content wise, what makes his motive-based view specifically centrally different to motivation ethics is that there is a conception of the virtuous individual embodying the good life – for him the agent with the right balance of motivations (notably the right balance of self-concern, a warm caring for close others and a broad humanistic concern) – who will also promote their own good. This is not necessarily why the agent does what they do – it is not an action-based egoism where one simply aims at one's own good – but rather is a consequence of having certain internal features. Indeed, Slote's goal in his Chapter 7 is to show how 'moral motivation follows out of a properly conceived self-interest and is therefore required by practical reason'.[23]

Motivation ethics lacks this, and in doing so flatly denies it should underpin agent evaluations. Motivation ethics as such provides scalar comparativist evaluations (see Chapter 4) and does not have evaluative unity between the good of the agent and their overall ethical evaluation: a morally heroic agent may not be an exemplary parent or enjoy close relationships that would personally enhance her life precisely because of the strength of her motivation to further the good of all others. And for motivation ethics the more one is motivated to promote the good of others the more morally one is motivated, but there is no necessary cut off level at which the strength of motivation is virtuous, it is simply more or less.

These differences are not accidental. If one seeks to determine what a virtuous individual would be like as partly an answer to the question of why be moral in that the virtuous individual would be expected to lead a good life, or at least a better life than the non-virtuous – then one is likely to end up with something close to a virtue ethics view, and if our case-based intuitions are central to furnishing the details and we focus on motivations, something perhaps close to a Slotean virtue ethics view.

If, by contrast, we hold that it is the good of all that should determine moral evaluations, that agents are the right object of primary evaluation, and that we reject any assumption that ethical agent evaluations need track the good of the agent, then we are likely to end up with something close to motivation ethics. The justifications of the two approaches, and the assumptions about how the moral life and the good life relate, are just fundamentally different.

2.8 So why motivation ethics?

So what then is the argument for motivation ethics given that it lacks the intuitive pull of virtue ethics, and does not even answer the question of 'Why act justly?' (or virtuously or morally?) if this assumes that doing so is normally better for the agent than unjustly.

Recall that the difficulties consequentialism faced were in simultaneously meeting four criteria:

(i) invulnerability to amoralism
(ii) evaluative coherence
(iii) evaluations dependent on the overall good
(iv) non-arbitrary agent evaluations

These conflict for an action morality such as consequentialism as for such theories the primary object of moral evaluations is actions. That is, roughly speaking, meeting (i) entails making agent evaluations. Meeting (ii) requires that these be based on the evaluation of what an agent does. Meeting (iii) entails that these be based on the overall good of what an agent does. But then (iv) cannot be met as an agent's comparative impact on the overall good is not determined by her features.

If we are to meet these four criteria then we will need to reject the assumption that actions not agents are the primary object of moral evaluation, and instead base evaluations on how motivated an agent is to promote the overall good. Coherent action and agent evaluations require us to evaluate agents by why they do what they do, that is by what motivates them. Since actions are motivationally heterogeneous (one can undertake them for a range of reasons) this in turn requires that we base it on their motivation aiming at what is objectively better or worse, that is our theory of the overall good. Thus motivation ethics follows quite straightforwardly *if one wishes to meet the previous four conditions.* This is the central argument in favour of the theory (one taken up further later).

Yet while preliminary arguments for conditions (i), (ii) and (iv) were offered in Chapter 1, condition (iii) – the basing of moral evaluations on the overall good – has so far not been at all defended, as it is explicitly adopted by consequentialism, and indeed is often taken to be a central virtue of the theory.[24] This, in particular, is directly challenged by deontological theories. Thus a further question is: why not adopt motivation ethics with a deontological conception of the good or indeed just adopt a normal deontological theory?

CHAPTER THREE

Deontology and the moral agent problem

The moral theory component of 'motivation ethics' can be thought of as the combination of the following two claims:

(1) Motivation ethics (general)
Agents are morally better the more motivated they are that X obtains.

(2) Motivation ethics (specific)
The moral goal – X – is that the overall good is promoted.

Claim 2 is based on the idea that it is the good of all that should determine moral evaluations, a premise shared with consequentialism, the difference being that consequentialism applies it to the consequences of what we do, whereas motivation ethics applies it to the content of a particular motivation. But why not adopt instead a version of motivation ethics with a deontological goal (such as 'to do one's duty' or 'to not do harm')? Furthermore, in discussing these choices, should whether some theory agrees with our case-based intuitions be an important consideration? These are the topics of this chapter.

Section 1 sets out the structure of deontological theories and the difference between harm- and will-based variants. Section 2 argues that harm-based variants suffer from the moral agent problems and should be rejected as such. Section 3 compares a will-based deontology with a potential harm-based version of motivation ethics, arguing the former has apparent advantages over the latter. Section 4 then asks whether instead of simply comparing structures of moral theories we should additionally compare how the theories fit with our intuitions or case-based considered judgements. Having surveyed a range of worries about the reliability of intuitions, the chapter concludes in Section 5 with the 'Intuition Regress Problem', a worry that it must be impossible to justifiably give weight to intuitions as a guide to correctness.

3.1 A deontological version of motivation ethics?

So why not a deontological variant of motivation ethics, such as for instance where moral agents are those motivated to not harm others? To see why ultimately this should be rejected, it's first necessary to step back and see why motivation ethics was required in the first place.

The case for motivation ethics rested initially on the observation that consequentialism struggled to address the moral agent question, and that overcoming the associated problems required us to reject a central feature of consequentialism – its action morality structure.[1] Motivation ethics was one way to do so while still retaining the focus on the good of all. Whether we need to do so with deontological theories will depend crucially on whether these are vulnerable to the moral agent problems or not.

So do deontological theories encounter the moral agent problems? Yes and no – this hinges on whether the theory is an action morality, in that it stipulates that certain acts are impermissible due to the harm they inflict (a harm-based deontology), or an agent morality in that it provides an account of the morally good agent and identifies duties by what such an agent would do or will (a will-based deontology). To see why, and subsequently why motivation ethics is right to adopt a universal (rather than harm-based) conception of the good, consider the basic structure of deontological theories.

While consequentialism holds that the right is that which best promotes the good of all, deontological theories, in contrast, hold that the right is prior to the overall good in that there are some acts that are forbidden or required irrespective of the *overall* consequences, typically that it is the *doing* of the act to a particular person that is key, not what may or may not subsequently follow. As Nagel notes, 'what absolutism forbids is *doing* certain things to people, rather than bringing about certain *results*. Not everything that happens to others as a result of what one does is something that one has *done* to them.'[2] Here for instance are adapted versions of several prominent thought examples that illustrate this:

Fat Man: A trolley car is out of control, heading towards five workers, and going to kill them. You can stop it by pushing on to the tracks a fat man who is standing on a bridge with you, killing him, but saving them. Is it permissible to do so?[3]

Shooting an innocent: Visiting a rural village in South America, Jim is told that if he shoots one villager four others will go free; if not, all five will be shot instead. Should he do so?[4]

Torturing a child: After a car crash on a deserted highway the only way to save one's fellow passengers is by getting an old lady living nearby to tell you where her car keys are, yet she has locked herself in a room, and the only way of getting her to tell you where they are is to twist her granddaughter's arm until her cries make the grandmother talk. Is it permissible to do so?[5]

Many people have strong intuitions that the answer to these questions is 'no', and deontological theories respect these by holding that there are some things that are a duty or forbidden irrespective of the overall consequences. Specifically, they hold that there are certain 'side-constraints' on what one can do, such that one cannot do some things to people *even if doing so will bring about the best consequences by promoting the good of all*. However, one can draw a distinction between two basic types of theory – a harm-based deontology and a will-based deontology – that differ greatly in structure, though it is often claimed that they would yield similar action evaluations.

A harm-based deontology stipulates that there are certain harms one cannot do to people (even if doing so reduces the overall amount of such harm) and this is what justifies the side-constraints.[6] A will-based deontology stipulates that morally good agents have a certain good will, and this will lead them to not violate certain side-constraints. In addressing the moral agent problem this difference in theory structure matters greatly.

There are of course a host of other ways of classifying deontological theories, the point of introducing the harm-based and will-based distinction is that both have a clear rationale and that the former will suffer from the moral agent problems while the latter will not. The taxonomy is useful in this context; I do not mean to suggest that it will be useful in all other contexts.

Furthermore, as well as harm- and will-based variants, there is an additional large set of theories that are in essence intuitionistic-deontology or what is often called everyday-morality or common-sense morality. Here our intuitive judgements – suitably considered – provide the ultimate justification, where these type of theories are deontological to the extent that such judgements would endorse some actions being forbidden irrespective of the overall consequences. This collection of theories is put to one side for now but implicitly covered by sections 3.4 and 3.5 on the role of intuitions.

3.2 Harm-based deontology and the moral agent problem

Harm-based deontological theories hold that there are certain types of harm to an individual's good that one should not do and it is this feature that makes actions impermissible (or, less commonly perhaps, if it requires the promotion of the relevant good, that makes actions morally required).

Such theories thus link the right to the good in a very particular way, they hold that there are some aspects of the good of the person to whom an act may be done – such as to not be murdered, not be tortured, have a basic standard of life, enjoy certain rights – that should be promoted or protected. There is a conception of the good underpinning moral evaluations here: there is a reason that no credible theory holds it is morally impermissible to aid someone starving, nor morally required to torture someone, this is because relief from starvation is good for the famished, and being tortured is bad for the victim.[7] The description of deontological theories as having the 'right prior to the good' may perhaps obscure this central feature. The point is that a harm-based theory *is* good-based. It is the good of the person *to whom an act is done,* however, that is central to a harm-based deontology, where as it is the good of all affected that matters to consequentialism.[8] With a harm-based deontology the relevant aspect of the good of to whom an action is done is potentially based on certain of their key interests, such as avoiding immense pain, suffering and death, or that they be treated in a certain manner, such as they have a right to not be non-consensually used in a certain way.[9]

Any harm-based theory is thus centrally going to need to give an account of how to identify to whom an act is done – in the morally relevant sense – and what it is that is done to them. The most prominent suggestion is that by allowing or enabling something one is not necessarily morally complicit in the doing of it ('The Doctrine of Doing and Allowing'). Thus when a women on the bridge does not push the fat man into the path of the runaway trolley it is not that she has killed the workers, even though the workers' deaths is the predictable outcome of doing nothing.

Secondly, a further distinction is sometimes drawn between intending or willing act or outcome A and 'doing' B that is a foreseen or foreseeable side effect ('The Doctrine of Double Effect').[10] Thus, if a trolley is heading towards five workers and can be switched to a siding where it will kill just one different worker, then doing so is not necessarily morally forbidden, as what is done is the saving of the five, even if an unfortunate side effect is the death of the worker on the siding. Importantly, the Doctrine of Double Effect does not always supply side-constraints in the cases where the Doctrine of Doing and Allowing would: diverting the trolley seems to be one such case – here, a consequentialist would also agree that the trolley should be diverted. Therefore in what follows the theory will be illustrated with cases where they do agree, such as the three initially outlined, in that they both impose a side-constraint on doing certain things due to the harm that is done (rather than allowed, or that arises as a side effect).

A harm-based deontology is an action morality as it evaluates actions based on their features, in this case the good of to whom an act is done.[11] For this reason such a theory is vulnerable to the moral agent problems.

As the action evaluations (a duty, permissible etc.) do not necessarily reflect motivational ease, difficulty and content, then if we assume broad evaluative coherence between the agent and her actions, then the moral agent problems arise. The identical agent problem, for example, was that identical agents may be evaluated in contradictory ways. Thus consider 'Deontology and the conformist'.

Imagine someone who has a major motivation, not to violate social norms, and a minor one, to do her deontological duty.[12] If she lives in a city where doing one's deontological duty is what most people do she will also do so and consistently act morally rightly. If she lives in a city where people disregard their duties then she will do so too and consistently act morally wrongly. She is identical in both cases and yet morally evaluated in contradictory ways.

The identical agent problem accrues to a harm-based deontology as whether someone does her duty (or not) is not determined by her features but rather by how doing her duty (or not) in that situation interacts with her set of motivations. Of two identical agents who face different situations in life one might always act rightly and the other always act wrongly and with evaluative coherence one thus be morally good and one morally bad even with identical constitutive features.

The comparative agent problem was that doing morally better actions seemed to fail to be linked to being a morally better agent in a consistent manner, specifically that such a judgement could be reversed overall even while the agents' features were retained. For a harm-based deontology this seems to arise too. To illustrate, consider again the case of the fat man on the bridge (who can be pushed in front of a runaway trolley, killing him, but saving five workers). Suppose there are two other people on the bridge. The first, the sadist, does nothing as he is excited at the prospect of seeing the speeding trolley hit five workers. If they were far away perhaps he would push the fat man, as that would be rather amusing too, but as they are close, the five of them being hit delights him more and thus he does nothing.

The second person – the family man – sees the workers, sees that they are his brothers and daughter and, distraught, pushes the fat man to save their lives. The family man does what is morally forbidden, the sadist does what is morally required (not to push the man). But not only is it troubling to think of the sadist in this regard as the morally better agent (and if such situations are common then typically), it would of course be very easy to think of alternative situations where the evaluation would be reversed but their features remain constant (say it is not the family man's family on the tracks, and the sadist actually thinks a fat man hitting a trolley would be more amusing).

Now what many, perhaps, will want to say here is that the reason why people do what they do matters for the agent evaluations, that in other words there are good motivations and bad motivations (the sadist has a bad motivation and the family man, perhaps, has a good motivation). This is discussed below. The point here rather is that *if we don't give an account of good or bad motivations (or a good or bad will)*, then a harm-based deontology seems to suffer from the moral agent problems, namely that the theory cannot simultaneously have (i) certain actions morally forbidden due to the harm done to whom one acts; (ii) evaluative coherence; (iii) agent evaluations based on the agent's features. This is a structural feature: consider a harm-based deontology that grounds some conception of our duties such that certain acts are morally forbidden and certain others morally required. Take two agents, one of whom – A – repeatedly does what is morally impermissible and also fails to do what is morally required. The other – B – repeatedly avoids doing what is morally impermissible and also does what is morally required.

If we assume evaluative coherence then B will be a morally better agent than A.[13] But of course since for a harm-based deontology motivational ease, difficulty and content do not form the determinants of what is morally required and impermissible (it is that some acts are simply forbidden due to the harm they inflict or required due to the interests they promote), then being morally good or bad will not be based on the agents' features, and the problems of Chapter 1 will accrue. That is, it is possible both (a) that A and B have identical features, the 'identical agent problem', and (b) that given a different set of life choices their comparative evaluations would have been reversed, the 'comparative agent problem'.

3.3 A will-based deontology or a harm-based variant of motivation ethics?

These problems are not endemic to deontology, however. They accrue only to a harm-based deontology where it is doing one's duty and avoiding doing what is morally forbidden that normally identifies morally good agents (or failing this that normally identifies morally bad agents).

An alternative however is to hold that *it is the possession of some motivation or will that identifies morally good or bad agents*, and then try to show that this will cause agents to do certain things (that are as such duties) and avoid doing certain other things (that are as such morally forbidden).

That is, there are two obvious responses to the agent evaluation problems of a purely action-based deontology: one is to adopt a will-based deontology with a conception of a good will identifying morally good agents, and the other is to identify some harm-based motivation focused on the good of to whom one acts (not the overall good) and evaluate agents by their strength of this motivation, that is to adopt a harm-based variant of what was earlier called motivation ethics.

The first proposal is a will-based deontology.

Will-based deontology
The morally good agent has a 'good will' that:

(i) identifies what actions are morally impermissible or required;
(ii) motivates the agent to avoid or undertake such actions (respectively).

Though Kant's is the most famous version of this,[14] the structure is an obvious response to the requirement that a theory (1) retain side constraints on certain actions; and (2) avoid the problems with arbitrary agent evaluations. For present purposes it does not matter whether there is a conception of the good will that can achieve these goals, although this is obviously central to the success of any proposed will-based deontology.[15]

Alternatively, however, one could adopt a version of motivation ethics – where agents are morally better the more motivated they are in terms of some motivation X – but hold that this X is not the good of all, but a harm-based conception of the good. Specifically:

'Harm-based' motivation ethics
Agents are morally better the more motivated they are to personally not do harm to others.[16]

(And compare this to what was earlier proposed, 'standard' motivation ethics: agents are morally better the more motivated they are to promote the overall good.)

Now a harm-based motivation ethics and a will-based deontology are agent moralities and as such clearly overcome the moral agent problems: agent evaluations are non-arbitrary as they are determined by agential features, there is a general evaluative coherence between an agent and her actions, and the theory is not vulnerable to amoralism. Yet a harm-based motivation ethics is going to face two problems that a will-based deontology might not, and thus the latter seems a more compelling structure of moral theory of the two.

Firstly, and most importantly, 'harm-based motivation ethics' has retained from deontology exactly the feature that seems most difficult to justify, namely why it is the good of to whom one acts that underpins evaluations, not that of all. If it is bad that people are harmed, it is prima facie problematic to hold that the harm of to whom we act is more important than identical harms to others (it is this problem that creates Scheffler's complaint that deontological restrictions are paradoxical in that they forbid us to do what is morally objectionable even when it would reduce the overall amount of morally objectionable acts undertaken[17]).

The motivation that is supposedly moral seems either unjustifiably arbitrary – in that harms to certain people are decisively morally bad but identical harms to others are not – or distinctly egoist if the real concern is that one *personally* not do harm to others rather than a concern that others are not harmed. A will-based deontology, by contrast, promises to overcome these problems by showing that the nature of rationally willing identifies one's duties, rather than focusing on the good of to whom one acts (this, incidentally, is why promise-keeping and truth-telling seem more likely to be duties for a will-based deontology than a harm-based one).

Secondly, a harm-based motivation ethics will not necessarily supply what we commonly think of as deontological action evaluations – that of certain acts that are morally forbidden irrespective of their overall consequences for the overall good. (I do not personally think this is a terrible problem: maybe our deontological intuitions are just wrong. It would however be a problem given certain commitments to the type of action-evaluations a deontological theory must supply).

The reason is that under 'harm-based motivation ethics' morally good actions are those that one would expect of someone with a significant motivation to not personally do harm to others, but this motivation might in a large range of situations be insufficient to counteract other motivations.[18] Consider, for example, the man on the bridge who sees his family in danger from the runaway trolley. Even with a strong motivation not to personally harm others, he might still push the fat man if his horror at his family dying was overpowering. For a harm-based motivation ethics, he does not act morally badly *even though he violates what is normally regarded as a side constraint* (if avoiding harming the fat man and sacrificing his family would require an immensely strong motivation to not personally harm others then it would, for a deontological motivation ethics, be morally heroic).

For a will-based deontology, however, he will have done what is impermissible. He may not be negatively evaluated as an agent – assuming that he acted due to weakness of will, but he did have a good will – yet his good will would have identified his duty.[19] A will-based deontology identifies duties and causes the agent with the good will to act on these as duties. A version of motivation ethics with the moral motive being to not personally do harm will not identify duties, it simply motivates the agent to care about particular features of the choices she faces, but she may have other motivations too.

A will-based deontology is thus, I think, a better deontological agent-morality rather than a version of motivation ethics with a harm-based conception of the good, as the latter incorporates a prima facie problematic restriction of moral concern (only to those to whom one acts), lacks the possibility that it is rationally willing something that creates this not a restriction in concern, and need not entail that certain types of act are strictly impermissible which has been taken to be a signal advantage of deontological theories, difficulties a will-based deontology promises to overcome.

Thus, stepping back, it's worth reviewing the choices of structure of moral theories sketched in the introduction. Firstly, we need to choose the primary object of moral evaluation: is it actions or agents? Specifically, whether we start with an account of the features of morally good actions (for 'action moralities') or with those of morally good agents (for 'agent moralities')? Secondly, we need to decide the determinant of evaluation, that is, *whose* good to base moral evaluations upon: is it all affected, to whom actions are done, or the agent themselves?

As such, we might hold that actions are right if they best promote the good of the agent (egoism); or that agents with certain character features will best lead a good life (virtue ethics); or that there are harms to people's good that are impermissible no matter what the overall consequences (a harm-based deontology); or that agents with a certain will would avoid and undertake certain types of action (a will-based deontology[20]); or that right actions best promote the overall good (consequentialism); or agents are more moral the more motivated they are to promote the overall good (motivation ethics). That is:

		Primary object of evaluation	
		Actions	**Agents**
	own good	egoism	virtue ethics
Determinant of evaluation	**good of to whom done**	harm-based deontology	will-based deontology
	good of all	consequentialism	motivation ethics

The overall argument has been that we can examine the choice between agent and action primacy, and think about which conception of the good is justified, and that these choices will manifest in substantive arguments for and against particular theories. The argument of Chapter 1, for instance, was that it was consequentialism's action-morality structure that created problems in how it might ground agent evaluations. One can, however, adopt an agent-morality structure and retain consequentialism's determinant of evaluation (the good of all), and that indeed is exactly the logic underlying motivation ethics (it is the conjunction of two claims: (i) that only agent-moralities can supply evaluations to actions and agents that are evaluatively coherent and non-arbitrary, and (ii) that the justified determinant of moral evaluations should be the good of all).

A harm-based deontology suffers from exactly the same problems as consequentialism did with agent evaluations, but the best response here is not a version of motivation ethics with a harm-based good (as discussed above), but a will-based deontology, as this promises to retain what is distinctive about deontological side-constraints while still grounding a conception of the moral agent.

The argument in favour of motivation ethics is thus two-fold. Firstly, that the right primary object of moral evaluation should be agents (and this thus counsels in favour also of a virtue ethics theory and a will-based deontology). This has been the subject of the first three chapters. And secondly, that moral evaluations should be based on the good of all as this is the only fully justifiable determinant of evaluation (this requirement, on its own, also counsels in favour of consequentialism). As noted in the conclusion, there are potentially good arguments for replacing the latter with a different requirement (for a will-based deontology that we act based on some conception of practical reason; for a virtue ethics theory that one lives a good life).

The goal so far has only been to sketch the structure of motivation ethics, and outline why it is right to adopt that structure in contrast to consequentialism, an agent-centred prerogative or a harm-based variant of motivation ethics. In doing so the choice of moral theories has been framed as a choice of different structures. Yet one prominent means of moral methodology has so far been largely ignored, and could undermine the entire approach; namely, if a significant weight should perhaps be given to our intuitive judgements in particular cases and examples (where such cases are more than an illustrative aid to exposition but a guide to correctness).

Furthermore, the approach has been to discuss and try to evaluate the core structural features of various prominent theories: so above, for example, the discussion looked at a harm based deontology where there are certain harms that are morally impermissible to inflict as this has a clear underlying rationale. But if a strong intuitionism is correct then any such iterative investigation of the structure of moral theories is going to be radically incomplete. One can, after all, simply modify or add to any theory where it has somewhat counterintuitive implications, or jettison its key features in those cases that seem problematic. Since theorists' intuitions and the cases considered presumably vary hugely, for any criticism there will be a modification to the theory that can remedy this, and someone, somewhere, is bound to have proposed it.

Intuitionistic deontology or common-sense morality will thus always be able to respond to a problematic case by ad hoc modification. Aside from moral philosophy becoming like evolutionary natural selection without the selection (adaption galore, but no dying of the duds), this possibility raises two more immediate worries: firstly, whether motivation ethics will survive such intuitive-testing, and secondly what weight we should give to such testing.

3.4 Is motivation ethics intuitive?

All the discussion so far has focused upon the conditions we might impose on moral theories and the type of structure such theories could take in response to various choices, notably: what should be the primary object of evaluation and what should be the determinant of evaluation? Yet a further issue might be whether motivation ethics supplies the 'correct' judgements in a range of cases. Is it typically, somewhat, frequently or barely intuitive? No sustained attempt has been made here so far to answer this, nor to evaluate what this answer should tell us.

Now, it might initially seem likely that it will be intuitive as there has been some impressive recent work on how motivation-based views may be supported by careful consideration of a range of cases.[21] Yet, for what it is worth, my own opinion is that there are likely to be cases where a virtue ethics theory, either focusing on motivations or some other more traditional conception of the virtues, is likely to be much more intuitively compelling, notably perhaps in our strong association of a range of behaviours – friendship, loyalty to family – with being intrinsically virtuous. And secondly, we do seem to have deontological-style intuitions about a range of acts, judging some the wrong thing to do even when they will best promote the good. As such I think it fair to assume that intuitive fit, while perhaps not decisively counting against motivation ethics, will sometimes count against the theory, and a deontological or virtue ethics alternative (depending on the case) may be more intuitively compelling.

Thus the goal in what follows is to implicitly defend motivation ethics by sketching some broad sceptical worries concerning the use of case-based intuitions. The more persuasive the reader finds them, the less the question of intuitive fit should influence theory choice (and, in contrast, the less persuasive the sceptical case is, the more important will be how the cases 'fall out' intuitively).

So should intuitive fit be a key test of the correctness of theories? There are two broad categories of argument that counsel, I think, for us being somewhat sceptical. The first, 'localized scepticism', is where we cast doubt on the *reliability* of certain intuitions by noting how they are potentially affected by considerations that seem irrelevant to their correctness. This is a bit like noticing that a sixteenth-century device designed as a compass points in markedly different directions based on whether it is a cold or hot day: as such we should be doubtful that on any particular day what it indicates is north really is so.

The second, 'fundamental scepticism', doubts that we could have any good grounds for giving our intuitions weight per se in evaluating the correctness of moral beliefs. This is a bit like discovering that the compass device tries to tell north based on air-pressure: these are things we have no reason to think are relevantly related (air pressure and localized longitudinal location are generally just unrelated).

Since a broadly sceptical set of theses is outlined below, it's worth before doing so perhaps just noting a few ways in which case-based examples are potentially immensely valuable in moral reasoning, even if intuitive scepticism is completely justified.

Firstly, of course, they may help us think through the relevant causal links: the question, for instance, of whether truth telling tends to help or harm those involved might be advanced by trying to be clear on the main features of a range of relevant cases.

Secondly, particular examples can clarify whether principles conflict: consider the proposal that, of a hundred thousand citizens convicted of speeding, every year one is selected at random and publicly shot. Will this reduce overall human fatalities and potentially highlight a conflict between desert-based punishment theories and consequence-based ones?[22]

Thirdly, cases may highlight apparent contradictions in our moral beliefs, prompting us to try to think through which has better arguments in favour of it.

All three roles could be accepted by the intuition sceptic. They might also, somewhat more controversially, accept that intuitive cases can be useful in winning arguments – if you can convince someone that some theory has an implication they don't intuitively accept, then perhaps that will help sway them against the theory. (This is a more controversial use of cases as we need a justification for why winning arguments is the goal. The mere pleasure of being victor seems too egoistic and trivializing of the subject matter.)

While potentially accepting all of the above, what the sceptic would clearly dispute, however, is whether cases can tell us more: by our reaction to certain examples, whether we can better approach correct moral beliefs.

Localized scepticism

Below is an outline of five types of localized scepticism. Since several of these have been well-explored by others and since they share similar structural features, the descriptions will be very brief, and will then merely note what an effective response would to seem to require. What the problems will thus serve to do is to prepare the ground for the more fundamental scepticism that follows.

Problem one: The origin of intuitions

To the extent they reflect the peculiarities of human evolution, our intuitions are likely to be shaped by a range of empirical contingencies. Furthermore, since people raised in different environments have wildly differing moral views of a wide range of cases, then there would be related worries that (i) none of us were raised in situations where our intuitions are likely to be accurate or; (ii) the intuitions themselves cannot speak to which of us was raised in better or worse situations.

As Singer, along with many other sceptics, has argued:

> There is little point in constructing a moral theory designed to match considered moral judgements that themselves stem from our evolved responses to the situations in which we and our ancestors lived during the period of our evolution as social mammals, primates, and finally, human beings.[23]

The problem clearly generalizes though as a range of different social and cultural factors also causally affect our intuitive responses, and these too will depend on various empirical contingencies.

A solution to this is not impossible: what it would have to do, however, is to give us grounds for believing that some intuitions are more reliable than others, and identifying which these were.

Problem two: The psychological determinant of intuitions

Even on a very basic understanding of our psychology, there are a range of different types of psychological phenomena that plausibly can influence how we respond to a variety of moral thought experiments: mood, emotional identification with the case, normative beliefs, what features we focus our attention upon, and so on. These will vary by cases, thus in some situations one may drive our response much more than in others, creating seemingly contradictory responses. As such we need to know which psychological determinant of intuitions is a more reliable guide to truth.

As Tadesco notes, 'Some situations engage one part of our brain, some situations another, and our intuitive response to any particular case is essentially captive to this evolutionary development.'[24] What we require to overcome this concern is some account of which 'parts of the brain' support better intuitive responses than others.

Problem three: The weight of intuitions

Perhaps the most common use of intuitions is via a 'Reflective Equilibrium'. Using a reflective equilibrium one takes a certain principle or structure and compares its implications with that of our judgements about a set of cases or situations. If these conflict we suitably modify them with the goal that they should end up agreeing. The idea is first introduced by Rawls, in his case that we shall find a description of the initial situation 'that matches our considered judgements duly pruned and adjusted' (he links the idea, but not the term, to Goodman).²⁵ Since the arguments made for motivation ethics have been theoretical, if reflective equilibrium were correct then we should be confident that, as it has not been through such a process, the theory – at least as outlined – is wrong.

The main worry about such an equilibrium though is, ironically, that there is no equilibrium here: there are no forces to be balanced, no common unit of currency to adjudicate the tipping point between a set of considerations (it is also, clearly, in no sense a strategic interaction). The metaphor seems inapt, and as such misleading in that it implies that it produces a justified determinate conclusion.²⁶

Consider for instance that we have a moral theory M that entails judgements in a series of cases. And we have differing intuitions about some subset of these cases (say ten of them). One 'equilibrium' is that we hold the cases correct and M not applicable in those contexts. Another is that we hold some of them correct and M sometimes correct in the other contexts. Or we hold M always correct. Or we apply a modification to M to make it cover some cases. Or we could apply a rival modification to make it apply to other cases. And of course, the more cases where M and intuitions clash the more such modifications are logically possible. Reflective equilibrium implies that our conclusion should not be weighted 100 per cent theory, or 100 per cent intuitive judgement, but since there is no common metric quite what the ratio should be – 80 per cent theory or 30 per cent? – is not settled by the method *as there is no equilibrium*, which leaves the very method potentially wildly indeterminate.

This is not an insuperable worry though so long as we can identify which of our intuitions are a better or worse guide to correct beliefs. But we need to do so, and merely the fact that they are intuitions cannot do so for us.

Problem four: The object of intuitions

Any inference from cases is going to face the problem that the judgements could be identifying the moral goodness or badness of the actions or the moral goodness or badness of agents who normally undertake them. That is, the empirical question of *psychological* action or agent primacy – are we normally implicitly evaluating first the act or first the agent – will impact what we can infer from intuitive judgements about cases (this is not the same as the normative question of what should be the primary moral object of evaluation).

Consider, for instance, that we have a general sense of there being certain features that make agents morally better or worse (and at certain levels morally bad, good or heroic etc.). Now if morally bad agents typically do a certain type of action, and morally good ones do not, then it would seem normal for us to acquire quite a robust sense of the actions in question being morally bad. That is, assume the following:

Premise one: Morally bad agents typically, in the situations we commonly face, do P.

Premise two: Morally good agents typically, in the situations we commonly face, avoid doing P.

Conclusion: Doing P is intrinsically morally bad.

This conclusion is not supported, but we might well have a remarkably strong feeling that it is correct if we almost always encounter doing P in situations where it is done out of motives we associate with moral badness.

Assume, for instance, that people normally lie to others out of a lack of concern for them and for selfish gain. Truth telling is normally reliably undertaken by people with at least a moderate level of concern for others. Faced then with a particular case of lying we may well have such a strong association between lying and moral badness that this leads us to feel strongly that lying is morally bad. But of course the inference that lying is intrinsically morally bad per se is unwarranted – it is that it is normally undertaken by egoists not by what we regard as morally good individuals. It would be easy, however, to construct exceptional examples where a morally good individual might well lie – and if our general intuitive sense of the badness of lying accrues to this case then our intuitions will mislead us as to the badness or goodness of lying (or promise breaking, or inflicting harm on others, or whatever it is that we normally expect of badly motivated agents but not well-motivated ones).

The question of psychological agent or action primacy thus needs to be settled for us to know what to infer from cases – that the action is an example of a good/bad action type, or that it is normally undertaken by good or bad agents. If our intuitions are structured by what we think of agents then these may well produce the wrong conclusions in cases that are sufficiently rarely encountered in everyday life. If alternatively intuitions are simply identifying features of actions then we risk making wrong inferences about the moral goodness or badness of agents in those cases. Until we know, as a psychological matter, what it is our intuitions about cases are typically responsive to, then it will be unclear whether we can make inferences about actions or agents from such cases.

The further problem – and the one relevant for fundamental scepticism – is that we might have both objects, and need to know, when it comes to intuitions, which should be prioritized or given greater weight in which situations.

Problem five: What type of agent's intuitions?

It seems plausible that exposure to moral thinking under reflective equilibrium may alter our intuitive judgements and thus our conclusions.

As Hardin argues, 'our intuitions, if they were ever somehow autonomous or real cannot be any longer after we have theorized enough to be doing moral philosophy'.[27] If so, we need an account of which is correct of the rival set of intuitions – those pre-reflection, post-slight reflection, and post-extensive reflection, or indeed those under different circumstances. The fact they are intuitions will not be enough. More generally we therefore need an account of what types of agents have better or worse intuitions.

All these problems create the same sort of difficulty. Namely that reasoning from moral intuitions can be affected by a range of factors: (1) different possible evolutionary histories and social upbringings that influence the intuitions; (2) different types of psychological causes underpinning the intuitions; (3) the range of weights we could give to intuitions vs. theories; (4) what it is that intuitions are actually picking up upon; and (5) what type of agents have better or worse moral intuitions.

The apparent solution is an account of which intuitions are better or worse. It is this that, according to fundamental scepticism, cannot be provided without undercutting the very role of intuitions.

3.5 Fundamental scepticism and the Intuition Regress Problem

All of the types of local scepticism could – at least potentially – be overcome if we could identify which of our different types of intuitions were a reliable guide to correctness. Then such intuitions would be informative. The 'Intuition Regress Problem' introduced below is a worry that this must be impossible.

Consider a particular type of intuition, 'P-type' intuitions (these might be those after careful reflection, those of experts, those in a calm state, those of a majority and so on), that someone regards as the good type of intuitions.

If accepting these intuitions as a guide to correct views is to be justified we need to be able to give the following type of argument:

Intuitionism 1: P-type intuitions are more reliably correct than non-P-type intuitions because they have feature X.

The feature X serves to justify giving weight to the P-type intuitions so that our belief in them is not arbitrary.

There seems to be two different types of ways X could provide justification. Firstly, it could refer to the way the intuitions are arrived at or produced (some aspect of their P-ness). Or, secondly, it could refer to their content. The difficulty is that such a justification is either going to be on the one hand circular or regressive, or on the other hand renders their intuitive status redundant.

That is, here are the obvious options:

1 X refers to some feature of the P-ness of the intuitions
2 X refers to the content of the intuitions

If (1) then the argument to be justified will need to be re-run, as follows:

Intuitionism 2: X type intuitions are more reliably correct than non-X type intuitions because they have feature Y.

And for Intuitionism 2 to be justified we need an account of why Y justifies the X-type intuitions. If this references their P-ness or X-ness then the overall argument is circular. If it references something other than their P-ness and X-ness but not their content then the regress continues (say it references their Z-ness, then we need an argument for accepting Intuitionism 3: 'Z-type intuitions are more reliably correct than non-Z-type intuitions because they have feature W'. And the regress continues ...).

Alternatively, we can hold intuitions justified purely based on their content and the regress stops. But if so, then the fact that the cases or statements are intuitive or not must be entirely redundant (if it has any weight then we can ask why it should have that weight, and the regress continues ...). The problem is not that justified moral beliefs should give limited weight to intuitions, it is that to be justified – to be non-arbitrary and non-circular – moral beliefs must give intuitive status no weight at all.

To illustrate, consider the following two generic rival moral beliefs, where P is some empirical entity (an action, an agent, an institution, a policy and so on) and where Q is some ethical or moral descriptor (a duty, a right, just, moral, virtuous):

A: 'P is Q'
B: 'P is not Q'

Our intuitive judgements are relevant to ethical reasoning if learning whether statement A or statement B is intuitive should influence whether we should accept or believe A or B to be correct. Imagine, for example, that someone argues for A by pointing out that B is absurd or implausible. Is this a justified argument against B?

To be a justified argument it would need to show why we should accept the following:

Claim 1: Plausible-sounding ethical beliefs are more likely to be correct than absurd sounding beliefs because they tend to have property X.

Now property X can reference some feature of the intuitive support for the beliefs, or their content. The former, for example, might be 'Plausible sounding ethical beliefs are more likely to be held even after sustained examination.'

But if so, then we need to justify Claim 2:

Claim 2: Ethical beliefs held after sustained examination are more likely to be correct than ethical beliefs not held after sustained examination because they have property Y.

If we justify Y based on some other property of how or by whom the beliefs are arrived at, or how we intuitively relate to them, then we face further regress. The alternative is to make property Y directly reference the *content* of the beliefs. For example, 'ethical beliefs held after examination are less likely to have content which is biased'. This – assuming that we can give a sufficiently explicit account of bias – would not necessarily result in an immediate regress. Yet, if this is the argument, then it entirely undercuts any weight for intuitions per se. A belief's plausibility or absurdity is irrelevant: what matters is whether it meets our criteria for being biased in its content. Absurd or counter-intuitive beliefs that are unbiased should be accepted, self-evident or intuitive beliefs that are biased should be rejected. That something is intuitive, in of itself, cannot be an argument for it.

Responses from the intuitionist

Appealing to all beliefs

One response, prompted perhaps by the nature of local scepticism, would be to hold that all of our intuitions about cases are some sort of evidence. It is not, as such, that there are good or bad intuitions, but rather all intuitions should be given some (perhaps small) weight.

This does seem in some respects to address localized scepticism, to the extent that localized scepticism is based on identifying a conflict between intuitions based on some seemingly irrelevant feature. Yet the response has no special resources to overcome the Intuition Regress Problem. For that problem can be applied to the claim that the set of intuitive beliefs is more likely to be correct than the set of non-intuitive beliefs. Such a claim can be justified by reference to some features of our process of finding something intuitive, setting up a regress (why believe that feature is truth tracking …?), or such a claim can directly reference the content of the beliefs, beliefs with content of type G are more likely to be correct than those without type G. But then the beliefs' intuitiveness becomes irrelevant, and the only question is: which beliefs have G-type content? Giving some intuitions weight is problematic, but so too is giving all intuitions weight.

The goal is not correctness, but some instrumental aim

Implicit in the above discussion has been the assumption that those giving weight to case-based intuitions are using them as a guide to correct ethical and moral beliefs (or, at least, beliefs more likely to be correct, or less likely to be incorrect). So that the claim 'X is absurd' or 'X is implausible' gives us a consideration against thinking that X is correct.

However, one alternative would be to argue that the aim is not correct moral beliefs, but some instrumental goal. Here are a few obvious candidates for such a response:

1. We want to have coherent beliefs because coherent beliefs are instrumentally useful for acting.
2. We want collectively to converge on some moral beliefs, and systemizing our case-based intuitions is one way to do so.
3. We function better psychologically when we have some sort of equilibrium between our reactions to cases and moral theories.

To the extent we really do have these aims, then this does seem to create a role for case-based intuitions. But importantly, for anyone caring about the correctness or not of moral theories this will tell us absolutely nothing.

Take, for example, someone considering the ethics of the factory farming of animals. If we adopt instrumentalism about intuitions then there is a role for case-based intuitions in thinking about this topic. But the role is in assessing the following: 'Does *having the belief* that animal suffering is morally bad help me have more coherent beliefs, help us collectively reach a consensus, or improve my psychological wellbeing?'

The difference is in two distinct roles for beliefs:

B1: Belief Y is correct.

B2: Holding belief Y is useful in achieving Z.

Now, if B2 is justified by reference to B1 – such that holding belief Y is useful in achieving Z because it is more likely to be correct than the belief 'Y is false' – then the intuitiveness of Y can have no role. If B2 is not based on Y's correctness, then the intuitiveness of Y can have a role, but obviously this can tell us nothing about Y's correctness.

So imagine, for example, that someone thinks it desirable that we have a general consensus on core moral beliefs. Here our case-based intuitions, particularly if very robustly held, might be useful, notably through some sort of social reflective equilibrium. But we should not delude ourselves that this process gives us better beliefs in terms of beliefs less likely to be wrong. There is no guarantee that using reflective equilibrium will not take us away from correct beliefs.

Ultimately though, the Intuition Regress Problem is only a problem if we care about the correctness of our moral beliefs where this relates to their content, not the consequences of holding the beliefs or our relationship to them. Pure instrumentalism has no role for intuitions as a guide to better or worse moral beliefs where better or worse refers to the content of the beliefs, rather than the causal effects of the belief-holding. However, it is only really meta-ethical views that hold moral beliefs truth-apt by content that are in trouble, and pure instrumentalism thus simply side-steps the difficulties (as does a range of other meta-ethical positions, for example an expressivist who held beliefs correct if they correctly capture our attitudes, not some truth-of-the-matter independent of our attitudes). It is only if we want to treat intuitions as a partial guide to correctness – *and thus its mild non-intuitive status as a potential problem for motivation ethics* – that we require a response to the Intuition Regress Problem.

Intuitions as a proxy for content?

The Intuition Regress Problem is that the intuitiveness of a claim cannot be any guide to its correctness unless purely referencing the claim's content, in which case its intuitiveness is entirely redundant. But what if intuitiveness is sometimes a proxy for better content? This would seem to be a bit like working out how someone voted based on certain of their demographics, such as age and income. This won't guarantee you the right outcome, but the fact they are younger should be some evidence that they are more likely to have voted for the left wing or liberal party. Similarly, absurd beliefs would, as such, be more likely to be incorrect.

The trouble with this suggestion is that for us to tell if some case or implication of a theory for a case is intuitive we have to know the content. Yet a proxy is only useful if we don't know the variable we are trying to track. So estimating how someone voted based on demographics is useful if we don't know how they voted. But this cannot be the case with intuitions, for it is the content that drives our assessment of whether something is intuitive or not. 'Claim X is absurd' might be a useful proxy for 'Claim X is incorrect' *if we didn't know what X is*. But our assessment of its absurdity depends on knowing what X is. Thus it seems that intuitions simply can't be a proxy for content, as their evaluation – intuitive / counter-intuitive – depends on knowing the content.

Isn't this a generic problem?

One possible further argument from the intuitionist would be to hold that the Intuition Regress Problem is in fact simply a localized version of the more general 'regress problem' in epistemology. Since that has several proposed solutions (notably foundationalism, coherentism and infinitism),[28] might these have similar analogues with regard to intuitions?

Although it is true that the problems have some similarity, there is one key difference: intuitive-status is not part of the content of a belief (or if we argue it is, then the content not intuitive-status is what matters). The general regress problem in epistemology arises from asking for a justification for the content of an empirical belief, and all of the proposed solutions directly address that (foundationalists argue the content should appropriately relate to the content of some foundational beliefs, coherentists argue the content should be coherent with the content of other beliefs, infinitists argue that the content should form part of an infinite chain of supporting beliefs). This is exactly what the intuitionist cannot appeal to however: if they specify that the content of the belief is what matters – in that justified content is X – then its intuitive status is irrelevant.

As such the Intuition Regress Problem is still a problem even for those who think that the more general regress problem in epistemology has solutions, because a key feature of all of the proposed solutions – direct content evaluation – is exactly what the intuitionist cannot appeal to when giving weight to intuitive status.

But what's the alternative?

A final response of the intuitionist might, however, be something along the lines of 'Well, what would you do?'

In part, Chapters 1 to 8 of this book are an attempt to respond to this request, since they try to offer arguments for all of the key claims without relying on case-based intuitions (there are plenty of illustrative examples to aid clarity, but they don't do the argumentative work at the key junctures). And even if this book fails, huge amounts of moral and political philosophy is undertaken without depending upon our intuitive responses to particular examples.

Yet, the intuitionist's complaint here should not be so easily dismissed. For although this book's arguments do not rely on case-based intuitions, they do rely on us accepting certain principles, and the intuitionist might charge that our acceptance of these is intuitively determined, and thus subject to all the previous worries.

As such the intuitionist could hold that we have simply smuggled in a bias: when the intuitions are case-based they are subject to the Intuition Regress Problem, yet when the intuitions are multi-case – such as based on some principle covering several situations – then suddenly all the problems are assumed away. There is, according to this response, simply different sites of intuitions: some find intuitions about a particular case compelling, some find intuitions about multiple cases ('principles') compelling, and there is nothing at root to distinguish these two. Ultimately, it is intuitions all the way down.

This, I think, is a potentially persuasive answer against some anti-intuitionist arguments. However, to have bite, the key principles that we are using to choose between moral theories have to themselves be moral beliefs whose only support is intuitive status. Yet this need not be the case, and in fact this book aims for it not to be the case: the key principles are not moral beliefs but rather *properties* of moral beliefs (specifically: evaluative coherence, non-arbitrariness and invulnerability to amoralism).

The book's overall argument is that these three – non-arbitrariness, evaluative coherence and invulnerability to amoralism – are sufficient to greatly clarify and whittle down the choice of moral theories, and that this reduced choice will minimally include motivation ethics and, to the extent the argument succeeds, comparatively support it. That is, in practical terms it is not that we start with non-arbitrariness and coherence and try to come up with a moral theory from scratch, but rather that we use these conditions to try to comparatively evaluate prominent theories and think through how they might be changed to overcome any problems that arise.

Our commitment to these principles need not be intuitively determined. The commitment to a moral theory rejecting amoralism seems a constitutive commitment of being a moral theory (in the same way that an account of some empirical beliefs being justified entails the rejection of scepticism about justification). Coherence and non-arbitrariness also seem to flow from the goal of reasoning about some moral beliefs being justified and others not: if we reject coherence or non-arbitrariness then in a sense anything goes, and all beliefs can be justified.

Now there is a further question about which meta-ethical views most directly support these conditions, and the Epilogue discusses one position as an example of what these might be like, though it seems likely that many meta-ethical views would endorse these criteria in one form or another. The point for here, however, is that the endorsement of coherence, non-arbitrariness and invulnerability to amoralism need not be purely intuitive in justification: there are possible independent arguments for adopting these. As such, to the extent we can use them to choose between moral theories we will potentially be justified in a way that, because of the Intuition Regress Problem, the intuitionist will not.

Many, however, do give weight to intuitions and it's possible there is an acceptable way around the Intuition Regress Problem, thus this book tries to note in the subsequent chapters when a particular conclusion or implication being discussed is absurd-seeming, as if intuitionism can be justified, this will be an important consideration. Doing so is not meant to endorse or rely upon a back-door intuitionism however: at every single point where intuitive status is implicitly noted a further entirely separate argument is provided for the overall position, one that relies alone on non-arbitrariness, coherence or invulnerability to amoralism.

CHAPTER FOUR

Moral demandingness and two concepts of evaluation

Motivation ethics holds that how motivated an agent is to promote the good of others should determine their moral evaluation. But how is the level of motivation determined? Specifically, on what basis do we arrive at the qualitative evaluands, such as something being morally good / bad / exceptional / heroic etc.? This chapter outlines a choice between two different determinants of qualitative evaluations: comparativist evaluations, where we compare an instance to a distribution (such as when we say someone is a good student and mean compared to their cohort), or absolutist evaluations, where the evaluations do not implicitly or explicitly track a distribution of others.

It does so by discussing the 'Demandingness Worry', the claim that if the requirements of a moral theory are too demanding then the theory should be rejected. In the literature this is typically framed as a choice between a powerful intuition and a general principle (and intuition sceptics thus point out: why not just reject the intuition?). According to this chapter, it is also potentially a worry about absolutist action evaluations from the assumption of comparativist agent evaluations, and thus a valid criticism if the latter are correct.

4.1 The demandingness problem

So how demanding is morality? Here is a very important view, what Kagan calls extremism:

Extremism
Morality requires you to do all you can to promote the overall good.[1]

It seems 'extreme' as 'there is no limit to what you might be called upon to sacrifice in the pursuit of the good. Your material possessions, time, effort, bodily parts or life-itself – all of these might be commanded by morality'.[2]

The most often cited example of such a theory is consequentialism,[3] though, as this is heavily disputed, extremism can in what follows alternatively refer to any moral theory that could require us to give to charity most of our material possessions for most of our lives.[4]

Many have intuitions that such a potentially demanding theory cannot be correct. However, as Kagan rightly notes 'if the intuition that consequentialism demands too much remains impossible to defend, we may have to face the sobering possibility that it is not consequentialism, but our intuition, that is in error'.[5] In particular, if we are to justifiably reject extremism, we will need to show both the principles (and arguments for them) that justify doing so, and plausibly why these do not entail a morality that is too undemanding, such as that of the pure egoist.[6]

To presage the strategy ahead for doing so, here are versions of two key principles:

Evaluative coherence
The moral evaluation of an agent and her actions should broadly cohere.

(Moral) comparativism
A qualitative moral evaluation applying to an agent is only potentially correct if in comparison to an implicit or explicit distribution of agents.

The core argument will be that, suitably spelled out, evaluative coherence and comparativism entail that we must reject extremism, and that there are arguments for doing so. That is, in outline: under evaluative coherence the basic demands of morality are what we would expect a morally good human being to undertake. Under comparativism, being a morally good human being means being morally good for a human being, that is compared to humans beings in general. And if both principles are correct, the basic demands of morality cannot therefore be things we would expect almost anyone recognizably human to fail to perform. Yet this is what extremism potentially entails. Hence we must reject evaluative coherence, extremism or comparativism (motivation ethics for instance rejects extremism, whereas consequentialism rejects comparativism or evaluative coherence).

The overall aim here is to set out the choice between comparativist and absolutist moral theories, and how the issue of moral demandingness is affected by this choice. The chapter thus proceeds as follows. Section 2 outlines the case against extremism, the need for broad evaluative coherence, and the nature of the problem of moral demandingness. Section 3 considers arguments the extremist might make against comparativism. Section 4 outlines some considerations in favour of comparativism. Section 5 concludes.

4.2 Comparativism and absolutism

Here again is extremism:

Extremism
Morality requires you to do all you can to promote the overall good.

For illustrative simplicity, in what follows it will be assumed that this would entail that anyone in a developed country with a moderate income or higher (say above the minimum wage) would be required to give most of his or her income to reduce suffering in developing countries. Of course, a person might not be required to give all their income, as doing so might undermine their future earning potential and not best promote the good in the long term, but for the sake of argument let us assume something like donating most would be required.

There are two ways in which this might be thought too demanding–either that doing so is very hard to undertake, or that it involves giving up interests that one is morally entitled to not give up. That is, here are two conditions that we might impose on moral evaluations both of which require rejecting extremism:

The Difficulty Condition (DC)
Moral requirements cannot be so motivationally difficult that almost anyone recognizably human would fail to meet them.

The Sacrifice Condition (SC)
Moral requirements cannot be so demanding as to require one to sacrifice key components of a good life.

Prominent suggestions for 'key components' have been one's own projects, particular relationships (such as with one's children or spouse), personal welfare or own integrity.[7] The precise specification will not be at stake here; all the sacrifice condition requires is that it is possible that sacrificing such components of a good life may sometimes conflict with best promoting the overall good.

The Difficulty Condition and Sacrifice Condition are importantly different. However, in terms of the rejection of extremism, in practice they may overlap, specifically in that if we think that humans are normally strongly motivated to promote some of the 'key components' of what makes theirs a good life then the Difficulty Condition may entail the Sacrifice Condition. This chapter will offer arguments for accepting the Difficulty Condition and rejecting extremism.

Now, consider someone on median income who, rather than giving most of her income to charity to relieve suffering, gives a quarter with that goal.

Under extremism she fails to act as is morally required. Is she a morally bad human being? This is going to be the key question. One way of deciding is by adopting evaluative coherence:

Evaluative Coherence
The moral evaluation of an agent and her actions should broadly cohere.

As noted in Chapter 1, the phrase 'broadly cohere' is intended to cover a wide range of specifications of the underlying idea, such as that they actually cohere, or tend to cohere, or mostly cohere, or are expected to cohere. The key point is that, when the extremist talks of fulfilling the 'demands of morality', or of performing one's duties, or of acting rightly, or of doing what is morally required then, given evaluative coherence, these are things that would be undertaken by a morally good agent (mostly, or typically, or normally, or in expectation). If you repeatedly fail the basic demands of morality then you should prima facie be morally evaluated negatively.

We could, of course, instead have evaluative coherence between doing what is 'morally required' and with being morally heroic. But this would undercut the whole notion of the extremist: it is for an extremist not doing what is superogatory or what is morally heroic that is demanding; it is doing what is required of a morally good agent. Extremism is controversial *precisely because* what is demanding is nonetheless required of a moral life, that of a morally good agent. Without assuming some sort of evaluative coherence there really is no problem: if living a morally good life and being a morally good agent is not that demanding, only the life of a morally heroic agent is, then there is nothing particularly extremist about 'the extremist'. Thus in what follows this chapter will assume evaluative coherence is roughly correct (though the possibility of rejecting it is revisited in section 3 response 5).[8]

If evaluative coherence and extremism are correct then the person who gives a quarter of her income to charity to relieve suffering is a morally bad human being (she does what is morally wrong, and does so every single day, and with almost every consumer decision she takes).

Now, this seems counter-intuitive. But this should not worry the extremist, because the principle itself – as its most perceptive defenders have recognized – is not founded on the attempt to systematize our everyday moral intuitions, and thus not shown to be false if it conflicts with these. What is problematic for extremism is the possibility that to be a morally good human being should mean to be morally good for a human being – that is, compared to human beings in general. The difficulties for the Extremist arise if the moral evaluation of agents should correctly be thought of as *comparativist*. Specifically:

(Moral) comparativism
A qualitative moral evaluation applying to an agent is only potentially correct if in comparison to an implicit or explicit distribution of agents.

For the moral comparativist when we say someone is morally good, or bad, or heroic, or depraved this is potentially correct if in comparison to some instance or distribution, or more vaguely some rough idea of relative human variance. That is, 'morally good' is only meaningful if 'morally good' implicitly means 'morally good compared to X' (X can be one instance or a distribution). What is incorrect about evaluating as morally bad someone who gives a quarter of her income to charity is that she is not morally bad compared to how we think people are in general – quite the opposite; she is morally fairly exceptional. That she fails to do what is consequentially optimal cannot, given comparativism, necessarily entail she acts morally wrongly and should be evaluated negatively morally.

To get a sense of comparativism consider perhaps the following examples of comparativist evaluands that are non-moral:

> C1: 'Sarah is a great swimmer for an eight year old.'
>
> C2: 'Jack is a good student compared to most who enrol in the course.'
>
> C3: 'Tom is an excellent manager compared to most in the company.'

We could state these as implicit comparisons, for example if simply by saying 'Sarah is a great swimmer' we implicitly mean that she is a great swimmer compared to her age-peers, not dolphins or Olympians. The central feature is that *the qualitative evaluations compare the object to an instance or a rough distribution, and that is what renders them potentially correct*. If it turned out Sarah was a worse swimmer than most eight year olds then the statement would be false.

And here perhaps would be some evaluative sentences that, prima facie, without further specification, are absolutist[9] (non-comparativist):

> A1: 'Barry is a great barber in that he never cuts his customers' heads off.'
>
> A2: 'Meghna is a very good student and the worst of the hundreds I have ever taught.'
>
> A3: 'David is a terrible comedian, and among the best comedians in the world.'

Absolutist evaluations are, perhaps, much less common, but not impossible. We could for example say someone is a 'good swimmer' and simply mean that he doesn't sink when put in water, or alternatively mean he can swim the English Channel, so long as the evaluation of 'good' is not implicitly referencing some rough distribution. Whether familiar or not, however, what matters is whether moral agent evaluations should be understood to be comparativist or absolutist: the above examples are meant to be illustrative, not represent argument-by-analogy.

The central comparativist–absolutist difference thus hinges on the determinants of the qualitative labels. For comparativism there are meaningful judgements of 'more X than' or 'less X than' but not qualitative properties of being Y or Z *that do not reduce to* 'more than' or 'less than' statements. We may use qualitative labels to pick out rough areas on an implied distribution, but ultimately this is shorthand for saying 'more than most Ps' or 'more than almost all Ps' etc. For absolutism, by contrast, qualitative labels refer to the presence of some property or feature without reference to other instances. Being tall is comparativist. Being right-handed is absolutist.

But aren't *moral* evaluations and the theories that supply them necessarily absolutist? Despite consequentialist, deontological and (Aristotelian and Platonic) virtue ethics theories appearing to be non-comparativist, an explicitly moral theory need not be so, however. Indeed if we frame the debate over moral demandingness as a conflict between consequentialism and deontology then the issue of comparativism is likely to be obscured. For illustrative purposes we can compare an absolutist good-based moral theory with a comparativist one. Here again is Extremism:

- Morally good actions are those that best promote the overall good.

- Morally bad actions are those that do not best promote the overall good.

(For convenience, 'morally good' is meant potentially to include a wide range of linguistic descriptions, 'right', 'a duty', 'a demand of morality', and, under 'morally bad', their negative siblings.)

This is absolutist, as undertaking the actions that best promote the overall good may be incredibly demanding and all may fail to do so, or it may be trivially easy and most would any way do so (it is possible doing morally good actions might be expected of pure egoists given the right empirical contingencies).

Here alternatively is the previously introduced comparativist moral theory, 'motivation ethics':

- Morally good (or heroic) actions are those only expected of an agent significantly (or exceptionally) motivated to promote the good of others.

- Morally bad (or depraved) actions are those only expected of an agent not even moderately (or even slightly) motivated to promote the good of others.

The level of motivation – moderate, significant, exceptional, etc. – is intended to refer to some implied distribution, provisionally here that 'for a human being'. This is comparativist as the moral evaluation of agents therefore tracks an implicit comparative distribution of human variance. The individual who gives a quarter of her income to charity to relieve suffering is, in that regard, morally exemplary and perhaps even heroic, and her actions are thus morally evaluated in a significantly positive way. For the extremist, by contrast, she consistently does what is morally wrong.

For illustrative purposes, this chapter will assume that motivation ethics is the right comparativist moral theory, though hopefully if another theory seems more appealing it can be easily substituted in the relevant examples. If we do think both (moral) comparativism and evaluative coherence are broadly correct, then we must reject extremism. For if anyone recognizably human would consistently fail to act morally and (with evaluative coherence) therefore be morally bad, they cannot be morally bad if this means compared to human beings in general. Given evaluative coherence we face a choice between extremism and comparativism. This is the focus in what follows, and in doing so this chapter implicitly therefore frames the problem of demandingness via the Difficulty Condition, that is as a problem of motivational difficulty. But why is the Sacrifice Condition – that there are some demands a moral theory is not entitled to make – not a better way of understanding this dispute?

The central difficulty, I think, is that the latter does not appear to advance the debate – important as a claim though it potentially is – since it simply asserts the incorrectness of extremism without any obvious potential argument for this (aside from the counter-intuitive nature of requiring great sacrifice, but the extremist should not and need not accept intuitive-fit as a valid criterion). If someone adopts a moral theory that entails the Sacrifice Condition then clearly they are going to reject extremism, but this is precisely because they have adopted a rival theory to the extremist.

The choice between absolutism and comparativism by contrast at least offers us a framework for assessing which is correct. What, as such, might the extremist argue in favour of absolutism and against comparativism?

4.3 Options for the extremist

Here are six potential arguments open to the extremist in arguing that comparativism should be rejected. (1) Moral evaluations are binary, not comparative. (2) There is no unique distribution with which to compare. (3) It is absurd that moral evaluations should depend on what other people are like. (4) Comparativist evaluations demonstrate an unjustified status-quo bias. (5) Comparativism confuses moral goodness with moral rightness. (6) Comparativist evaluations are too indeterminate. (7) Comparativist evaluations are arbitrary.

1. Moral evaluations are binary

For the comparativist, moral evaluations track a distribution on a scale of more-moral and less-moral. While this distribution can be roughly qualitatively labelled at various points – such as that of being morally heinous, depraved, bad, good, exceptional and heroic – these ultimately simply divide it up much the same way that letter grades can divide up the marks students obtained in an exam. In the case of motivation ethics the distribution is possible strengths for human beings of a motivation to promote the good of others, and there are no necessary unique dividing points.

But if we frame the key question as establishing the 'demands of morality' or of our 'duties' then this suggests instead a stark binary (or tertiary) divide, and it could be argued that we as such have strong intuitions that morality should conform to these categories.

There are perhaps two initial problems with this response from the extremist however. Firstly, that these intuitions do not appear remarkably robust nor necessarily supportive of absolutism: we can easily talk of strong and weak duties, of some demands having a greater moral salience than others, and this not seem absurd, and thus even within stark linguistic categories have a much more scalar sense of moral evaluations. Murdering someone for fun or alternatively giving only half of one's income to charity may both be morally wrong for the extremist, but there does seem to be some background sense of them differing in how wrong they are, and this gestures towards a more scalar understanding, even if submerged. Our intuitions do not seem overwhelmingly decisive. (Furthermore, for non-intuitionists, the fact that the debate over demandingness is couched in terms of 'the demands of morality' should give us pause that there is not a framing effect present that obscures the issue of comparativism vs absolutism.)

Secondly, and perhaps more importantly, however, if the key argument for moral evaluations being binary is that some people have intuitions that all actions should be cleanly and robustly divided into right and wrong (or, perhaps, a duty, impermissible and neither), then this cannot be the key argument in favour of extremism, because the position is by its very nature counter-intuitive, this after all is the point. If the extremist adopts 'coherence with intuitions' as a necessary condition for moral theories then she has undercut her own position. She requires a principled reason why comparativist evaluations may be problematic. Linguistic intuitions are not enough.[10]

2. There is no unique distribution with which to compare

The previous formulation used the idea of someone being highly or significantly or exceptionally motivated to promote the good of others 'compared to human beings in general'. But why is this the only possible comparator distribution? Surely we could also compare people to other distributions, such as that of their society, or similarly situated agents, or all human beings who might live in the next hundred years. So why is a rather crude notion of human variance the unique distribution?

The comparativist should reject this critique as wrongly premised. For the comparativist, qualitative evaluations can be meaningful *in reference to any distribution*. Consider for example the question 'Is Bill Clinton tall [at about 6 feet and 2 inches]?' Well, compared to his contemporaries, somewhat. Compared to thirteenth-century peasants, he is very tall. Compared to professional basketball players, he is decidedly short. The question 'Is Bill Clinton tall?' cannot be correctly answered without reference to an implicit or an explicit reference group, but can be meaningful as a statement in reference to any particular clearly specified distribution. So too for the comparativist with qualitative moral evaluations.

What is open to the comparativist however is that some particular distribution is either conventionally or contextually privileged, and with moral evaluations this seems plausibly to be some sense of contemporary broad human variance. But at the same time, even if so, *we can still make meaningful statements compared to other distributions*, and indeed, if we were to disagree about the precise type of privileged human variance so long as we were clear on our distributions then both would be valid potential reference sets in order to make potentially correct or incorrect statements.

Thus the possibility of meaningful evaluations in reference to different distributions is not problematic for the comparativist, it is exactly what the theory explicitly entails. It is not a critique of comparativism, it is a feature of the view. That this is sometimes mildly counter-intuitive need not be surprising: it may be that the existence of a shared social context provides a dominant implicit comparator set, such as perhaps when we casually describe someone as tall and are implicitly referencing her or his contemporaries, and this may lend an appearance of absolutism, even if ultimately the reference is comparativist.

3. It is absurd that moral evaluations depend on what other people are like

As discussed above, comparativist moral evaluations reference someone as being more or less moral compared to some distribution. Qualitative evaluands may roughly pick out a point on the implied distribution, such that giving a quarter of income to charity is morally exceptional, giving none is morally bad, seeking to harm others is morally heinous, and devoting one's life to aiding the worse off morally heroic for a human being. But these only make sense because of the comparison, such as to contemporary psychologically normal human beings. In this sense the evaluations depend on what other people are like. One consequence, however, is that multiple comparisons, such as to those in a *particular* society or time, can be meaningful. But doesn't that risk giving us absurd results, such that someone's moral evaluation will vary depending on to which subset they are being compared?

One consideration against this being absurd is that there does seem to be a common sense in which we can both compare people to human beings in general, and also to some particular explicit subset, in particular that we can regard some figure as morally good for their society, even if they would not be morally good for a human being simpliciter.

It is possible for instance to think of a society where selfishness is venerated, children are taught the importance of unflinchingly pursuing their own interests, and social norms celebrate maximizing wealth for personal gain, and as such there is widespread unfettered egoism. In such a 'Selfishistan' someone consistently giving 10 per cent to charity to relieve suffering might be morally exemplary *for a citizen of Selfishistan, that is compared to most citizens in Selfishistan*. If however he lived in a more decent society – 'Alturistan' – where a concern for others was encouraged and widespread, then his actions might only be morally good (and not exemplary) *compared to most citizens of Alturistan*. Both could also in principle be evaluated in reference to a broader conception of human variance, such that someone acted simultaneously morally exemplarily compared to the citizens of Selfishistan, and yet only in a morally good manner for a human being. That these judgements vary because the comparator sets vary does not seem absurd, even if it is not the usual way of conceiving of such evaluations.

Yet the more radical possibility not only of qualitative evaluations differing in scale (good / exemplary / heroic) but rather of multiple *conflicting* evaluations based on radically different comparator sets is a bullet the comparativist needs to bite. That is, the following two judgements could, under comparativism, in principle be both potentially correct.

Someone who is a mild misanthrope[11] is:

(i) morally good compared to a society of significant misanthropes
(ii) morally bad as a human being

To the extent this really is counter-intuitive, then this would be a consideration against the comparativist, at least for those (unlike the extremist) committed to intuitive-fit as a key condition of theories of morality. My personal opinion is that this is not that absurd, that since we can readily distinguish differing comparative judgements in other areas – 'tall for a contemporary human being; short for a basketball player' – that it does not seem at least very cognitively or linguistically difficult to do so with regard to moral evaluation. But the possibility of different even conflicting qualitative evaluations given different comparator sets is something the comparativist has to accept.

Doing so, however, does not involve the rejection of evaluative coherence, since the evaluations are perfectly coherent *given any reference set*. To illustrate consider the following. Bob is tall compared to pygmies. He is small compared to basketball players. Whether he is tall in the first case or small in the second depends on his features in that anyone with identical height features would be evaluated identically, and if Sarah is taller than Bob then it is *impossible* for there to be some comparison where she is small and he tall compared to the same comparison set. Yet it is true we could say that Sarah is small (compared to giants) and Bob is tall (compared to pygmies) while it is still true that Sarah is taller than Bob. This is perfectly coherent as the referent comparison sets designating Sarah as small and Bob as tall are different. Yet their comparative evaluation will always be consistent: Sarah is taller than Bob period (this, remember, was exactly what action moralities such as consequentialism could not achieve with comparative moral evaluations).

4. Comparativist evaluations – in referencing contemporary human beings – demonstrate a status quo bias or excessive conservatism

If we are normally (without further clarification) evaluating people compared to contemporary human others wouldn't this implicitly endorse contingent and potentially unjustified current norms or habits, and represent as such an unsupported conservatism or status quo bias in moral evaluation? Even if we concede that the right privileged comparator set is that of broad human variance and not some subset, there might still be the worry that this is privileging a particular time.

There is something to this, but the force of this critique is going to depend significantly however on the *content* of the distribution to which agents should be morally compared. That is, comparativist evaluations need not be based on current behaviour, instead they might track some underlying psychological feature whose behavioural expression is conditional on a series of potentially true or false normative and empirical beliefs (as with motivation ethics).

One need not, for example, comparatively morally evaluate charitable giving based on the actual amount people give, but on what they would give with true beliefs and different strengths of a hypothetical motivation even if very few people's actual broadly altruistic motivations correctly aim at the right good. As such, a comparativist moral theory can reject a status quo bias *where current behaviour is contingent on false empirical or normative beliefs*.

If, for instance, giving to charity is highly effective in promoting the overall good, but most people believe it is not, then we should expect most people in society to act morally badly in their charitable giving, and this still be a correct comparativist evaluation, as if they had had correct empirical beliefs then they might have given much more. The reason for this is that, aside from the familiar problem of execution errors – we aim to do X but end up doing not-X – there are at least three ways for a comparativist moral theory that one could fail to undertake what is morally good (or exceptional or heroic). Namely due to:

(i) false empirical beliefs
(ii) false normative beliefs
(iii) an insufficient level of the relevant psychological feature (for motivation ethics: a motivation that the lives of others go well)[12]

Even if the third category is comparatively determined, by for instance our judgement of the possibility, patterning and variance of human egoistic versus altruistic motivations, it need not be that in assessing the status quo we should defer to conventional beliefs on the first two. As such comparativism may not be conservative in its evaluation of current practices at all. That is, consider the following three individuals:

1. A semi-altruist who believes (wrongly) that climate change is not a real threat to mass human welfare.
2. A semi-altruist who believes (wrongly) that the suffering of people from her own country or of her own race is objectively more important than that of other human beings.
3. A pure egoist who is simply unconcerned with the interests of others.

All three individuals could be expected in a series of situations to act morally badly, but their reasons for doing so will vary, and to the extent that false normative or empirical beliefs predominate then social norms reflecting these will be criticizable and negatively morally evaluated even if comparativism is true. If, for instance, it is correct that animal suffering is objectively bad, and if this isn't widely recognized, then significant altruists could be expected to frequently act morally badly, even morally depravedly.

A comparativist moral theory can reject a status quo bias where this bias is contingent on false empirical or normative beliefs, and this may render it from conventional standards a really quite radical theory indeed – the charge of an excessive conservatism seems prima facie that it can be met.

5. Comparativism confuses moral goodness with moral rightness

In framing the problem above, different ways of describing positive and negative evaluations were treated as largely synonymous (what is right / good / a demand of morality / a duty etc.). But what if, however, evaluations of moral goodness and badness apply to agents, and moral rightness and wrongness to actions, *and there is no systematic expected relation between the two* (it is not that doing what is right is expected of morally good agents etc.)? Actions could be evaluated in terms of right / wrong and be absolutist, and agent evaluations consist of goodness / badness and be comparativist.

This response in effect rejects 'evaluative coherence' and will suffer from the same problems as any such rejection, notably that of phenomenological misfit and prescriptive ambiguity. Consider, for instance, that giving 10 per cent of one's income to charity would be what we would expect of a morally good agent, as this judgement is comparativist, but simultaneously it would be the morally wrong thing to do, as this evaluation is absolutist. Here are two problems with this.

Firstly, that when we normally describe someone as acting consistently morally wrongly we typically imply a negative moral evaluation of them. Thus in rejecting the connection between acting morally wrongly and being a morally bad agent we are at a minimum going to be misleading in our deployment of moral terms. This phenomenological misfit is, from the point of view of advancing clear debate and discussion, undesirable, and as such the proposal needs to provide some positive argument for it.

Secondly, and more importantly, however, severing the general connection between the moral goodness (of agents) and acting rightly or fulfilling one's duties leaves us with widespread prescriptive ambiguity, for the question 'As a morally good agent, what should I do?' now has two answers. One should, as a moral human agent, give 10 per cent to charity. But one should also do what is morally right, which is to give 80 per cent. So too with the negative evaluations: one should not give only 20 per cent as this is clearly morally wrong, but one should give 20 per cent as a highly moral human being, as this is morally exemplary. If extremism determines rightness and comparativism determines goodness then this conflict need not be occasional, it may occur all the time (the potential repeated demandingness of acting morally for the extremist is after all why the view is controversial).

Furthermore, it is not, if we make them entirely separate, that these two concepts of evaluation – rightness based on absolutism and moral goodness based on comparativism – are equally useful. Goodness gives us coherent agent evaluations *and* action evaluations – it tells us what it is like to be a morally good or bad or exceptional or heroic agent and what actions would accompany this. Rightness tells us what is right or wrong to do but not what type of agent would so act. As such it is not clear what its purpose is (unlike if the evaluation of agents and their acts broadly cohere, in which case rightness helps us understand what is required to live as a morally good agent).

Denying an expected or typical connection between the rightness of actions and the goodness of agents is not only potentially misleading but risks severe prescriptive ambiguity. Given the costs, we need some very good reason to overturn rough evaluative coherence between an agent and her actions. It is not immediately clear what this would be, and certainly observing the lexical distinction between rightness and goodness is not it.

6. Comparativist evaluations are too indeterminate

For comparativism there is not some tidy formula one can simply apply: making moral evaluations requires a judgement of the distribution of the feature upon which comparisons are based.[13] In many cases this may be easy, but it need not always be so. In particular, since they depend on a judgement of various human phenomena we might expect comparativist evaluations to sometimes be decidedly indeterminate, and problematic as such. There are perhaps two potential worries here: firstly that they are as such incorrect; and secondly that they are as such unhelpful, as we require relatively determinate evaluations.[14]

The first worry assumes that making correct evaluations should be perfectly determinate given the knowledge usually available to human beings. But why should this be the case? Judgements of whether someone is guilty given a certain evidential set are often under-determined, in that they rely on some broad psychological theories that themselves are not strictly logically entailed by the evidence. But that does not entail that it is not, in principle, correct that someone is innocent or guilty. To give this criticism bite we need some principled reason why conclusions based on partial information sets should be as determinate as those based on complete information sets, something that is far from obvious.

And secondly, if we *pragmatically* require some threshold of determinacy in our everyday moral evaluations – if, for example, it is instrumentally useful to have certain moral judgements clear, simple and widely understandable – then that is an argument for taking what we regard as the correct evaluations and simplifying and generalizing them (such as that proposed in section 2.3). It does not indicate that they are incorrect, rather that they are insufficient for a certain purpose. This is commonplace however: we can use Newtonian physics or simple election-prediction models for practical applications without having to concede that relativistic physics is false or voter complexity absent, the former are rather useful but crude versions of the latter. Even if we think that perfect actual judgements of moral goodness and badness would require much psychological information and understanding, we still may find it useful to adopt certain social norms or general evaluations based around acts we are pretty confident are morally bad or good, even if we admit that there are possible currently unknown psychological facts that might qualify this judgement.

Comparativism after all is an argument about the nature of correct moral evaluations and the information we would need to form correct beliefs about these. With less, uncertain or hesitant information such judgements may be hard. But this indicates that moral judgement, in some situations at least, will be difficult. It cannot, without assuming or demonstrating the necessary correctness of crisp, simple determinate evaluations, be an argument against comparativism.

7. Comparativist evaluations are arbitrary

The critique of consequentialism in Chapter 1 was that the agent evaluations were not determined by features of the agent and were thus arbitrary (so that for example two identical agents could be evaluated in contradictory ways overall, and two different agents could be evaluated in divergent ways depending on something unrelated to their features). But doesn't comparativism entail the same problem? By advocating it and the critique of consequentialism isn't this book self-contradictory?

Well, no. Moral comparativism is an account of the nature of qualitative agent evaluations (morally good, morally heroic, morally depraved etc.). It holds that *quantitative* agent evaluations are basic and determined entirely by scalar features of the agent. *Qualitative* evaluations are simply one way of descriptively referencing these underlying agential facts. But the agential facts are based on agential features, in motivation ethics' case, for instance, how motivated the agent is to promote the good of others.

Here, for instance, are four possibilities:

1. Qualitative moral agent evaluations are basic and determined by agential features.
2. Qualitative moral agent evaluations are basic and not determined by agential features.
3. Quantitative moral agent evaluations are basic and determined by agential features.
4. Quantitative moral agent evaluations are basic and not determined by agential features.

An example of (1) would be a will-based deontology where the good will would be either present or not (and thus determine the presence of moral worth or not). Motivation ethics is an example of (3). Neither (1) nor (3) raise arbitrary agent-evaluation worries, however, since the basic evaluations are entirely determined by agential features.

Comparativism in general is the view that the evaluation of X should track a scalar feature potentially possessed by things like X, and thus that qualitative evaluations are derivative (and comparative). So – if comparatively determined – to call someone 'tall' does not mean she has some qualitative feature, 'tallness'. What it means is that she has some amount of a scalar feature – height – and we can label it qualitatively in reference to some distribution (say the heights of people in general). There is nothing arbitrary here if we remember that the ultimate evaluative facts are scalar, hence why you need comparativism to make rough qualitative references. For motivation ethics agents can be more or less moral based on how motivated they are to promote the good of others. We can use qualitative evaluands (morally good, morally heroic etc.) to try to describe rough levels on this scale in comparison to other levels, but these are ultimately derivative of facts about how morally motivated agents are.

4.4 Arguments for comparativism

None of the previous arguments against comparativism are self-evidently decisive. But are there considerations that count in favour of comparativist evaluations and against absolutist ones? To an extent this will depend on our broader arguments for particular moral theories. But there are also considerations specifically in favour of comparativism. Here is an outline of three.

Firstly, if we adopt absolutist action evaluations then the demand for comparativist agent evaluations does not necessarily go away. Many of us want to know what it would be like to live a morally good, or exemplary or even heroic life *for a human being*, that is with some sense of the possibilities, limits, difficulties and temptations that structure and pattern human nature. The extremist answer is to describe the morally ideal human being with falling below this being morally bad, or to deny the relevance of the question. But for many of us, in contemplating what we do with our lives and the different things we seek to pursue, having some sense of what a good or even morally exemplary life would be like does seem desirable. Yet absolutism cannot derive this from its evaluations, and if it concedes separate grounds for producing agent evaluations it risks both prescriptive ambiguity and undercutting its action evaluations (the 'demands of morality' would not typically be fulfilled by a morally good human agent, and to lead a morally good human life would not entail meeting such demands). Comparativism by contrast can not only help us evaluate human behaviour compared to a broad notion of human variance, but also conditioning on the age in which a person lived. To the extent one thinks these important questions, absolutism will, prima facie, lack the conceptual resources to answer them.

Secondly, for a particular meta-ethical stance – that of moral realists – comparativism may in a certain sense help render the view less mysterious, or at least less mysterious than under absolutism. One thing that has seemed problematic to some people about moral realism is the precise nature of our duties or of rights: what, in a sense, such qualitative entities are made of, most famously that they would be 'entities or qualities or relations of a very strange sort, utterly different from anything else in the universe'.[15] Part – only part, but part – of this stems from the assumption of moral entities as having distinct qualitative properties such as 'wrongness', 'rightness' or 'being a right' etc. This seems most striking with absolutism.

For comparativism, by contrast, all we need is a scalar feature that the moral evaluations are to supervene upon, and that this can vary between human beings. For example, with motivation ethics, once we accept that people's lives can go better or worse (that is our theory of the good), then we can describe agents as being more or less motivated to promote this without requiring the existence of any other special moral entities (such as duties, or rights, or right and wrongness), while still capturing that some of these terms may derivatively be useful as referencing some rough points on a distribution.

For the comparativist there is no such thing as a good swimmer simpliciter or a good essay simpliciter; rather this evaluation makes sense in reference to some implied distribution (healthy adult humans, students in a class cohort etc.). So too with qualitative moral evaluations, in this case, at least with motivation ethics, based on their level of motivation to promote the good. In both sets of cases there appears something less puzzling about the notion of a good swimmer or a morally good agent where these are comparativist rather than with the latter in contrast to the independent existence of duties or rights or moral wrongness where the precise metaphysical status of such entities is decidedly unobvious.

This is partly a concern about the 'mysteriousness' of duties as entities, something that might only be problematic for some meta-ethical stances. Yet comparativism can also be seen as imposing weaker requirements of justification in general. If, for instance, we understand 'tall' to be comparativist, then all we need to do is establish that there is some metric of more of less – in this case of more or less height – and then be clear about which particular distribution we are referencing. If, however, by 'tall' we mean over 8 feet as opposed to over 7 feet then as well as establishing the metric of height we additionally need to establish that the 8 feet cut-off is the right cut-off for 'tall', not the 7 feet one. Absolutism as such seems to impose a greater burden of justification. So with moral entities, even if we do not worry about the status of absolutist moral entities, we may well still face a great justificatory burden if absolutism is true.[16]

Thirdly, if an action morality is absolutist, it will be vulnerable to the moral agent problem of Chapter 1. That is, consider an action morality where acting morally is not comparatively determined, i.e. in principle does not track how demanding the action is (and thus where on the distribution of agents the line between its likely performance and non-performance would be). And take an agent reasonably motivated to do whatever this theory regards as morally right, and to avoid whatever this moral theory regards as morally wrong. We can think of potential choices she would face, some of which where it would be very demanding to act rightly – D choices – and she would likely not do so. Alternatively there would some choices where it would be fairly easy to act morally – E choices – and she would likely do so.

If whether or not she typically or generally acts rightly or wrongly affects her moral evaluation, then that evaluation will be contingent on whether she mostly faces demanding D choices or easy E choices. That is, if these are a set of possible choices:

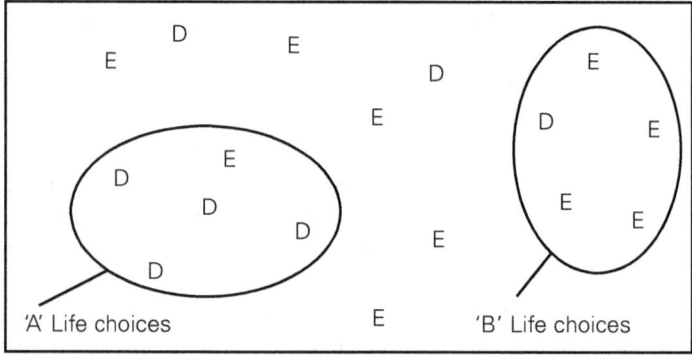

As such her agent evaluation will depend on whether she faces A life choices or B life choices, even if she would in both sets of situations have the same features. This simply follows because the motivational ease or demandingness of the actions does not determine their moral evaluation. In other words, that if we have absolutist action evaluations then we should expect to encounter the earlier moral agent problems.

Thus although this chapter has focused on extremism, Chapter 1 on consequentialism, and Chapter 3 on a harm-based deontology, we can see that the rejection of comparativism by all three is part of the reason for the moral agent worries. If the demandingness of doing what is morally better does not potentially affect the evaluation of an agent's doing so, then the evaluation of agents will be dependent on whether they face demanding or non-demanding situations, something that might be consistently different even with identical agents, or at a minimum radically contingent on things unrelated to the agents' features.

To thus put this in the context of extremism, take the following two agents and facts:

'Rightly Richard' consistently fulfils the demands of morality.

'Wrongly Ryan' consistently fails to fulfil the demands of morality.

Now assume extremism and rough evaluative coherence are correct. If so, Rightly Richard is a morally good agent, Wrongly Ryan is a morally bad agent (or, at least, Rightly Richard is a much more moral agent than Wrongly Ryan). However, if extremism is true then it is perfectly possible that Rightly Richard and Wrongly Ryan have the same constitutive features as agents, and indeed that each would act identically facing the same situations. Richard, of course, simply faced situations where fulfilling the demands of morality was much less demanding than Ryan.

What is the extremist to hold here? Well, they face exactly the same problematic options as consequentialism did in Chapter 1.[17] They can maintain that two identical agents can be evaluated contradictorily, and generally that the evaluation of agents should not be determined by agential features, and then face the charge that such evaluations are arbitrary and should be rejected (along with the theory that entailed them). Or they can hold that rough evaluative coherence should be rejected, in which case they appear to have substantially undercut their own theory's action evaluations: living as a morally good agent doesn't involve generally fulfilling the demands of morality, an agent who consistently fails the demands of morality can be morally good, one who consistently meets them can be morally bad.

Or perhaps they can appeal to hypothetical sets, naively hope that these problems won't occur too often, or suggest moral agent evaluations simply can't be meaningful. Each option will encounter the previously surveyed problems (so one simple way to see the choices is to ask: is there a good response to the moral agent question available to act consequentialism? If so, then this is available to extremism. If not, then there is no good response available to extremism.)

Not only does the extremist need to offer a compelling argument against comparativist qualitative agent evaluations, but she needs too to do so in a way that still permits a persuasive response to the moral agent question. Doing so is not straightforward.

4.5 Conclusions

The demandingness worry is not solely a conflict of intuition and theory. Rather, it also arises from two competing conceptions of the nature of qualitative moral evaluations: comparativism and absolutism. These are in tension if we adopt absolutist qualitative action evaluations while implicitly retaining comparativist qualitative agent evaluations, and this plausibly creates most of our disquiet over the extremist – to imply that someone is morally bad for failing to do what is incredibly demanding clashes with our sense that we should evaluate people as human beings, that is in comparison to some rough idea of human variance and based on agential features.

The choice between whether moral evaluations are best thought of as absolutist or comparativist is as such a fundamental one. The dominant position in the literature is that of absolutism and indeed the very way the debate over demandingness is framed – that of identifying the 'demands of morality' or of 'our duties' – implicitly pushes us towards an absolutist framework. If this position was self-evidently correct then this would be a problem for motivation ethics. Yet, as the discussion here has tried to indicate, even though the comparativist position is seemingly the more radical, it has arguments in favour of it, and the prima facie arguments against it on examination are not decisive.

That motivation ethics makes comparativist evaluations makes the theory unusual (and, as far as I know, unique in this respect compared to our most prominent moral theories). Yet such a feature does not obviously make the theory incorrect, and if the demandingness worry is at root a worry about agent evaluations, then if anything it indicates a strength of comparativism in being able to non-arbitrarily and coherently supply these.

CHAPTER FIVE

The problem of special relationships

On an almost daily basis, most of us favour our children, our families and our friends over those in much, much greater need. The partiality of such 'special relationships' is typically a large, consistent and dominant motivation in much of what we do. Moral actions, however, are often held to be impartially justified, in particular in being based on an equal concern for all. Such bias towards one's family and friends thus appears at first glance to be morally unjustified. This, very roughly, is the problem of special relationships. But what type of problem is it?

One way of viewing it is as a conflict between a general moral principle and our fallible intuitions, and that as such we could simply reject the intuitions. This chapter argues, however, that the problems are more basic and, in particular, arise as a consequence of a specific semi-latent assumption: that the primary object of moral evaluations should be actions. The argument of part one is that this assumption should be rejected. Part two then outlines the motivation ethics approach and its account of 'quasi-moral duties'.

5.1 The problem of special relationships

Let a 'special relationship'[1] be a relationship that motivates an agent to promote the interests of some particular person[2] – parent, child, friend, spouse, etc.[3] Now, consider generic actions, or sets of actions, such that choosing the 'impartially-justified actions' would better promote the morally relevant interests of all affected impartially assessed and such that choosing the 'partiality-caused' actions would better promote the interests of the object of the agent's special relationship (the spouse, the child, etc.) and what someone reasonably motivated by such partiality would do. Each of these actions might be single acts, or the sets of acts arising from some rule, virtue or motivation.

If we directly morally evaluate these acts or sets of acts, and if moral actions are those justified by an equal concern for all, then it appears that we should do the impartially justified actions.[4] To do the partiality-caused actions would involve not treating everyone as equally worthy of concern, to be partial. If we morally ought to do the impartially-justified actions, then the special relationship seems to risk creating four prima-facie troubling problems:

1. Demandingness: acting morally is made more motivationally demanding as a result of the relationship, and we will sometimes fail to act morally as a result.[5]
2. Corrosion: we may have a moral reason to reduce the importance of the relationship in our lives as it makes it harder to act morally, and reduces the probability we will do so.
3. Alienation: even if we cannot or do not reduce the importance of the relationship, we should morally evaluate its presence negatively: its existence is morally bad in that it makes us less likely to act morally. What is extremely important to the agent, and valued greatly by them, is simultaneously something they should evaluate negatively (morally), and see as morally undesirable.
4. Impoverishment: it would be morally better if we lacked the special relationship, but doing so could make our lives unfulfilling.[6] To the degree one attaches importance to these types of relationships, then the problems of impoverishment will seem more or less troublesome.

These problems correspond to four potential general schematic features of any motivation – P – that primarily motivates us to show partial concern, in that: (i) it makes acts based on an equal concern harder to do; (ii) if P was reduced or weakened we would likely do more such acts; (iii) P can be evaluated as harmful to those potentially benefited by an equal concern; and (iv) a life without P seems morally desirable but possibly very bad for the agent.

Now someone might claim that the choice between the impartially justified actions and the partiality-caused actions was rare or impossible, that it just happens that our partial special relationships turn out to encourage impartially justified actions.[7] This option is discussed below. Yet the more fundamental initial question arises as to why demandingness, corrosion, alienation and impoverishment are indeed potential problems. Someone could hold that they are simply features of special relationships and morality; morality really can be incredibly demanding, corrosive of deeply valued relationships, alienating from them and emotionally impoverishing.

Underlying why they may indeed be problems is an implied clash between the evaluation of two different potential objects of moral evaluation: the action and the agent. Consider these two evaluations:

E1: Consistently prioritizing the interests of some children over those in much, much greater need, and much more easily helped, is to act morally wrongly.

E2: A father who deeply cares for and loves his children is not a morally bad agent for so doing.

Many hold E2 (or judgements like it) and would appeal to some of the considerations underpinning demandingness, corrosion, alienation and impoverishment in doing so: to say the agent was a morally bad person would be to hold them to too high a standard given the burdens, difficulty and sacrifice of living without the relationship or not caring for the other person in it.

Yet the idea that moral actions are those that demonstrate an equal concern for all seems to imply E1 or similar judgements. Thus we seem to have two conflicting evaluations: those in the special relationship are not morally bad for so being; those in the special relationship are likely to act morally wrongly for so being (E1 may be the dominant result of the relationship). The problem of special relationships arises because of our contradictory evaluations of the agent and of the actions the agent is likely to undertake as a result of the relationship. To generalize, the 'Problem of Special Relationships' occurs if, and when, we hold the following:

SR1: Having special relationship – S – entails that the agent will generally undertake actions that reflect an unequal concern for all.

SR2: The agent is not morally bad for having special relationship S.

Combined with the following two moral principles:

M1: Of two or more actions, (or sets of actions arising from a virtue, rule or motive), the morally right action (or set of actions) is that which reflects an equal concern for all.

Evaluative Coherence: In general, the moral evaluations of actions and agents should roughly cohere.

The 'Problem of Special Relationships' is that these premises conflict: an agent cultivating or maintaining the special relationship acts morally badly as a result (SR1 and M1) is not a morally bad agent as a result (SR2), and yet the moral evaluations of agents and their actions should cohere (EC).

Because he or she is a loving parent, for instance, it seems someone may consistently do morally unjustified acts, evaluative coherence implies that he or she is thus a morally bad person for so doing, but we don't think being a loving parent makes someone a morally bad person. We cannot simultaneously hold SR1, SR2, M1 and Evaluative Coherence without contradiction: one of them must be wrong.

To address the problem of special relationships we need to decide which should be rejected. Here are four possibilities:

(i) Hold that cases under premise SR1 cannot occur: special relationships always lead to actions that reflect an equal concern for all.
(ii) Hold that premise SR2 is false: having the special relationship really does make one morally bad in this regard.
(iii) Reject Evaluative Coherence: the moral evaluation of actions and agents need not generally cohere.
(iv) Reject M1: moral actions are not necessarily those that reflect an equal concern for all.

By arguing against (i) to (iii), the first part of this chapter will argue that we should adopt (iv) and reject M1, in other words reject the idea that the primary object of moral evaluation is actions (and moral actions are those justified by an impartial concern). It is this idea that ultimately creates the 'Problem of Special Relationships', and section 5.2 therefore implicitly argues we should reject it because of its inability to be consistent with an acceptable account of agent evaluation.

The alternative is to hold that the primary object of moral evaluation is agents – that is we start with an account of morally good and bad agents and derive action evaluations from these – and to hold that moral concern is impartial concern for all. This is the motivation ethics approach. Section 5.3 therefore sets out how the theory approaches special relationships, and its accompanying account of 'quasi-moral duties'.

5.2 Arguments against the initial problem

The first response to the Problem of Special Relationships, (i), was to claim that the actions arising from partial relationships will always happen to be impartially justified based on an equal concern for all. This response is typified by the consequentialist who holds that it just so happens that – overall – loving one's children, spouse and friends actually does lead to the best consequences impartially judged. The chief considerations in favour of this are epistemic (one's superior evidence of the local effects of one's actions) and causal (that local impacts are frequently greater in size and require less multi-agent coordination).[8]

Now, this seems prima facie empirically extremely dubious. After all, the reason people normally enter into the relationships is not from impartial motives or out of a concern for all; rather, it's because they fall in love, or develop an attachment for some other person, or share experiences and come to care about the other person. The claim that actions stemming from partial concern might be impartially morally justified seems dubious in particular as the phenomenology and causal chains bear little relation to the evaluative impartiality: no one loves his or her parents due to reflection on the demands of morality but rather due to an extended history of love, affection and concern. As such we *might* live in a world where the actions stemming from such relationships were directly justifiable based on an equal concern for all, but it seems incredibly unlikely, as this concern had nothing to do with the main causes of the relationships.

Furthermore, in a world as unequal in economic distribution as ours, showing partiality to those in the developed world, as most of us with special relationships there do, seems spectacularly unlikely to be impartially best on almost any plausible reading of the relevant empirical claims.

Yet the greater problem with option (i) is that the overall worries being raised are structural: they assert that in choosing between two alternate acts (or sets of acts) one may be justified by an equal concern for all, the other based on giving extra weight or consideration to a particular person and what we would be more likely to do if we had a special relationship with that person. To claim that it has just turned out that we don't as a matter of fact face such situations, as well as seeming plain false, is to fail to respond to the worry that we might do so.

One way to capture this is to accept for argument's sake that some special relationships – say towards our children – can be impartially justified somehow. Now think of one of the relationships that fails this test – say our relations with our elderly but non-poor and non-vulnerable parents. We still need an answer to the question of how to morally evaluate the actions these relationships typically entail. Thus even if, despite the apparent empirical implausibility, some relationships can be justified by an equal concern, the question remains of how to morally assess those other relationships that cannot be justified by an equal concern. At a minimum SR1 remains possible, that is, it remains possible that strong partial motivations will lead agents to not do what is impartially justified. If so we need to assess which of (ii) to (iv) to reject when this happens.

Claim (ii) is that special relationships do not raise a problem for moral theories that accept M1, as if it really is the case that the actions encouraged by such relationships are not justifiable by an equal concern for all then by still doing them we act morally badly and should be morally evaluated negatively as a result. The moral evaluation of agents is derived from that of their actions, and in those situations where the relationship causes one overall to act morally badly then the agent should be morally evaluated negatively for having it, and thus that demandingness, corrosion, alienation and impoverishment may simply be things that morally good agents have to live with; they do not represent valid criticisms of a moral theory that entails them.

The view of moral evaluations underlying this option is perhaps the pre-eminent if implicit stance of theories that focus upon the direct moral evaluation of actions (that is they don't first give an account of the features of a moral agent and derive action evaluations from what such an agent would do). Under (ii) if one morally ought to do X then not doing X means one should be morally evaluated negatively; if one does X one should be morally evaluated positively (or at least not negatively). Similarly, if action P is morally preferable to action Q then the agent who does P is prima facie morally better in this regard than the agent who does Q.

The first difficulty with this view, however, is that if we morally evaluate actions impartially, based on an equal concern for all, then this can exclude a range of agent based considerations because actions are frequently motivationally over-determined (in that agents can do them for a variety of reasons), and heterogeneous in difficulty (the ease of one action compared to others will vary greatly). Specifically such a method of morally evaluating actions can fail to take into account why an agent does an action, and how hard it is to do an action or group of actions. For anyone who gives weight to intuitions this is clearly a problematic stance (for those, like myself, that are sceptical of giving intuitions such weight the option is still deeply problematic, as subsequently discussed).

Consider, for example, Jack and Peter, two similarly wealthy old men. Jack writes a will leaving all of his estate to a well-known charity in order to upset his children, whom he detests. He cares nothing for charity, nor the poor, but delights in the thought of his children's distress. Peter on the other hand writes a will leaving most of his estate to charity but reserves a third for his adult children, whom he loves dearly. Peter gives most of it to charity out of a desire to reduce the suffering of others. Evaluated impartially, or against the criterion of an equal concern for all, Jack's action seems morally better: he causes better outcomes (given global inequalities he produces much more utility/wellbeing/suffering-avoidance even factoring in that of his children), he follows a better rule (give all your estate to charity), and has a consequentially better motivation (had he shared Peter's motivations the world would have been a worse place).[9] And if agent evaluations are derived from action evaluations then Jack is more moral than Peter. Yet this seems wrong for a very good substantive reason: in judging an agent we partly judge why they do what they do. Yet if the evaluations of an agent are merely based on what they do then this will be excluded.

Additionally, agents' differing difficulty in undertaking impartially justified actions seems like it should affect our evaluation of them. Consider a variant on a classic example from Williams. A sudden storm threatens two row-boats out at sea, and a sailor has to choose what she should do: should she stay in port, try to save the row-boat containing four people, or try to save the other containing six (trying to save either carries a small risk to herself).[10] Impartially judged, or showing equal concern for all, if she can only save one boat she should save the one with six in. Yet the one containing four contains her husband, brother and parents.[11] If she saves her family and not the strangers she will thus have done the morally wrong thing. While it is psychologically possible that she could save the strangers, her love for her family makes it much harder to do so. Should that affect our evaluation of her if she manages or fails to do the right thing? If she saves her family should we evaluate her similarly to someone who saved the four because they thought that might be more likely to lead to a reward? I think most will have a strong intuition that, given it is her family at risk – as it changes how hard it would be to do the impartial act – our evaluation of her should not simply be derived from the impartially justified moral evaluation of what she does.

Such a case of itself cannot be decisive however: a defender of claim (ii) could simply hold our intuitions wrong or non-informative (a position I currently personally think has the best arguments in favour of it). Yet the deeper difficulty with proposal (ii) is that it cannot co-exist with the more general normative principle that:

The agent evaluation principle
If agent X is subject to normative evaluation, then the normative evaluation of X should be determined by features of X.

Under option (ii) – evaluating agents based on the evaluation of the actions they do, and actions based on the impartial justification of their features alone – then we must violate the agent evaluation principle. Consider, for example, someone who is utterly selfish: whatever situation he faces he looks out for himself, he intrinsically cares not one whit for others (he may have special relationships, but he does so merely to make him be happy, and cares nothing per se for those in such relationships). Is he a morally good agent?

Well, given certain empirical contingencies all his actions will be justifiable based on an equal concern for all and thus right: sometimes, for instance, focusing on our own wellbeing will cause us to do actions that will also best promote the interests of all impartially judged (we may be in a better situation to further our own interests, through causal or epistemic asymmetries).

If for instance someone lives in a very poor but egalitarian country then even if she is utterly selfish she may actually do what is impartially justified, her working hard to make her own life better might actually be the best thing to do viewed by an impartial spectator or based on an equal concern for all. Yet in other situations such untrammelled selfishness could lead one to act morally badly all the time: if one is wealthy and many are poor then relentlessly and unflinchingly seeking to look after one's own interests could cause one to always act wrongly. However, by stipulation, the individual in both situations shares exactly the same features: they have the same inclinations, emotions, attachments, feelings, beliefs, virtues, and so on. Thus to morally evaluate them based on the moral evaluation of their actions, where this evaluation depends on the situations they happen to face, must entail that we are not really evaluating them: they could be identical and yet be correctly evaluated in completely contradictory ways given a different set of life situations or of empirical relationships. To adopt option (ii) is to be forced to reject the agent evaluation principle.[12]

Perhaps we should: maybe agents shouldn't be evaluated based on their features, but based on what situations they happen to find themselves in.[13] Someone who is utterly selfish but happens in his life to face situations A, B, C is a morally good agent, but of course had he faced situations D, E and F then he would be a morally bad agent, even if he had no potential control over which set of situations he would face. This is coherent and allows one to hold that agent evaluations are derived from action evaluations, which themselves are determined by impartial features of the actions (what best promotes the interests of all, what represents an equal concern for all, what treats all as equally valuable moral ends etc.). Yet it seems in an important way to leave such a moral theory vulnerable to a particular type of amoralism. For when our theory indicates that the amoralist is a morally bad agent (or morally good), they can reply that this is simply a feature of the situations they happened to face, and had they faced different ones they would have been evaluated completely differently, despite having had the same features. Thus it doesn't seem to be a compelling evaluation. If an agent has features P, Q, R, S, T, where these features are what we take to be the constitutive features of the agent, and we claim that having P, Q, R, S, T makes one morally good given that empirical fact X obtains, but morally bad given that fact Y obtains, and the agent has no control over whether X or Y obtains, then the amoralist can complain, with justification, that our moral evaluations of P, Q, R, S, T are not compelling.

Thus as well as having very strong intuitions that the evaluation of agents should be partly based on why they do what they do, and how difficult it is to do what they do, even intuition sceptics like myself have a broader substantive reason to reject option (ii), namely that in morally evaluating agents we should evaluate features of them else we run into all the problems discussed in Chapter 1.

Option (iii) – that the moral evaluation of actions and agents are not derived from each other – initially seems attractive: it can meet the agent evaluation principle and solves the Problem of Special Relationships because it can concede that as a result of such relationships one may consistently act wrongly, but that someone should not be morally evaluated negatively as a result.

Being a loving parent, for example, could cause one to act consistently morally wrongly – due to the partiality of the concern – but if so this would not indicate any moral failing on the part of the agent: she would not be morally evaluated negatively for consistently doing what is morally wrong. On this view, the evaluation of actions can be based on features of them (are they impartially justifiable, do they reflect an equal concern for all?), the evaluation of agents is just based on a different non-related set of considerations.

The difficulty, however, is that for a moral theory that lacks evaluative coherence – where for example, one ought to do P, but a moral agent would do not-P – there need be no systematic link between living a moral life, that of a morally good agent, and acting morally (and the same holds for negative moral evaluations: doing the wrong thing and being a morally bad agent need not be related). One consequence is prescriptive ambiguity: the theory tells us both to do what is right, and to live like a moral agent, and these recommendations do not cohere.[14]

Now, a response to this might be that although our action and agent evaluations are not derived from each other they might still draw on the same considerations: thus acting rightly tends to be what a morally good agent would do; acting wrongly tends to be what a morally bad agent would do. While this seems plausible so put, what this response does is to trade off the problems of option (iii) – roughly that of how arbitrary the agent evaluations are – for those of option (iv), roughly of how coherent such evaluations are when scrutinized against our action evaluations. In other words, the more we make our agent evaluations better cohere with our action evaluations the more we reduce how compelling such evaluations are by ignoring or removing from consideration features of the agent (such as what motivates them to do what they do, or how hard it is to do what they do) and instead introducing arbitrary (non-agential) considerations. Yet if neither option (iii) nor option (iv) are persuasive on their own, then a mix of them will not be either.

Thus the Problem of Special Relationships – that the partiality they represent may cause one to consistently act wrongly, but that we do not necessarily think an agent is morally bad for having such a relationship – is a symptom of the broader underlying difficulty in relating the moral evaluation of agents to the moral evaluation of actions when the latter is determined based on impartially justified features of the actions (this last clause is met by M1).

The obvious ways of addressing this difficulty are not without problems of their own. The claim that partial relationships always happen to encourage impartially justified actions is both empirically implausible and does not address the worry that they might not. The claim that agent evaluations are derived from action evaluations excludes salient features of the agent, and is difficult to reconcile with the view that agents should be evaluated based on their features if the evaluation is to be non-arbitrary. The claim that agents and the actions they undertake should be evaluated on unrelated grounds left us lacking evaluative coherence and thus with prescriptive ambiguity. To address the problem of special relationships we should thus consider rejecting M1, doing so because it struggles to permit non-arbitrary and coherent agent evaluations.

But how should it be rejected? What undermined M1 and more broadly the view that agent evaluations should be derived from action evaluations was that we failed to evaluate agents by why they did what they did (what motivated them), and how hard it was to do what they did (what alternative motivations were in play): in other words, based on their motivational set. It was, after all, that special relationships radically alter how we are motivated – that they entail being strongly motivated to promote the interests of particular individuals – that created the problems in the first place. The next section discusses how motivation ethics retains this insight, and the claim that morality consists in an equal concern for all, but applies this concern to a particular motivation agents may have, rather than directly evaluating the actions they might undertake (as with M1).

5.3 Motivation ethics and special relationships

Motivation ethics holds that the moral evaluation of an action depends on the level of moral motivation required for the action to be performed or avoided. The moral motivation is based on an equal concern for all, specifically that the good of others is promoted. Such good is determined by the correct value theory (if welfarism is correct this would be their welfare, if desire-fulfilment is correct then this would be that their most valuable ends are achieved and so).

As such, a morally good (or exemplary) agent is one significantly (or highly) motivated to further the good of others. A morally bad (or depraved) agent is one not moderately (or even slightly) motivated to further the good of others. Crucially, this does not exclude, however, that a morally good or morally exemplary agent will have other motivations, such as a specific concern for particular individuals. We can also infer action evaluations from these, deriving these from an agent's potential motivations, for instance, an action is morally good (or exemplary) if it requires being significantly (or highly) motivated to further the good of others.

As the formulations above indicate, motivation ethics thus avoids the structural problems that were said to accrue to moral theories that directly evaluate actions based on M1. Firstly, it bases the agent's evaluation on why they do what they do, and how hard it is to do what they do, since it is evaluating the agent's motivations (both moral and others when they conflict with it). This meets the worry that theories that do not do so are not compelling in their evaluations, and is compatible with the agent evaluation principle since an agent's motivations are features of them. Secondly, it demonstrates evaluative coherence since morally good (or bad) actions are those that would be expected of morally good (or bad) agents.

What though specifically of the 'Problem of Special Relationships'? The problem arose if we accepted M1, namely that 'of two or more actions, (or sets of actions arising from a virtue, rule or motive), the morally right action (or set of actions) is that which reflects an equal concern for all'. Now motivation ethics rejects this, as the morally right (or, in the terms discussed here, 'morally good') action is that which would be undertaken given a significant motivation to further the good of others, *but potentially with other non-moral motivations too*. Among those non-moral motivations could be a motivation to promote the interests of some particular individual (a child, parent, spouse, friend etc.).

Thus whether a father acting partial to his own child acts morally badly will depend on whether he would still do so if he also had a moderate motivation to further the good of others in addition to his love for his child. His concern for his child is not prima facie morally suspect, however, unless having a moderate level of motivation to further the good of others would have caused him to not have the child or to undermine the relationship. To evaluate him morally does require psychological judgement – what is it like to be a father with the attendant feelings and so on. But this is right: if we derive action evaluations from those of agents, and the agent evaluations by comparing the different motivations humans do and may have, and how they interact, then some empirical judgement of our normal human motivational nature and patterning is germane.

Consider again the woman who faces a choice between staying in port, trying to save six strangers, or trying to save her family (of four), where trying to save anyone carries a very small risk to herself. Under motivation ethics, for almost any person, staying in port is morally bad, as any agent with a moderate motivation to further the good of others would try to prevent them from dying when the risk to herself was very small (an exception is perhaps someone with a deep fear of water, for them to try to save anyone would be morally exemplary). If her love for her family is strong, saving them might not however be to act morally badly, and indeed if the threat to herself was significant could be to act in a morally good manner. Saving the six strangers, despite her love for her family, would be to act in a morally exceptional manner, for it really requires a strong motivation to protect the lives of all others no matter who they are.

Yet while motivation ethics seems, within certain constraints, to allow for motivations showing concern for particular individuals, and how these can make our actions seem partial yet still be morally good, what of the explanatory demand that we account for what we often think of as 'special duties'?[15] According to the logic being set out here, these reflect other evaluands than the moral, that is they reflect the potential strength of other good-based motivations sustained by relationships – that of a parent, child, sibling, spouse and so on. Someone reasonably (or highly) motivated that their child's life goes well is on this account a good (or exemplary) parent, but note that this also includes an assessment of the general motivations we expect of parents (to be reasonably motivated is to be reasonably motivated given that one's love for one's child is normally expected to be deep and compellingly felt).

Such a judgement includes what we think is normal for such a relationship among humans in general: true friends do care for each other and for what happens to each other, parents normally love their children not out of some deference to the demands of morality but as a normal part of their relationship with them. As such our different motivations – a love for our children, the caring of friendship, the affection and concern of romantic partnership – can be used to evaluate actions we expect of those with such motivations at varying strengths. The advantage of separating out the moral motivation – to further the good – from other motivations, such as that one's children's lives go well, is that we can be conceptually clear on how and when such motivations make a difference to what one does, and thus evaluate those actions without having to cram the differing concerns – the good of all, the good of one's children – into a single evaluation or notion of morality.[16]

To be clear: it is not that our non-moral concern as part of a relationship is not indirectly morally evaluable. Such relationships can be evaluated by whether they would have been cultivated and retained by the agent with previous different strengths of moral motivation. For this reason, while morally good agents may have a range of such relationships, morally heroic agents might well not, precisely because of their overwhelming focus on the good of all.

But isn't there something badly wrong here? Under motivation ethics someone's concern for their family (say) is not necessarily moral, yet some such motivations are often seen as an important part of morality, notably when it comes to concern for one's children. Surely good parents are, in this regard, morally good?

Now motivation ethics does partly account for this, in that it would hold that someone's concern for specific family members might usually *be good evidence* that they will also have the type of motivational set that contains a more general concern for others. Those who make good parents, for instance, might reliably have their egoistic impulses in check, and this indicates a greater potential for giving weight to the interests of others in general.

That is, implicit in the idea of evaluating agents by their strength of moral motivation is the possibility that being more morally motivated will impact or entail having a certain type of non-moral motivational set too. Consider again the motivation ethics notion of basic moral duties:

- There is a basic negative duty to not do X if doing X would normally require being less than moderately motivated to promote the good of others.

- There is a basic positive duty to do Y if doing Y would normally require being significantly motivated to promote the good of others.

Here it is the level of moral motivation that makes the difference, hence how the evaluation of such actions tracks the evaluation of how morally motivated the agent is. However, we can also think of what we might call 'quasi-moral' duties: actions that we would expect of morally motivated agents not purely due to their strength of moral motivation but due to their associated non-moral motivational set.

- There is a quasi-moral negative duty to not do P if not doing P would typically only be undertaken by those at least moderately motivated to promote the good of others even if the action itself does not require being so motivated.

- There is a quasi-moral positive duty to do Z if doing Z would typically only be expected of an agent at least significantly motivated to promote the good of others even if the action itself does not require being so motivated.

This is a rather clumsy way of formalizing the idea that having a moderate or significant concern for others may entail or typically accompany a range of other changes to our motivational sets. Performance of quasi-moral duties is thus evidence of moral agency, but defeasibly so. Perhaps the most obvious candidate for a change to our non-moral set is the checking and moderation of a range of egoistic impulses. As such, for motivation ethics the association of good friends and those considerate of and caring for their family with being morally good agents stems from the evidence that such people are not overwhelmingly selfish and as such much more likely in their actions to show concern for people in general.

Yet, this is importantly a contingent claim. It is perfectly possible under motivation ethics for someone to have a significant sincere concern for their children or family and not to be a morally good agent at all. It is in theory possible for such a person to be morally heinous, to seek to harm others all the while having a loving relationship with their children.

Now, for a pure or semi-strong intuitionist this account will still be lacking: most people, after all, have intuitions that we have moral duties to various family members. Yet even for intuitionists, there is going to be the problem that people's intuitions about the scope of these duties is plausibly wildly variant: some will hold that our main duties extend to parents, siblings and offspring, others that they also encompass neighbours, aunts, uncles and cousins. Thus even for intuitionists we may need to assess whether and when such duties can be justified. This, admittedly, is not a major problem if one is prepared to simply introduce ad hoc modifications on moral theories to meet any intuitively problematic case: here the ad hoc theorist could perhaps say such duties varied by context, or by how much concern one typically felt, or that the agent actually felt. Ultimately, pure intuitionism with ad hoc theorizing can absorb any problem (except, perhaps, the Intuition Regress Problem).

But what, under motivation ethics, justifies labelling a general concern for others 'moral' but not a specific concern for a particular individual with whom we have some special relationship (spouse, parent, child, friend etc.)?

The argument for the specialness of moral evaluations (and one not necessarily confined to motivation ethics but rather any theory based on the overall good) is that moral evaluations track a value that is objective in the sense that it is not contingent on the agent's particular evaluative mental states or beliefs. With a concern for the good of others it is not our contingent relationships with the individuals in question that identifies why they are valuable but rather it is simply their possession of certain features – the ability to suffer, to have aims, etc. – that comprise the good that makes them valuable.

In contrast, any justification of why I care for my friend will need to make reference to features of our relationship, our history and my personal psychological states. Yet a claim about the badness of someone suffering needs no such reference, rather being based on features of the victim in question. To be motivated to promote the good is to be motivated to make the world better. To be motivated to help one's friend is to be motivated to make their life in some regard better. But the latter need not make the world better, and indeed that is not normally why we do so: we care for our friend because we care for our friend, the particular person with whom we have a relationship of affection and concern and a shared past.[17]

Yet in tracing the evaluation of actions to that of features of agents' hypothetical motivations, where these include considerations of their relationships, is there a worry that the richness of these judgements detracts from their decision-theoretic usefulness? In other words, are answers to moral dilemmas that do not require much in the way of psychological judgements ipso facto superior at least as a decision-theoretic tool, namely, as something that helps us in choosing?

This seems partly correct, and to some extent the motivation ethics account of general duties supplies such 'generalized' evaluations. However, to the extent there is a valid worry here, it is not a criticism of a theory that in principle makes evaluations based on a rich set of psychological considerations. Instead it is merely the unobjectionable observation that we may have to trade off the accuracy of some of these evaluations for their ease of use when we have constraints of, or costs in gaining, (i) information, (ii) time, or (iii) deliberative capacity. To the extent that it is desirable that we have simple theories giving unambiguous advice then we have a reason to take those that rely on more complex judgements and when necessary use them rather crudely. If the correct judgements really are complex then doing so is a trade-off, one that we cannot even begin to assess, however, if we stipulate that the correct judgements must always be straightforward or easy to make.

To illustrate with an earlier example consider again Jack and Peter. Jack writes a will leaving his estate to charity, though he cares nothing for others, he does so to cause upset to his children. Now according to motivation ethics, in so writing his will, even though the act of giving all of one's money to poverty-alleviating charity potentially leads to the best consequences impartially judged, he does not act in a morally good way: as his actions are entirely explained by his non-moral motivation to upset his children. More generally, though, Jack should be morally evaluated negatively, and expected to act morally badly when given the chance, and indeed to act morally heinously when given the chance, such as if he can gain some small benefit even if inflicting widespread pain and misery.

Peter, on the other hand, leaves most of his estate to charity out of a desire to reduce suffering, but gives a significant proportion to his children out of a love for them. The moral evaluation of Peter's action is more involved, although he is clearly a much more moral person in general than Jack, as he demonstrates a concern that the lives of others go well: this is why he gives so much of his estate to charity. To evaluate his actions we need to make some rough judgement over how much of his money he would have given had he had differing strengths of a motivation to further the good of others: if he had this at a level that was high for humans in general would he have given so much, or would it require a level that is exceptional for humans in general?

The evaluation of his action will also depend on how much he loves his children and what the effects of each alternative (of giving some money to them, or some to charity) will have on those receiving: if the world is grossly unequal then acting morally requires giving more, if his children face real hardship without his support (say one has a severe disability) then giving more to them becomes more morally acceptable.

Given the paltry amounts most people give to charity, even in their wills, my own sense is that giving most of his estate to charity out of a desire that the lives of others be better entails he is plausibly acting in a highly moral manner. To give such money to charity in those situations where it is even harder motivationally – such as during one's life when alternatively it might be spent on a better house, more trips, or other goods for oneself – would potentially be to act in a morally exemplary manner. To make these judgements requires some judgement of how hard or easy the actions would be given different strengths of motivation to further the good of others. Peter's case illustrates how, even if we are clear on the relevant determinants in principle, some difficult work needs to be done in assessing the particulars of the case, the psychological influences agents are subject to, and the range of ways normal human motivations affect what we do. Motivation ethics provides a framework for thinking through these issues.

Thus three of the earlier problems – of demandingness, corrosion and impoverishment – if they occur at all for motivation ethics occur as features of the difficulty of living a morally exemplary or even morally heroic life (that demonstrating a high or exceptional level of motivation to further the good of others). It really may be that to demonstrate an exceptional level of motivation to further the good of others may mean acting in the face of, and reducing the importance of, our special relationships, and may mean leading a life so focused on the good of others that it lacks many of the ties of family and friends that might otherwise enrich it.

For motivation ethics morally heroic actions are typically incredibly demanding and involve sacrifice, as this is precisely why they are heroic. To live a morally heroic life need not necessarily involve alienation, however, if our decision to be, or remain, so motivated is one we endorse. Unlike with a morality that focuses first on actions not agents, where the alienation arises from a clash of evaluations, for someone who is morally heroic there need not be such a clash: they have chosen to live with the possibility of furthering the good of others dominant in what motivates them, even if this comes at the expense of other more egoistic goals or relationship-based feelings. Changing the primary object of moral evaluations from actions to agents and to their different strengths of motivations to promote the good of others removes the requirement that partial acts be either necessarily morally bad or that moral concern be unequal concern.

5.4 Conclusions

This chapter has argued that the problem of special relationships arises from a clash between two claims: that agents that have certain relationships are not morally bad for so doing, but that when considering what they do from an impartial perspective it seems that they might act morally badly from so doing. The principle underlying the latter claim, of evaluating actions based on features of the actions such as whether they could be justified by an equal concern for all, led to at least one of three problems – vulnerability to amoralism, arbitrary agent evaluations or a lack of evaluative coherence. None of these problems, however, necessarily arises from the claim that moral concern is equal concern for all, as the proposal of motivation ethics sought to illustrate. What they arise from is the assumption of action primacy: in other words, they are structurally analogous to the difficulties discussed in earlier chapters.

CHAPTER SIX

Global duties and the state

Introduction

The current inhabitants of all democratic developed countries provide massively more domestically focused rather than externally focused collective welfare goods. Yet those outside their borders are vastly more in need. If all humans are worthy of equal moral concern then there seems to be a problem here, in that the bias towards co-nationals appears to represent starkly unequal concern. There are three main ways the issue has been addressed:

The left-cosmopolitan approach
A significant provision of welfare goods only to co-nationals is unjust in that we have a duty to provide such goods (so long as feasible) to all, irrespective of where they live.[1]

The right-cosmopolitan approach
A significant provision of welfare goods to co-nationals is unjust in that we do not have a duty to provide such goods to anyone, we should instead be respecting the rights of everyone (such as of freedom of movement or contract), irrespective of where they live.[2]

The political-associationist approach
One has additional duties to those with whom one is associated under the coercive authority of the state, for example due to group membership,[3] being part of the same people,[4] joint authorship of and subjection to the state[5] or co-liability to state coercion.[6]

Although political associationist approaches arguably better cohere with many people's intuitions, they have faced two prominent challenges. Firstly, to show that the relational feature that identifies why we owe extra duties to co-nationals or co-residents really does coalesce with state borders, and secondly to show that this relationship plausibly might entail extra duties (a common way is by analogy with the relationship in other contexts).[7]

Yet any view supporting political associationist-like conclusions must surely do more: for the default option really belongs to the cosmopolitan, who bases duties on the good of those affected and does not in principle discriminate by location (save for practical issues). Political associationists ideally need to show not only that their view is plausible, but *why* cosmopolitanism is not correct, and presumably the argument for why it is not correct will help identify the right political associationist view, and the content and nature of the duties it supports.

For it is noteworthy that although most political associationist views begin with markedly variant premises – duties based on reciprocity, co-coercion and law authorship represent very different conceptions of morality indeed – they seem to end up with surprisingly similar conclusions. Thus an argument for why cosmopolitanism about duties is incorrect may also rebut the worry that political associationism's appeal is partly merely a conservatism about current arrangements and behaviour. This is the goal of part one. Specifically, it argues that cosmopolitan duties do not reflect the motivational ease and difficulty of promoting or protecting the relevant interests, notably that affected by the presence of coercive state-based institutions, and that a credible account of our basic duties would need to do so. Part two discusses how motivation ethics responds to this need and how adopting such a stance radically reframes the debate over our duties to non- and co-nationals. The chapter concludes by discussing what such a reframe implies about duties and the impact and evaluation of institutions more broadly.

6.1 A difficulty with cosmopolitan duties

What is a basic moral duty? This chapter will assume – initially – that a basic moral duty identifies what a morally good agent would typically be expected to do, but a morally bad agent might not (we might, note, have a duty to do one of multiple things). These potentially contrast with supererogatory duties – those that a morally heroic or exemplary agent would be expected to do, but a morally good agent might not.[8] Our basic duties are those things that as basic moral agents we should undertake, even if there are possibly some things that go beyond this and might be done by highly moral agents. Now, cosmopolitans hold that our basic moral duties are owed equally to all human beings (at least human beings, maybe also to non-human animals), specifically:

Cosmopolitanism about duties
One has a basic moral duty to do what will protect or promote the relevant good of all humans irrespective of where they live, so long as feasible.

Left and right cosmopolitans disagree on the *content* of the relevant good: is it positive welfare goods (left-cosmopolitans) or liberties/rights (right-cosmopolitans). Cosmopolitans and political associationists, by contrast, disagree on *whose* good: is it all humans (cosmopolitans) or with extra duties owed to those with whom we share some relation under the state (political associationists)?

As an illustrative example, consider better-off citizens (those earning above the average income) in developed countries. Such people contribute very, very roughly a quarter of their income through taxation to the provision of welfare goods – health, education, social security, pensions etc. Do they have a basic moral duty to do so? And if so, to whom are such goods owed?

If such basic moral duties are cosmopolitan, then they are prima facie owed to whom they could benefit most, or to whom is most in need: in principle being a co-national or non-national does not matter, though in practice investing in some national expenditures, such as education, might be the more effective way of providing such goods to non-nationals in the longer term.[9] Even with this pragmatic qualification, however, the disparity is stark. Citizens provide significant domestically focused welfare goods, but scant externally focused ones, the former is commonly thought of as a moral duty (for both left-cosmopolitans and most political associationists) yet the status of the latter is then the source of a moral puzzle: to say we should also provide such a level of goods internationally seems breathtakingly radical, but at the same time to say that we owe more moral concern to co-nationals is hard to justify. What is the potential problem with the radical conclusion?

A basic moral duty was earlier defined as what we would expect of a morally good agent but potentially not of a morally bad one (and superogative duties – if they exist – as what we would expect of a morally exemplary agent). But if cosmopolitanism is right about the content and determinants of our basic moral duties then the demandingness of fulfilling such duties will be primarily determined by factors outside the control of the agent, and thus whether an agent is potentially morally good or bad will depend almost entirely on external contingencies.

Assume, for instance, that we have a basic cosmopolitan duty to provide 20 per cent of our income to help those most in need, wherever they may be. Now, imagine we live in a benevolent dictatorship where this is enforced through the taxation system, with credible threats of punishment for non-payment. In such situations we would expect almost everyone to undertake such a duty. In a next-door nationalistic dictatorship, where taxation is spent only on national goods, almost everyone would be expected to fail to fulfil their basic cosmopolitan moral duties. But is it really true that the citizens living under the benevolent dictator are morally good and those living under the nationalistic dictator morally bad? For if their dictators died and were succeeded by sons with widely varying aid-preferences the evaluation of the citizens might apparently be reversed.

This is not a problem of a clash between these duties and our intuitions. The difficulty for cosmopolitan duties is that there doesn't seem to be any conception of a morally good (or bad) agent either underpinning or derivable from them. If you were to take all the agents that fulfilled some conception of such duties in one group, and all the agents who failed to fulfil such duties in another, the people within each of the two groups need not internally have any features in common nor there be any systematic difference between them in terms of their character. What would presumably be the only thing highly correlated among the groups was birth-location. Someone born into a very poor country is likely to expend their resources on those globally in greatest need, and fulfil their basic cosmopolitan duties.[10] Someone born in a very rich country is likely to expend their resources on those quite well off (themselves, their family etc.), and fail to fulfil their basic cosmopolitan duties. But if such duties are what we would expect of a morally good agent but not necessarily of a morally bad one, then we seem to make being morally good or bad depend on birth-location, to depend on something someone has no control over, and not on what the person is actually like.

Cosmopolitanism – assuming it links fulfilment of one's basic duties to being a morally good agent – is therefore going to either have to abandon cosmopolitanism about duties or make borders relevant to the moral evaluation of agents. That is, assuming a broad link between the evaluation of agents and what they do, then these two views are mutually incompatible:

'Cosmopolitanism about duties'
One has a basic moral duty to do what will protect or promote the relevant good of all humans irrespective of where they live, so long as feasible.

'The moral irrelevance or borders'
Whether an agent is morally good or bad should not depend on their location (*unless* this affects their internal features).[11]

If someone lives in a very poor country, or in a country where the coercive power of the state heavily incentives giving to the world's poor via taxation, or in a community where there are very powerful social norms supporting charitable giving, then she may fulfil all of her cosmopolitan duties readily, even with no level of concern for the world's poor. If, however, the same person lived in a wealthy country, one where taxation revenue is focused domestically, and one where there are weak or no social norms promoting charitable giving, then she may fail to fulfil any of her basic cosmopolitan duties. Whether she is a morally good agent will, as such, be almost entirely contingent on where she lives.

Now one could of course deny the link between being a morally good agent and fulfilling one's basic duties, either (i) that one can consistently act morally wrongly and still be a morally good agent or (ii) being a morally good agent requires fulfilment of one's supererogatory duties, not merely one's basic moral duties. Yet both options are problematic – the first undermines the force of duties being basic, one can after all disregard them and still act as a morally good agent would. The second only pushes the problem back one stage – one could simply replace 'basic duties' with 'supererogatory duties' in the previous discussion and re-run the argument. Either we reject that duties are cosmopolitan or we have to accept that borders are morally relevant in that where an agent lives will likely almost entirely determine their moral evaluation, even if where they live has no impact on any of their internal features. This at least is the agent evaluation problem that cosmopolitan duties face (namely, that it is the same structural problem as with the earlier discussions).

The right solution to this problem is not, however, to adopt political associationism about duties. The agent-evaluation problems are not caused because co-association creates new normative relationships that cosmopolitanism cannot reflect, rather they arise as the presence of coercive state institutions typically radically alters the ease or difficulty of a range of other-impacting actions. For this reason, the worry over agent evaluations is going to apply to political co-associationism about duties as well. Consider the following thought experiment involving three possible dictatorships: Poor-cosmostan, Rich-cosmostan and Nationalstan:

Poor-cosmostan
Citizens fulfil via their taxes their duties according to cosmopolitanism, which primarily benefit the welfare of the citizens of Poor-cosmostan.

Rich-cosmostan
Citizens fulfil via their taxes their duties according to cosmopolitanism, and thus these resources are spent on the inhabitants of other countries.

Nationalstan
Citizens fulfil, via their taxes, their duties according to political associationism, and thus these resources primarily benefit the welfare of their own (middle income) citizens.

If morally good agents are those who consistently or typically fulfil their basic duties, then the following holds:

- The citizens of Poor-cosmostan are overall morally good for both cosmopolitans and political associationists.

- The citizens of Rich-cosmostan are overall morally good for cosmopolitans but morally bad for political associationists.

- The citizens of Nationalstan are overall morally bad for cosmopolitans but morally good for political associationists.

The problem, however, is that the citizens might have exactly the same features – the same beliefs, the same levels of altruism and egoism, the same attitudes – and thus it seems arbitrary to morally evaluate them overall in directly contradictory ways. What the thought experiment highlights is that undertaking actions that benefit some group and not some other can be motivationally over-determined: people can pay taxes for instance purely for selfish punishment-averse reasons.

That is, the apparent problem surrounding our duties and national borders was that the citizens of developed countries seemingly showed much greater concern for co-nationals than non-nationals in the provision of welfare goods. But this need not be the case at all.

From the fact that citizens contribute significantly to domestically focused welfare goods and not to externally focused ones *we cannot necessarily infer that they typically show greater moral concern for co-nationals rather than non-nationals and thus that in justifying such a provision we need to justify partial concern*. They might, for instance, actually be utterly unconcerned about all other people. This may hold true in a democracy too: even a democracy of egoists might end up forming political coalitions whereby there was support for large-scale domestic public goods. We cannot simply infer from behaviour that benefits one group rather than another any necessary level of concern for that group rather than the other. A basic puzzle of global justice – how to evaluate the great difference in moral concern represented by extensive goods provided to co-nationals and hardly any to non-nationals – may be mis-premised: it may not be *moral* concern at all that underpins this disparity, and, as is set out below, the justification (or evaluation) of this disparity therefore not require showing that moral concern is partial.

We seem superficially to be faced with a tension between the principle that moral concern is owed to all humans equally, and the observation that if this entails equally owed duties then our provision of welfare goods to co-nationals is either grossly excessive (it should be closer to that provided to non-nationals) or required to be replicated in large part abroad (erasing much of the distinction between what we give to others based on whether they reside within or outside our borders). But cosmopolitanism about moral concern – that all humans are worthy of it equally – need not entail cosmopolitanism about the impact of our actions or the content of our duties. Whether it does or does not will crucially depend on which is correct of the following two views of the determinants of duties:

Action-primacy: There are basic moral duties to do X based on features of X; and morally good agents are those generally expected to do X, morally bad agents those who might not do X.

Agent-primacy: Morally good agents have features Y, morally bad agents have features Z; and our basic moral duties are those things generally expected of morally good agents but not necessarily of morally bad ones.

Cosmopolitanism about duties, and political associationism, are both framed in terms of the action primacy of duties, *and this is what creates the difficulties*: for cosmopolitans that such duties cannot permit a non-arbitrary conception of morally good or bad agents, for political associationists that such duties seem predicated on an unequal concern that is hard to justify.

6.2 Overcoming the problem

But what would global duties be like with agent-primacy and retaining the claim that moral concern is equal concern for all, irrespective of where they live? To illustrate, here again is the motivation ethics account of agent evaluations:

- Morally good (or heroic) agents are those significantly (or exceptionally) motivated to promote the good of others.
- Morally bad (or depraved) agents are those not even moderately (or even slightly) motivated to promote the good of others.

And derivatively, there is the account of duties:

- There is a basic negative duty to not do X if doing X would normally require being less than moderately motivated to promote the good of others.
- There is a basic positive duty to do Y if doing Y would normally require being significantly motivated to promote the good of others.
- There is a supererogatory duty to do Z if doing Z would normally require being exceptionally motivated to promote the good of others.

As noted previously, the 'good of others' crucially refers to all others – that is at least to all human beings – moral concern is not partial, it does not discriminate based on location (a central cosmopolitan principle, in this case however applied to the particular motivation of moral agents, not actions).

To see how motivation ethics contrasts with cosmopolitanism about duties, even though they agree moral concern is equal concern for all, consider two democratically ruled countries whose citizens have different levels of moral motivation. Citizens in Egoistan are purely self-motivated: that is they are motivated solely by considerations of what will be in their individual self-interest, they are unmotivated by the good of others (they neither seek to promote nor harm it). Citizens in Moralistan have a significant level of motivation to further the good of others, along with the other self-regarding and particularistic motivations they have. What institutions and outcomes might we expect from these two countries?

Given that Egoistan is a democracy, it is possible we could expect a significant welfare state and provision of public goods built on somewhat redistributive taxation, assuming that the wealthy do not wield dominant and pervasive political influence over the less wealthy. It is at least highly plausible that with certain democratic arrangements – notably a competitive party system and the need to build majoritarian coalitions to wield executive and legislative power – that we would have an outcome that secures a range of public primary goods and a degree of wealth transfer from the richest to the less well off. One can change the assumptions (make the wealthy more politically influential, such as by having electoral success depend significantly on campaign donations or candidate personal wealth) and end up with outcomes that result in many more people being much worse off. But what is worth noting is that *with no moral motivation among citizens at all* the structure of democratic policy making may ensure we have a significant provision of domestic goods to the overall benefit of the good of that society.

What – however – we would almost certainly only have a very limited provision of would be goods to those outside the state's borders, because they wield almost no direct influence over the choice of democratically determined social and economic policies. There might be self-interested reasons to provide some goods to outsiders – to gain diplomatic influence for instance – but this would be limited, and probably aimed at a few countries (say those with significant natural resources such as oil, or those with ties to large domestic voting blocs) not at the world's poorest where it might be easiest to do the most good. Egoistan, though producing less good outcomes than many existing countries, could still manage to produce more good than one might initially expect, but this being predominantly domestically focused.

Now consider Moralistan, whose citizens have a significant level of motivation to further the good of others. What policies and institutions might they adopt? Domestically, one big difference might be the provision of goods to non-politically influential groups (say the homeless, or politically non-active poor), along with a greater likelihood of securing good-promoting domestic economic institutions (for a welfarist conception of the good, for example, these would be those institutions that result in the greatest expected collective welfare).

The biggest difference with Egoistan, however, would almost certainly be in the provision of goods and adoption of policies likely to benefit those outside the borders. Here is where the moral motivation makes a difference because self-regarding motivations are not normally salient. The most obvious candidate is global-good promoting aid and trade policies that could be collectively enacted, and thus merely require citizens being motivated to support political candidates espousing aiding those globally in need, rather than having to be motivated to make repeated voluntary direct sacrifices themselves.

Such a country, I believe, would not only pursue a significant provision of welfare aid (that aimed at relieving suffering, such as by fighting various diseases) but also push for development trade (that aimed at best improving long-term living standards in poorer nations). Others may judge the optimal causal mechanisms to promote the global good differently. What is notable however is that, even in a country where all the citizens are significantly motivated to promote the good of others, we should expect a greater collective provision of domestic goods than externally focused goods, even if the latter is significant. Domestically both other-regarding and self-regarding motivations will be in play, and thus may support policies helping very large coalitions of citizens; in foreign aid and trade policy it is normally only other-regarding motivations that will be supporting policies promoting the good of others (indeed, it may be that some self-regarding motivations are undermining them).

What the above thought experiment aims to establish is that not only is a greater provision of domestic goods rather than externally provided goods compatible with a morality that holds that all human beings are worthy of equal moral concern, it is exactly what we should expect to occur in a democracy were citizens to be moderately, significantly or not-at-all morally motivated, that is motivated to further the good of others. Even significantly morally motivated human beings have self-regarding motivations, and these by virtue of the nature of democratic decision making will promote policies aimed at providing more to those influencing such decisions.

The judgement that (arguably) political associationists generally adhere to – that a disparity between collective goods focused domestically and internationally need not be morally indefensible – is I believe correct, but its correctness lies not in new moral duties somehow created by special normative relationships with co-citizens, but by the special empirical nature of these relationships: namely how outcomes that promote the good of citizens are motivationally much easier to secure *no matter what one's level of moral motivation* than those that promote the good of non-citizens. The moral motivation remains, however, a motivation to promote the good of all other human beings, and is thus compatible with cosmopolitanism's principle of equal concern for all.

One way to illustrate this is to compare how a traditional moral action-theory and motivation ethics would analyse the actions of the wealthy in developed countries. On a theory with action primacy we would note that the wealthy provide a significant (or moderate) level of financial support through taxation to co-citizens, but not to non-citizens, even though the latter group seem vastly more in need. On such a theory there thus seems to be a moral puzzle: how can such domestic economic institutions – or anything vaguely resembling them – and the actions that fall under them be just when they demonstrate an unequal concern based simply on which side of the border a person lives? Such institutions and behaviour are thus either unjust (for left cosmopolitans) or the provision of the extra domestic goods is excessive (for right cosmopolitans). Driving the analysis of this injustice, or over-provision, is the fact that the action of giving more to co-citizens rather than non-citizens seems morally unjustified *judged as an action*.

Motivation ethics, however, would start by asking how the particular citizens, in this case the wealthy, are motivated. The fact that they provide goods (via taxation) to less-well-off co-citizens is no guide to them being at all morally motivated: one can pay one's taxes due to a fear of being punished for not doing so, and vote self-interestedly but simply be out-voted (given the large economic inequalities in modern societies what is remarkable is how the very wealthy do not generally get more starkly outvoted in self-regarding policy preferences: political influence is evidently not evenly dispersed).[12]

In thinking about the morality of these actions we need to assess what actions would be avoided by them were they moderately morally motivated (identifying what they have a basic duty to avoid), and what actions would be positively undertaken were they significantly morally motivated (identifying their basic moral duties).

On such an analysis the morality of the wealthy would not be identified by whether they paid their taxes – such action, assuming effective compliance threats, is motivationally over-determined – but by the degree to which they sought themselves through voluntary actions and political influence to promote the good of others.

Giving a moderate share of one's income to charity (with the aim of promoting the good, given the scale of global economic disparities almost certainly most effectively that of the world's poorest) would in this case be required to avoid living a morally bad life. Giving a significant share of one's income to charity would be to go beyond this and be part of a morally good life. Giving a high share of one's income would be to act morally exemplarily. To devote one's life to relieving such suffering, to live with it at an exceptional level of motivation, would be morally heroic.

These judgements – moderate, significant, high and exceptional – are judgements of how motivationally difficult the actions are and how much moral motivation they would hypothetically involve, a judgement that requires some grasp of what it is like to be a human being and the range of influences, inclinations and pressures we are subject to as such.

Part of the appeal of political associationist views is, perhaps, that they implicitly focus on what life as a contemporary human being is like, and as such what we might (at best, and at minimum) expect of such people. Their judgement over institutional outcomes and duties reflects this. Part of the appeal of cosmopolitan views stems from their adherence to a compelling moral premise. Thus both sets of theories are bringing different insights: cosmopolitans stress the fundamental nature of moral concern as universal and equal; political associationists highlight the relevance to normative evaluation of our expectations of human agents and their range of potentials.

These are in tension if we frame the problem primarily in terms of the direct evaluation of actions: for then political associationists must find new normative principles to make the evaluation of actions track various implicit agent judgements; cosmopolitans will charge in response that this conflicts with an equal moral concern for all. Yet we can reject the premise that pits the key insights of the two sets of theories against each other: we can primarily ascribe moral evaluations to agents.

If we do so, how are we then to evaluate how those with potential influence over institutions might alter them, or have altered them, with varying levels of moral motivation.[13] My own opinion, based on the relatively trivial amounts most developed countries give to help those in developing nations, and on how they use their global influence to support trade and economic policies that are biased against the global poor rather than biased toward them, is that most developed countries, and most of us in them, do not demonstrate much moral motivation at all. We give scant amounts to charity, and when we do, we often do not focus this on what will do the most good. On the scale between Egoistan and Moralistan the former seems to me much closer to our current state, as evidenced by the way we treat the world's poor, and future generations via our environmental policies.

Avoiding Egoistan is not that difficult, but were we to seek to live morally good lives a much greater motivation to promote the good of others, notably the world's poor, would need to be shown. We would need to live with this goal significantly motivating us in the range of situations we find ourselves in, as shoppers, citizens, income-earners, voters, activists, employees and a great deal more. This is demanding, and that is the point: to live a morally good life, and to aspire to a morally exemplary life, is to live significantly motivated to respond to and to further the needs and interests of our fellow human beings, where this level of motivation is significant given our human nature and the egoistic temptations and pulls to which we are vulnerable. If we focus our attention purely on actions then these concerns are obscured.

Thus a key question is whether we wish to be cosmopolitan about our duties or about political institutions (and moral concern) – for these need not cohere. Consider the following three claims:

1. All humans are worthy of equal moral concern.
2. Institutions are morally better the better they protect or promote the relevant good of all affected, no matter where they live.
3. One has a basic moral duty to do what will protect or promote the relevant good of all humans irrespective of where they live, so long as feasible.

As the argument above, and the example of motivation ethics, has tried to demonstrate, accepting claim one and claim two in no way requires one to accept claim three, and indeed accepting claim three requires one to accept that the moral evaluation of agents be radically contingent on where they live, not on what they are like (or one must sever the link between fulfilling one's duties and being a morally good agent).

As such, assessing the justness or morality of agents, of actions and of institutions will crucially depend on which of these is primary in evaluation. There is a natural affinity between the view that actions are primary and the view that the justice of institutions tracks the evaluation of actions – that if we have duties to others then just institutions are those that fulfil or reflect these duties, but it is this that causes the discussed problems. Rejecting it allows us to retain the claim both that moral concern is equal concern, and to still base agent evaluations on features of the agent.

6.4 Conclusions

This chapter has tried to show that the apparent tension between cosmopolitan concern and political associationist judgements is partly due to the assumption that actions, not agents, should be the primary object of moral evaluation, and to offer arguments for why we should reject this assumption. One way to do so is the motivation ethics approach: to hold that the moral evaluation of agents should be based on how motivated they are to promote the good of others, and then derive action evaluations from what they would and would not be expected to do as a result. Doing so integrates into our action-evaluations a range of judgements of human nature and potential, and thus where the very existence of a geographically bounded coercive state alters the motivational ease or difficulty of a range of actions this alters our evaluations of the actions of agents living under it (and those with sway over it).

Motivation ethics naturally suggests an instrumental account of institutional evaluation, as the moral motivation is that certain ends obtain (that the good of all is promoted). The most prominent rival approach is that of intrinsic institutionalism, whereby political institutions are *legitimate* or not based on their intrinsic decision making features – how or by whom decisions are made – not just on the content of the decisions and outcomes.

Why must motivation ethics reject this? The ultimate reason, according to the next chapter, is that there is an underlying clash between legitimacy-based normativity and good-based normativity. To adopt a good based moral theory, as with motivation ethics, may have to entail abandoning political legitimacy as a justified separate realm of institutional evaluation.

CHAPTER SEVEN

Political legitimacy and the good[1]

Many believe that it is important people's interests are not harmed, that their good is promoted. However, many also think that if laws are democratically passed, or coercion democratically authorized, then this confers a legitimacy that means that we have a duty to obey such laws and hold such coercion justified (both, usually, within bounds).

The problem of this chapter is how to reconcile these two potential ways of evaluating institutions, one good-based (on the interests they affect, such as with motivation ethics and many theories of justice) and one legitimacy-based (on how decisions are arrived at or by whom they are taken). The claim is that they are in necessary conflict not harmony, and it is as such very hard to demonstrate the value – that is the moral desirability – of political legitimacy.

7.1 Outline of the problem

Theories of political legitimacy normally focus upon and defend certain *conditions of legitimacy*, that is, they specify the features a state or polity must possess for it to be considered legitimate, and try to show how and when these may be met.[2] Yet there is also a second question of the *value of legitimacy*: that is, of the normative features a legitimate state has by virtue of it being legitimate (such as it being owed obedience, having a right to use coercion or enjoying a general justification in the use of force).

The problem discussed here relates to this latter question, as in that legitimacy, if it has any such value, seems to only change how we should overall act or judge in those situations where, prima facie, we should not want it to. As such, it seems to have apparent moral disvalue. That is, it requires moral agents to cause or to justify harm, with no outweighing benefit.

Now, as a conclusion this seems absurd. Many anarchists need not accept it.[3] But it is much harder to avoid than it might initially appear. The basic problem arises from what we can think of as the 'counter-factual import' of a duty or justification. That is, we can ask: which are the situations where a duty or justification alters overall how we should act or judge? These are the situations where it 'makes a difference'. Legitimacy-based duties or justifications appear to only have a counter-factual import in situations where they justify, or require, the infliction of a harm that cannot be justified by reference to anyone affected.

For example, assume we have an obligation to obey the law of a legitimate state. There are, logically, three possibilities here for any particular law, interpreted as 'Do X':

1 Obeying the law 'Do X' is justified on its merits, and you should do so whether in a legitimate or illegitimate state.
2 Disobeying the law 'Do X' is justified on its merits, and you should do so whether in a legitimate or illegitimate state.
3 Disobeying the law 'Do X' is justified on its merits, but you should still do X if passed by a legitimate state.

What difference does a duty to obey make? It creates category three, *and changes nothing else*. The problem is why we would want this. Similarly, the counter-factual effect of a state enjoying a general justification in the use of coercion because it is legitimate appears to be to permit, excuse or justify acts that are, based on their nature, morally undesirable.

Section 7.2 discusses some standard accounts of the value of legitimacy and 7.3 the overall problem that these create. Section 7.4 then surveys six seemingly promising responses. (1) That a legitimate state's right to rule is necessary not merely sufficient for justified coercion. (2) That a legitimate state enjoys the right to enforce pre-existing rights. (3) That legitimacy is crucial in those situations where there is reasonable disagreement. (4) That obligations based on legitimacy only apply to acts that, on their merits, are morally optional. (5) That government is legitimate if it is a reliable epistemic authority. (6) That the concept of legitimacy may promote institutional improvement, such as in spreading democratic reform. Despite their apparent appeal, all face serious difficulties.

7.2 The potential value of legitimacy

What is the value of political legitimacy? That is, what normatively desirable properties does a legitimate state have by virtue of it being legitimate? Simmons characterizes a standard moral conception of a state's legitimacy (and one underlying the Lockean account) as:

> the complex moral right it possesses to be the exclusive imposer of binding duties on its subjects, to have its subjects comply with these duties, and to use coercion to enforce these duties.[4]

Estlund states that:

> By authority I will mean the power of one agent (emphasizing especially the state) to morally require or forbid actions by others through commands. (To forbid x is to require not-x, and so I will usually simply speak of the moral power to require). By legitimacy I will mean the moral permissibility of the state's issuing and enforcing its commands owing to the process by which they were produced.[5]

Despite differences in usage, there are two basic ideas here, and we might accept one, the other, or both: that legitimate government has a right or general justification in the use or threat of force, or that one has a duty to obey the commands – commonly assumed to be the laws – of a government that is the legitimate authority or where the commands stem from a legitimate procedure.

Initially excluded in the discussion here will be purely instrumentalist accounts of legitimacy whereby laws and institutions are legitimate only when, and only to the extent that, they bring about desirable outcomes, where it is the desirability of the outcomes, not how or by whom they were produced, that lends them legitimacy (see, though, 7.4(5) and 7.4(6) for problems even with this).

7.3 The counterfactual problem: Force, coercion and duties

If the use of force or coercion is partly or wholly justified because it is done by a legitimate state, then this changes the overall assessment of such acts only in those situations where the use of force or coercion would be unjustified on its own terms.

For example, consider perhaps the most common and prominent use of the state's coercive apparatus: to punish, or threaten to punish, some particular individual. Here are three possibilities if one holds a desert theory of punishment:

D1. The individual deserves the punishment (or to be coerced) and any state would be justified in punishing him or her.
D2. The individual does not deserve the punishment (or to be coerced) and no state would be justified in punishing him or her.
D3. The individual does not deserve the punishment (or to be coerced) but a legitimate state is still justified in punishing him or her.

Here are the same three possibilities if instead one holds some sort of consequence-based theory of punishment:

C1. Punishing (or coercing) the individual produces relevantly good consequences, and any state would be justified in punishing him or her.[6]
C2. Punishing (or coercing) the individual produces relevantly bad consequences, and no state would be justified in punishing him or her.
C3. Punishing (or coercing) the individual produces relevantly bad consequences, but a legitimate state is still justified in punishing him or her.

One possible example of both D1 and C1 would be someone who committed murder or rape – even an illegitimate state would be justified in using its organized force to lock up, or to try to coercively deter, such an individual. An example of D2 or C2 would be someone who was criminalized for being Jewish – no state would be justified in punishing him or her simply for being Jewish.[7]

Thus a theory of legitimacy only matters for punishment or coercion if, and to the extent that, it entails that there are many and important cases where individuals do not deserve to be punished or doing so brings about relevantly bad consequences but a legitimate state is still justified in punishing them. The puzzle is why we should want this, namely that category D3 or C3 have cases that fall within them and these are significant.

Here is the same type of worry for a duty to obey a state or polity by virtue of its legitimacy. Consider a particular law that is interpreted as requiring us to 'do P'. A crude division of cases might be as follows:

L1. Doing P is required by reference to those affected, and thus I should do P whether commanded by a legitimate or illegitimate state.
L2. Not doing P is required by reference to those affected, and thus I should not do P, whether commanded by a legitimate or illegitimate state.
L3. Not doing P is required by reference to those affected, and I should thus not do P, unless commanded by a legitimate state.[8]

An example of L1 for many might be refraining from murder: whether it is illegal under a legitimate or illegitimate state one should not murder, this being justified by reference to the person affected, the would-be victim. An example of L2 might be torture: even if a legitimate or illegitimate state passed a law requiring citizens to capture and torture Muslims if the opportunity arises, this is not morally what citizens should do. Thus the puzzle is why we should want a duty whose sole counter-factual import (the difference it makes) is that there are many cases that fall into category L3. Why would we want there to be acts of obedience that – considered on their merits one ought not to do – but because they are commanded by a legitimate state one should do them?

This isn't a problem of intuitions. *It's a problem of evaluative coherence between our evaluation of an institution and of what it does.* Our account of the good or of justice allows us to evaluate what is done 'on the merits'. Legitimacy thus only changes the overall evaluation when, on the merits, the acts are morally evaluated negatively. Since the action evaluation is based either on promoting people's relevant interests, reflecting their desert or not harming them, then legitimacy cannot appeal to such interests, desert or harm in justifying why it changes the overall evaluation.

This concern is distinct from the two dominant classic anarchist worries. The first argues that a duty to obey conflicts with certain individual rights or moral powers, thus Wolff, for example, claims that obeying an authority because it is an authority is incompatible with moral autonomy.[9] The second casts doubt on particular arguments in favour of legitimating a political structure. Thus, one can argue against voluntarism that even if consent to a legitimate polity could create obligations to obey the law, that (almost) no one has so consented, and that tacit, coerced or hypothetical variants do not bind.[10] The problems raised above are distinct in that they do not require a strong commitment to a particular notion of moral autonomy and hold across legitimacy-grounded theories independent of their specific arguments for why we are obligated or force justified.

Illustrating the problem with democratic legitimacy

The counter-factual problem relies on comparing obedience or coercion in a legitimate state with such actions in an illegitimate one. This seems both rather abstract and has the notable danger of normative over-determination – in other words that when comparing these two state forms our background awareness of the range of ways a 'typical' illegitimate state may be bad may hinder us in cleanly assessing the role legitimacy should and should not play. Dictatorships, for instance, may be inescapably dominated in the minds of many with the expectation of egregiously bad laws and bad actions and therefore the specific impact of their illegitimacy is hard to discern.

Thus we require examples of states that, under particular prominent legitimacy theories, would be illegitimate, but who might in expectation produce many or at least some laws similar to a legitimate state. For the sake of argument let us assume that legitimate government is somehow democratic, and by this refer either to those theories that emphasize democracy's fair or equal procedural features or alternatively to those that emphasize the role of consent via voting.[11] What might we use to illustrate an illegitimate state? For such proceduralists – those who focus upon the equal concern or fair treatment a legitimate democratic state would afford all citizens – here would be an example of an illegitimate state:

Fridocracy: Only citizens born on Fridays are allowed to vote and the political authority is otherwise constituted as a regular democracy.[12]

Alternatively, for a democratic consent theorist, it might still be the case that in a Fridocracy people born on a Friday had political obligations, as they are electorally enfranchised.[13] Thus for these theories let us use for our illustrative illegitimate state a Lottocracy (which might, notably for a proceduralist, be legitimate):

Lottocracy: The upper and lower houses of the national legislature, and all state or regional assemblies, are chosen by lot of all adult citizens. Executive offices are chosen by these houses.

To return to the problem, the key question about coercion is: when would the general justification of force or coercion enjoyed by a legitimate state make a difference to our overall assessment of an act of force or coercion such that a Fridocracy or Lottocracy would not be justified in doing so (because it was undeserved, caused unwarranted harm etc.) but it would be normatively acceptable for a democracy to do so? For if there are no such cases, then the general justification of coercion enjoyed by legitimate states must have no or negligible normative weight: it is always over-ridden by considering what is done.

Thus there must be some cases, considered on their merits, where most governments would have been unjustified in so acting, but the general justification of the use of force or coercion enjoyed by a legitimate democratic state made, for them, the causing of such harm acceptable. Why though would we want it to be morally acceptable for democracies to harm citizens when we freely admit it is unacceptable for governments in general, such as Fridocracies, to do so?

Or with regard to duties to obey legitimate states, consider someone deciding whether to provide home-grown marijuana to her grandmother who has arthritis. For empirical simplicity let us assume that she is justified in believing that it will ease her grandmother's pain. Doing so is illegal.

She considers what is best for all those affected – including potentially her risk of punishment – and on these grounds concludes that she should grow and provide the drug. She now factors in, however, that the law was passed by a legitimate democratic government. Should she change her assessment of what to do? If a theory of legitimacy that grounds an obligation to obey the law has counter-factual import then the answer must sometimes be yes (her grandmother's pain or the danger of punishment can be altered if the specific empirics are not quite right).

These, after all, are exactly the cases where a duty to obey is not redundant: we do not have sufficient independent reason to obey (such as when we do not murder), nor is obeying heinous and thus we should not do so even with such a duty to obey (such as when commanded to torture). A duty to obey matters counter-factually if, and only if, consideration of the interests of those affected means one should disobey, but the obligation to obey outweighs this. Yet such a duty cannot be founded on the interests of those affected, because these do not vary depending on the providence of the law and are already part of our deliberation. The consequence is that, by living in a democracy, she is morally required to produce a harm (to her grandmother) that she would not be required to produce living in an illegitimate state, such as perhaps a Fridocracy or Lottocracy.

The overall structural worry is as follows. Consider coercive, or use-of-force backed, action X that is undertaken by a state: it may be imprisonment, the threat of going to jail, a range of other sanctions or whatever. The overall challenge for a theory of legitimacy is to show why a legitimate state being normatively justified in doing X is desirable if it is morally undesirable that states in general should do X.

In other words, why is it good for a democracy to be able to justifiably do X when it is bad for all other states – such as a Fridocracy or Lottocracy – to do X because of the type of action X is (doing X harms the relevant good of those affected)?

Similarly, a theory of legitimacy-grounded duties needs to establish why it is desirable for moral agents to obey a law to do Y if doing Y is something that moral agents in general should not do, and would not do in an illegitimate state because, on its merits, doing Y is morally bad.

Which laws should we (morally) disobey in a Fridocracy or Lottocracy but obey in a democracy? Which bad, unjust or unwise laws does an obligation to obey a legitimate state render deserving of obedience? For we already normally have reason to obey those that are good, just or wise, and this holds in any state.

7.4 Possible responses

Are there ways to address or circumvent the problem? Here are six that initially seem promising. (1) That a legitimate state's right to rule is necessary not merely sufficient for justified coercion. (2) That a legitimate state enjoys the right to enforce pre-existing rights. (3) That legitimacy is crucial in those situations where there is reasonable disagreement. (4) That obligations based on legitimacy only apply to acts that, on their merits, are morally optional. (5) That government is legitimate if it is a reliable epistemic authority. (6) That the concept of legitimacy may promote institutional improvement, such as in spreading democratic reform.

1. A right to rule is a necessary requirement for justified coercion

What if the right to rule enjoyed uniquely by the legitimate state is *necessary* not merely sufficient for justified coercion? The value of legitimacy, under this counter-argument, is that it provides a government with the required permission to undertake a range of coercive acts, and this, overall, is potentially going to be very desirable indeed (in overcoming collective action problems etc.).

The central difficulty with this account of the value of legitimacy, however, is that it has a double impact – it provides a legitimate state with the right to coerce, but it denies it to an illegitimate state. And while we would not want an illegitimate state to have a general right to coerce, if legitimacy's impact is to deny it and its agents the potential to ever justifiably coerce then a range of avoidable harms are going to be morally required.

Concretely, if a right to rule is both *only* enjoyed by legitimate states and is *necessary* to justifiably coerce then this is going to have the consequence that anyone in an illegitimate state with influence over state coercion will be morally required to not coerce. Police chiefs should not enforce the law; legislators should always vote against an action backed by force; prison wardens should leave doors unlocked; judges and juries should not convict; tax officials should never threaten those who do not pay and so on.

Of course, if they could make the state legitimate that would be best, but for jurors, judges, police officers and a great many more the option of acquitting or not arresting murderers is the more realistic way to avoid violating the murderers' right to not be coerced by an illegitimate state.

While there are often few individuals with direct influence over whether an illegitimate state becomes legitimate, there are always going to be a great many involved in its coercion, and in many of these cases if the lack of state legitimacy entails that all coercion is normatively unjustified then moral agents should as a result be complicit in causing a great amount of harm: not coercing would be murderers and rapists will have predictable, and horrible, consequences, ones that cannot be justified by reference to anyone's interests since it is not the acts of coercion themselves but facts about their origin that make them morally unacceptable for this concept of legitimacy.

If only a legitimate state can ever justifiably coerce, then those in the coercive apparatus of illegitimate states, were they to take this fact seriously, would potentially move their citizenry much closer to a Hobbesian state of nature with the immense suffering that may entail, suffering they are morally required to cause because of the value of legitimacy.

2. Holding that legitimate states are entitled to enforce existing rights

What if the value of legitimacy is that we confer to a legitimate state the right to enforce certain rights *that exist independent of the presence of the state*, where this right is also a right against other claimants to be in such a position?[14] Under this recognizably Lockean stance it is not that legitimacy creates new rights and duties but rather that it identifies the potential authority who could legitimately enforce them, presumably overcoming what Locke termed the 'inconveniences' of the state of nature. In an illegitimate state these rights remain decentralized and can be enforced either by no one or alternatively by everyone.

The difficulty with this conception of the value of legitimacy, however, is that it either morally forbids a range of actions that are, on their merits, deeply morally desirable or it merely confers onto the legitimate state the capacity to undertake the enforcement of certain rights in situations where it is on its merits not justified in so doing.

For example, consider a right to punish attempted murderers stemming from our natural right as owners of our own bodies. A legitimate state enjoys such a right as we (so the argument goes) have transferred it to overcome a range of practical difficulties with effectively using such a right ourselves. But consider those cases where an illegitimate state could effectively enforce such a right. Should it do so? If legitimacy is necessary for such action then we forbid what is, on the enforcement theory, eminently desirable: that we have our rights respected. Illegitimate states often have the capacity to coerce would be murderers, and in so doing solve a range of problems present in both the Hobbesian and Lockean states of nature, notably our physical vulnerability as individuals. But if the concept of legitimacy entails that illegitimate states lack a right to coerce and as a result should not ever coerce, or that they are not able to justifiably enforce those rights that we already possess even when doing so is of immense benefit, then this will leave the inhabitants of illegitimate states decisively and maybe horrifically worse off.

If, alternatively, the illegitimate state would be justified in so acting, *as all such states can justifiably enforce our basic rights*, then in transferring to a legitimate state the capacity to generally enforce such rights we either transfer nothing (if such a right only extends to the capacity to do what is just) or we provide it with an extra capacity to be justified when acting wrongly (and this is all we do). Again, legitimacy seems to either have a redundant or undesirable – that is good-harming – impact.

3. Reasonable disagreement

A third response might be to claim that legitimacy's justificatory role or deserved obedience is crucial in precisely those cases where it is uncertain or debatable whether the state action is justified or obedience due. A legitimate democratic state is justified in using coercion or owed obedience *because* there is a lack of consensus, some controversy or reasonable disagreement.

Given the pluralism inherent in modern states, reasonable disagreement seems inevitable. But its presence does not address the specific worry. To see why, for the sake of argument let us assume the following is true. (1) There are multiple individuals in the society with conflicting moral doctrines, all of which, however, are reasonable. (2) That the means by which the state arrives at decisions are both just and legitimate. (3) That all the individuals should and do accept that the means by which decisions are arrived at are both just and legitimate. These may be very demanding conditions (notably the combination of 1 and 3), but they are the assumptions most sympathetic to the disagreement-theorist, so let us grant them. Our question is: given these facts, should the individuals accept the desirability of a general duty to obey such decisions, or of the state having a general justification in the use of force and coercion.

Take for instance a particular law, 'do Q', about the merits of which the individuals have differing opinions based on their comprehensive moral doctrines. Here again are the three salient possibilities:

(i) Doing Q is required by reference to those affected by doing Q, and thus one should do Q whether commanded by a legitimate or illegitimate state.

(ii) Not doing Q is required by reference to those affected by doing Q, and thus one should not do Q, whether commanded by a legitimate or illegitimate state.

(iii) Not doing Q is required by reference to those affected by doing Q, and one should thus not do Q, unless commanded by a legitimate state

Now assume there are some individuals in the society who think that, for this particular law, case (i) obtains. There are some other individuals who believe that case (ii) obtains. There are some other individuals who believe that case (iii) obtains. All are reasonable, but they disagree.

However, what they should be able to agree upon is that, if case (i) or (ii) obtains then legitimacy, via a duty to obey, is having a redundant impact. If case (iii) obtains it is having an undesirable impact. In other words, they (reasonably) disagree as to whether in this particular case a duty to obey is redundant or undesirable. But the counterfactual problem is that a duty whose impact is either redundant or undesirable seems to have potential dis-value. Exactly the same problem will accrue to the evaluation of coercive acts.

The underlying worry is that not only does the presence of reasonable disagreement not establish the value of a duty to obey or right to use coercion, but the fact that that such a duty or a right are undesirable should potentially be something recognized as part of the overlapping consensus between reasonable people. Here, after all, are two types of questions ('A questions' and 'B questions') we might ask:

A1. Is an obligation to obey the law of a legitimate state desirable?
A2. Is a legitimate state enjoying a general justification in the use of force and coercion or having a right to so act desirable?

Or:

B1. Is this particular law – X – judged on its specific merits something we should act in conformity with?
B2. Is this particular act of coercion – Y – judged on its specific merits justified?

Reasonable people will often disagree about the B questions. But the presence of such disagreement does not represent an argument that answers the A questions. If a state is justified in using coercion because it is legitimate, then the undesirability of the counter-factual import of this justification is a *conceptual* consequence of the nature of the justification. We may lack agreement, for instance, on which of the three possibilities – (i), (ii) or (iii) outlined previously – obtain in a particular case. Yet whichever one obtains legitimacy is having a counterfactual import that is either redundant or normatively unattractive.

That is, whether we disagree if a particular law is bad, unjust or unwise does not impact on whether it is desirable that a law that *is* bad, unjust or unwise should be obeyed if a legitimate state commands us to, but disobeyed when all other states so command. Similarly, that we disagree *if* a particular act of coercion is on its merits morally unjustified does not show why it would be desirable for a legitimate state to justifiably do, or have a right to do, those acts which *are* on their merits morally unjustified.

The problem arises from the very notion of legitimating acts based on their providence rather than normative facts about the acts, and holds even if in particular cases the normative facts about the particular acts are disputed or unclear. (Point five below responds to the very important claim that a legitimate government is a more reliable *authority* about the normative facts, and thus is prima facie justified in its use of force or owed our obedience to the law.)

4. Distinguishing moral requirements and permissions

Previously, in setting out the problem as it relates to obligations, all acts of obedience were parsed into those that – based on their merits – either one morally should or should not do. But what if legitimacy makes a difference in precisely those situations where obedience is, on its merits, morally optional. That is, if both a legitimate and illegitimate state command one to obey a law X then the difference legitimacy makes is that, *if* obeying such a law is on its merits morally optional, then you should do so if commanded by a legitimate state but not necessarily if by an illegitimate state.

There are three possible cases here:

O1: Obedience to law X would harm the relevant human interests at stake but not sufficiently to be normally morally forbidden.
O2: Obedience to law X would promote the relevant human interests at stake, but not sufficiently to be normally morally required.
O3: Obedience to law X would neither promote nor harm the relevant human interests at stake.

Now, O1 does not circumvent the earlier worry, for legitimacy requires one to produce a harm that morally one would otherwise not be required to produce: it may be a marginal harm, but it is a harm nonetheless, legitimacy is having apparent moral disvalue and the counter-factual problem accrues. In cases of O2 however, obedience owed to a legitimate state requires one in such a state to do what is generally morally desirable but not normally required: it may for instance involve providing some benefit to others in the society or some deserving group that goes beyond one's normal moral duties, such as supporting museums via taxes, volunteering to help the needy or obeying the bylaws of a park. Under this option it is not that legitimacy requires one to do something that is morally bad, as it does with a general duty to obey, merely to go beyond one's basic requirements.[15] This avoids the previous worries as what the legitimate state commands is something that is advantageous overall, to some others, to civil society, or some co-citizens etc. The difficulty with this however is the following.

Double punishment: If we owe duties under a legitimate state and they are to the benefit of all or some deserving group, then we have a reason to fulfil these duties whether the state is legitimate or not, fulfilling them simply depends on considerations of efficacy and practicability. Thus if we have less duties under an illegitimate state then we potentially cause its subjects to suffer from double punishment: they suffer from a worse government, *and* from the lower level of concern represented by less duties owed to them.

For example, if we have additional duties to pay taxes to support various cultural public goods under a legitimate state, and this benefits the very poor for instance, then if we were to suffer some bad fate – say a coup – then the poor would end up being doubly punished: they would have the bad luck to be ruled by an inferior government, and the wealthy would additionally now have less of a duty to them. (Now, it might be that some of the duties of the wealthy under an illegitimate regime would be practically less easy to discharge as the government cannot be trusted to spend tax money wisely or justly, but this is a contingent argument for efficiency: we just cannot reliably fulfil our duties to help those worse off, but if we could we should do so.)

The problem is that legitimacy-based duties have the potential to harm people in two ways: they can require one in a legitimate state to do something that is on its merits morally bad; or they can permit those living in an illegitimate state to avoid helping others even though this might be

– given the sub-optimal government – even more desirable. Perhaps the perversity of this can be reduced if we restrict the scope of legitimacy-grounded duties to things sometimes considered low-impact so that being morally required to do so if commanded by a legitimate but not an illegitimate state leaves those generally subject to illegitimate rule only marginally harmed by our account of the value of legitimacy. But even if so, the fact that we may need to restrict duties of obedience to those things normally merely morally optional and of low impact in order to minimize the harm legitimacy does implicitly confirms the substantive point: legitimacy has normative disvalue.

But what about in cases of O3 where obedience would neither promote nor harm the relevant overall human interests at stake? Here it seems that subjects of the legitimate state and illegitimate state are morally unaffected by the counter-factual import of legitimacy: neither group is harmed by what is required unlike with options O1 and O2. We may have had to restrict the impact of legitimacy to a very small set of cases, but it seems here to at least not have any moral disvalue. This, however, is too quick, for imposing duties on agents is plausibly a burden on them at least. We normally take this burden to be greatly outweighed by the importance of the duty, but in cases of O3 this is precisely what cannot be the case. It is true that being required to obey a law or edict where obedience neither harms nor helps those affected is likely to be a small burden, but if this is all legitimacy does then we have both restricted the concept's import to a tiny subset of laws, and still imposed (in the imposition of a moral duty) a cost not justified by reference to any human interests at all. The disvalue may be small, but it exists, and even if only applying to what is neither morally required nor forbidden legitimacy fails to have any positive normative impact.

5. Appealing to epistemic authority

A much more promising response is to argue that, properly constituted, legitimate government is a more reliable authority about what we ought to do, and about when force is justified, than illegitimate government. Now, to overcome the counterfactual problem, such an epistemic approach is going to need to hold that legitimate government does not create duties per se, and does not have a general justification in the use of coercion nor a general right to coerce.

Thus the approach of someone like Estlund is still going to be subject to the counterfactual worry as his theory combines a thesis about the epistemic reliability of democracy with a substantive theory of the value of legitimacy, specifically that in a democracy the 'authority and legitimacy of its laws often extends even to unjust laws, though there must be limits on this'.[16] As such the concerns raised previously accrue to the theory as he rejects a *pure* epistemic route (what he usefully calls a 'correctness theory'), seeking instead 'to show how democracy yields moral reasons to obey the law and a moral permission to enforce it'.[17] The counterfactual problem is that such reasons and such a permission seem to be normatively undesirable, and a theory that assumes they are desirable will be subject to the previous worries.

But a pure correctness theory – most famously perhaps that of Raz's service conception – would potentially overcome the counterfactual problem because it quite explicitly does not hold that legitimate government creates additional new reasons to obey or to judge force justified, rather that it might sometimes be a better judge of when someone should obey or when force is justified based on the reasons that already apply.

The central difficulty with a purely epistemic account of obedience and deference to the assessment of force of legitimate authoritative institutions, however, is that it may not be able to establish any very clear relationship with legitimate institutions in expectation producing better laws than illegitimate ones. To see why, consider the underlying logic of epistemic authority.

Raz, applying his 'Normal Justification Thesis' to states, writes that 'The main argument for the legitimacy of any authority is that in subjecting himself to it a person is more likely to act successfully for the reasons that apply to him than if he does not subject himself to that authority.'[18] Such an argument is not vulnerable to the type of counterfactual worries outlined previously as it does not claim that the fact of a government being legitimate creates new additional reasons to obey, rather that you will have a 'pre-emptive' reason to obey if the government is a better judge of what you ought to do than you are. As he observes, sometimes this may be the case, sometimes not.

Raz gives us a coherent and cogent account of authority. To link it to the claim that one has a pre-emptive reason to judge force generally justified, or obedience due, to a legitimate state then it seems like we need the following, not utterly implausible, claim:

Epis1: A legitimate government's commands are likely to be a better guide to what a person has reason to do (or to the true assessment of justified coercion) than that person's own judgement.

At first blush this gives a person a general reason to obey the commands and accept the claims of justified force made by a legitimate state. Democracies would be legitimate on this account if and when they normally better judge when coercion is justified, and when one ought to obey, than citizens themselves do.

This, of course, is a contestable claim. But even if true it is not enough. For there is an ambiguity between being an authority *relative to the agent* and an authority *relative to other potential authorities*. If two 'experts' offer someone advice on what to do, even if both are better judges of what the person has reason to do, if one expert is a better judge than the other, then the person has a reason to take the advice of her alone.[19] Similarly, if a state commands one to do X, or claims that its coercion is justified, one should accept this not only if one thinks the state is a better judge than oneself of whether one should do X, or whether its coercion is justified, but if it is the *best* judge available.

There is, after all, no such thing as an epistemic authority simpliciter, the concept is only meaningful in comparison. That is, 'belief-holder J is an authority about Q' is under-specified, and only potentially correct as a claim that 'belief-holder J is an authority about Q compared to belief-holder K'. Thus for a government to be legitimate as an authority what we require is for the following to be true:

Epis2: A government's commands are likely to be not only a better guide to what a person has reason to do (or to the true assessment of justified coercion) than the person's own judgement, but the best guide of *any* of the potential authorities available.

I personally doubt that this is often the case, but we each must decide. However, what such considerations highlight is that, rather ironically, it may be that subjects often have more pre-emptive reasons to accept the commands of, and claims over force made by, oppressive states rather than democratic ones, even if the latter more reliably produce good laws and justified coercion.

If democratic states are often accompanied by relatively open societies and political processes, such that those who disagree with the government from outside, and those within the governing system opposing the official policy, can communicate their views and have them disseminated, then we will have a great many potential authorities to contrast with the state's claims. If legitimate states are democratic, for instance, we may thus face the following.

The irony of authority and legitimate states: If obligations to obey, or justifications of coercion, are epistemically justified, then the more open the political process and public sphere, the less likely it is that the state will be the pre-eminent authority for a given agent on a given issue. If legitimate states result in open societies, then legitimate states may be less likely to be the pre-eminent authority for subjects on whether one should obey the law or accept that state coercion is justified than oppressive illegitimate states, even though the latter may be expected to produce more bad laws and use unjustified force more frequently.

For example, if an oppressive illegitimate state passes a decree that one must observe a curfew, not eat fish, or temporarily evacuate one's town due to an imminent threat then – if the media is controlled and dissenting views are hard to find – one may be left with deciding whether the state is likely to be a better judge of what one has reason to do than oneself. In those cases where it is – and government does have structural advantages over private citizens in judging national threats in many situations – one seemingly has an epistemic and pre-emptive reason to obey.

Under a legitimate state, if one has access to a wide variety of potential authorities and dissenting views, the state is extremely unlikely to be the pre-eminent normative authority for an agent. Whether a state's commands or claims are authoritative depends not merely on the extent to which it is a better judge than the agent, but also on whether it is a better judge than other potential epistemic authorities. This crucial second clause highlights why even the view that legitimate states do not create duties or are not per se justified in the use of force, but merely are more reliable at identifying what one should do and when coercion is justified, does not entail any general presumption in favour of obedience or acceptance of their coercion as justified.

If legitimacy depends upon, or accompanies, open political processes and open societies, then any general presumption is likely to be undercut by the state's loss of pre-eminent epistemic authority. Even the very contingent and limited epistemic duties and justifications potentially grounded upon Raz's Normal Justification Thesis fail to underpin any necessary connection between legitimacy, good governance, one's duties, and the general justification of force.

The initial challenge for epistemic accounts is that they need to establish not only that legitimate government is a better authority than illegitimate government, and that it is a better authority than the citizen, but that it is also *the best authority of all those available*. This seems very unlikely to be true of the decisions of majorities in open societies where there are a very large number of alternative potential authorities. But there is one notable theory, Condorcet's Jury Theorem, that if it applied to voters could make such epistemic superiority near inevitable.[20]

Under the famous theorem, if each voter has a probability of being right greater than a half[21]; voters are voting truthfully on the same binary question[22]; and votes are statistically independent, then the probability the majority is right approaches 1 as the group size approaches infinity, and more relevantly, it quickly approaches 1 if the voters are a little bit better than a coin flip and fairly numerous, or at least as numerous as in all modern states. Does this establish the value of legitimacy? It seems on the surface it might, as if true the theorem would establish the near infallibility of majority decisions, and thus that as fallible individuals we should defer to their judgement.

Now clearly there is an elephant in the room: the basic CJT model makes a series of predictions – that majorities in two large jurisdictions will almost never disagree; that voting choices are not significantly correlated with income, race, age and religion etc.[23] – that are testable and, at least for all existing democracies, demonstrably false.[24] Thus the theory obviously has an apparently fatal hurdle to clear in that it appears directly refuted by pretty much all of the main psephological findings of the last hundred years (a possible good example of the 'bad-premise, pretty maths' problem discussed in Chapter 8.)[25]

That is, while almost every theory in empirical political science has at least some evidence in favour of it, one of the few exceptions is Condorcet's Jury Theorem as a model of human voting. The evidence against it is universal, widespread, consistent, robust, long-standing and truly unequivocal. CJT, as an empirical theory, is just false.

But even if someone could show that it somehow did apply, and thus that majorities are in fact near infallible, perhaps the more fundamental point is that it is not the state's legitimacy (as we commonly conceive it) that does any work here: it is the expectation of majorities almost never getting any decisions wrong. That is, the concept of legitimacy does not obviously add anything: it has no value in of itself.

Still, if someone did believe that majorities were close to infallible and as such a superior judge to all others in society then they would have a reason to defer to their judgements and it might look like such deference represented establishing the legitimacy of such governance, even if on examination it is their infallibility that is key. This is what an account of an epistemically grounded legitimate authority requires: that the legitimate institutions be the very best judge of when obedience is due and force justified of any of the agents and groups that can provide such judgements. This seems to me implausibly demanding of any realistic modern institutional form, but we do have a theory – CJT – that if it were true of human voters would potentially establish this. Such a theory does not, however, really establish the independent value of legitimacy, only the usefulness of deferring to a (supposed) near infallible decision maker.

6. Legitimacy and institutional improvement

Finally, even if legitimacy-based duties and justifications are normatively undesirable in principle it still might be that the belief in them, and by implication a belief in the importance of legitimacy, was desirable in practice, most notably perhaps by encouraging the spread of democracy. On this psycho-political view, the value of legitimacy is in labelling one set of institutional features as qualitatively better than any other and thus encouraging people to strive for those features. This is an empirical claim about how our normative language motivates agents with influence over institutional change. I am somewhat sceptical about it, but for the sake of argument let us assume it is plausible.

Does this demonstrate that legitimacy is normatively desirable? It does not. What it highlights is the potential instrumental value of some people believing it is, not that it is. The belief in a vengeful God, for instance, may make some people behave morally better and therefore promote certain good consequences: that does not demonstrate that God is vengeful, or exists. Thus even if we have some expected benefits from the widespread belief that legitimacy is normatively desirable, and an equating of this with certain democratic state structures – such as electoral executive and legislative selection – this does not show that legitimacy is in of itself normatively valuable, only that popular belief to that effect in certain situations may be, and in others may not. It is a very contingent and weak account of the value of legitimacy.

It is also one with risks. For while a widespread belief in the unique legitimacy of democracy may plausibly encourage transitions to this state form, it may also provide excessive authorization to what it subsequently does: the fact that an unjust, unwise or unconscionable act is undertaken through a democratic procedure may lend it an apparent legitimacy that distracts from its injustice, folly or moral egregiousness. It may therefore serve to give a normative veneer to those undesirable practices that seem entrenched features of democratic nation states, notably the low or negligible level of concern systematically afforded to those outside the state's territory, to future generations influenced by what it does and to those with few economic resources.

Not only does the psycho-political defence of democratic legitimacy identify not the correctness of a belief in the value of legitimacy but rather merely the potential instrumental utility of such a belief, there is also a real possibility of it fostering a sort of normative confusion whereby we conflate popularity with justice. To normatively mislead people has dangers.

And it may additionally be that the very nature of the notion of legitimacy as currently construed will unjustifiably prejudice us toward certain types of institutions and not others if we make it primary in institutional evaluation. While a Fridocracy enjoys no obvious advantages over the representative democratic republic, a Lottocracy or some variant thereof might, at least in that it is less likely to show bias toward the wealthy, well-born and well-known.

Yet the popular identification of legitimacy with consent, and conflation of that with voting, may hinder a clear-headed widespread assessment of the relative merits of a range of state forms. This is not a hypothetical worry. Manin has chronicled the really striking historical transformation from lot being viewed as inherently democratic and election as aristocratic to the equating of democracy with voting, and the latter with consent. 'There is every reason to believe', he writes, 'that it is this view of the foundation of political legitimacy and obligation that led to the eclipse of lot and the triumph of election.' The implication of this chapter is that this enormous change in political thought and institutional evaluation was potentially mis-premised.

7.5 Conclusions

The core problems highlighted previously have the same basic structure. If the fact that a state is legitimate creates duties or justifies coercion then we can ask the counter-factual question: when does this change what we should do, or when does it change our overall assessment of an act of force or coercion? In both cases it does so when the balance of more general reasons we have – based on people's interests or on what they deserve – is outweighed by the new duty or justification. That is, it only makes a difference when it 'tips the scale' against people's interests all things considered, or justifies what is – on its own terms – unjustifiable. This is because the institutional source of laws and coercion does not necessarily remake people's interests, nor alter whether they deserve punishment or if coercion produces relevantly good consequences.

The overall problem of political legitimacy is commonly treated as a dispute about what would need to be true of a state or polity so that it would have a right to use coercion and be owed obedience. This assumes that such rights and obligations are normatively undesirable when held by non-legitimate states but normatively desirable when enjoyed by a legitimate state. Yet this requires justification and, as this chapter has tried to show, that is not straightforward at all.

The ultimate source of the problem is disarmingly simple, namely that if 'the good' captures how people's interests are affected, either directly or via a notion of justice, then legitimacy is either going to clash with this if it establishes different grounds for normative evaluation (such as by creating duties or conferring coercion-rights), or if legitimacy reduces to the good (as with epistemic or instrumentalist accounts) then it will simply lack the conceptual resources to establish a separate realm of institutional evaluation, and potentially mislead in the attempt. The problem is a failure of evaluative coherence between the assessment of what a legitimate state does and the legitimacy of it doing it.

If we adopt a good-based moral theory – such as that of motivation ethics – then merely by doing so we may have to abandon most common assumptions about the value of political legitimacy.

Ultimately, we should ask of any approach to normative evaluation focused on one type of object – agents, actions, outcomes or institutions – that it be capable of supplying a coherent and justified account of the evaluation of the other objects (or deny the need for such an account).

We can as such ask of theories that evaluate institutional procedures and then actions what this entails for the good. If the sole counter-factual effect of some duty, right or justification is to require or justify harm to people's interests, then it becomes hard to establish the moral desirability of the duty, right or justification. This is a problem for our most prominent accounts of political legitimacy.

CHAPTER EIGHT

Interpersonal comparisons of the good[1]

Motivation ethics holds that agents should be morally evaluated by their strength of motivation to promote the overall good, and that institutions are morally better the better they promote the overall good (the latter a feature shared with consequentialism). But almost all actions, policies and institutional changes involve some people benefiting and some losing, so to be of prescriptive value we need some way of adding these costs and benefits. We need to make interpersonal comparisons of the good.[2]

According to overall-welfare sceptics, this is impossible, or meaningless, or indeterminate. There seem to be three distinct worries here.

The first type of scepticism draws upon what we might call the 'can't see the values' problem. Imagine there are several people in a room and someone wants to know whether he is personally the tallest, and if not who is. Well, one way of estimating this is to go around the room and stand near people. The person can then directly compare his amount of height to that of others, so to speak. This might not be perfect, but it will provide a reasonable estimate. What makes this work is that with height it's possible, in a sense, to 'see the values' (i.e. to directly compare the relative quantities).

Overall-welfare sceptics, however, point out that with welfare we can't do this, it's not that you can look into someone's head and see that a certain outcome will give them '25' welfarons or utils or whatever the measure of the good is. We might have a sense for ourselves how options compare – whether one possibility will make a big or small difference to how our lives go. But as we can't get into the heads of others, according to the sceptic, we can't make interpersonal comparisons.

Robbins, for example, rejects interpersonal comparisons because 'Introspection does not enable A to measure what is going on in B's mind, nor B to measure what is going on in A's. There is no way of comparing the satisfactions of different people.'[3] We can't see the values.

The second worry is slightly different. It notes that we can have ranking information for individuals and that if we are to make interpersonal comparisons this is going to represent, in effect, combining these rankings.

However, what the rankings don't tell us are the magnitudes, that is how far apart the options are, nor where on the scale they lie. So knowing that someone has more welfare in A rather than B doesn't allow us to know how much more (it might be a little or it might be a lot) and it doesn't allow us to know B is low or high in absolute terms. When we then compare these rankings across individuals, we cannot be certain that we are giving people the right weight: what if the welfare gaps between their rankings are really huge, or someone's ranking overall is just higher up the scale?

This is a long-standing worry and perhaps the most prominent justification for rejecting interpersonal comparisons. Writing in the nineteenth century, Jevons approvingly summed the view up nicely, noting that:

> the susceptibility of one mind may, for what we know, be a thousand times greater than that of another. But, provided that the susceptibility was different in a like ratio in all directions, we should never be able to discover the profoundest difference. Every mind is thus inscrutable to every other mind, and no common denominator of feeling is possible.[4]

A hundred years later, Nozick re-popularized the worry with the concept of a 'utility monster'.[5] Utility monsters look like other people but satisfying their preferences contributes much, much more to overall welfare than satisfying the preferences of other people. But we cannot know this, and in fact neither can they. Similarly, if there are utility monsters there might well be 'utility-waifs': people for whom satisfying their preferences contributes relatively little to overall welfare compared to other people. For convenience, let us call this set of problems the 'utility monster' worry.

Both the 'utility monster' worry and the 'can't see the values' worry are relatively clear. The final thing sceptics often appeal to is somewhat harder to pin down but seems to be a general sense that the very concept of the overall good (or overall utility / overall welfare) is somehow suspect or indeed meaningless.

Thus witness Arrow's summary of his overall stance, that 'the viewpoint will be taken here that interpersonal comparisons of utilities has no meaning and, in fact, that there is no meaning relevant to welfare comparisons in the measurability of individual utility'.[6] His justification is partly due to the type of problems behind the 'utility monster' worry, and partly the claim that 'it seems to make no sense to add the utility of one individual, a psychic magnitude in his mind, with the utility of another individual'.[7]

Arguments of this type, usually simply asserting that something is meaningless or makes no sense, seem to take the conclusion as self-evident once stated. This makes it hard to scrutinize the justification. However, sympathetically, we can perhaps identify three possible justifications:

1. That overall welfare would only be a meaningful concept if the 'utility monster' worry and the 'can't see the values' worry could be overcome. They can't, so it isn't.

Under this interpretation, it is the fact that we can't know overall welfare that renders it meaningless as a sum of individual welfares (this then suggests we instead examine the way we arrive at social choices or some other decision based construct). This is straightforwardly addressed if the utility-monster and can't-see-the-values worries can be addressed, and not if not.

The second possibility is that the implied analogy between individual and social welfare rests on a mistake. That is:

2. That individual welfare is only meaningful because there are individual minds, social welfare would only be meaningful if there was a social mind. There isn't, so it isn't.

This gains its plausibility from the well-evidenced biological fact that humans don't have a hive mind or share thoughts. While we might have a range of metaphors suggesting we do – 'we think' etc. – and we might sometimes speak this way– 'the jury has decided' – on this view what we are in fact doing is simply using a short-hand, it's not that we're asserting some sort of telepathic unity. As such, any account of social welfare that requires a group mind or social brain is premised on an empirical falsehood.

The final justification for thinking the overall good meaningless would be that the stuff it is potentially composed of is of the wrong type. Namely:

3. That to 'add up' some metric it has to have an absolute quantity, and welfare doesn't.

This view could of course just be the worry that we can't know the quantity (i.e. see the values). However, an alternative way to justify it would be to hold that individual welfare isn't an absolute quantity but a relative weighting. As such, it's not meaningful to think that someone has a 'certain amount' of welfare in A, but only meaningful to think of them having more or less welfare in A *compared to* B. Since there's no absolute individual welfare values or facts there's no truth to what the sum of the values or combination of these facts would be. To be meaningful, overall welfare would require absolute individual welfare values.

These three concerns all seem to support scepticism about the overall good (or overall welfare) being meaningful, thus we can perhaps call them collectively the 'what is the overall good?' worry.

The epistemic approach

The argument of this chapter will be that if we treat the problem of interpersonal comparisons as an epistemic problem then these worries can all be explicitly and fully addressed. In other words, that it is scepticism about interpersonal comparisons that lacks any clear justification.

The epistemic approach, at root, draws upon three observations. Firstly, that the 'can't see the values' worry and 'utility monster' worry both arise because of our epistemic situation: we can know some things but we can't know others. Secondly, that this doesn't just happen in the welfare case, there are lots of possible everyday empirical situations in which we both know and don't know the same sorts of things (we can know the rankings but not know the underlying values), *and that in those situations forming justified beliefs about the overall underlying values is relatively straightforward*. Thirdly, that not only can we then use in the welfare case the same techniques we would use in the empirical cases, but that we are justified in doing so: the areas where welfare and empirical-cases differ do not undermine the comparisons, in fact they support them.

To get a sense of the overall idea, consider the following situation. Imagine we have a group of students in a room, and we get them each to write down their birth city (or nearest city to birth location), species of first pet, mother's maiden name, most recently played sport, and favourite author's surname. They are not to show anyone else. So, for instance, someone could have:

Cambridge, Dog, Aziz, Football, LeCarre

All the students are then asked to put them in a ranking based on word length. So the aforementioned words would be:

Pet < Surname < Author < Sport < City

We then learn the rankings for each of the students. The question we want to answer is: can we form a justified belief about whether there are more letters in all the city words combined or in all the pet words combined?

The answer is straightforwardly yes: this is, in fact, a tractable epistemic problem. To do so you need to assess two questions:

1 Do we have evidence about the underlying values apart from the evidence of the rankings?
2 What weight should be given to factors other than the ranking information?

So under 1 it might be that we have looked over someone's shoulder and seen her author word, or maybe we know that a bunch of the students were born in Manchester, or maybe we know that the most popular pets are dogs and cats. Integrating such background knowledge, in the empirical case, complicates the task slightly, but not much (you just treat it as additional evidence). However, in overcoming welfare scepticism we can happily ignore the problem of integrating non-ranking evidence, as this is exactly what the sceptic asserts is impossible: that scepticism is warranted precisely because we cannot have any direct evidence of the underlying values.

Under question 2 we need to decide, in effect, what relative weight to give the information of different people. The following principle is one way of doing it:

Unbiasedness: Beliefs that are justified should be unbiased in the inclusion and treatment of information from individuals unless there is evidence supporting, or a positive reason for, such bias.

What this means is that, in addition to the ranking evidence, if we have no further evidence that someone has longer words than someone else, and have no further evidence that a particular type of word is longer, then to give certain people's evidence more weight would be unjustified.

So, in the welfare case, if we only have ordinal – that is ranking evidence – this entails:

The ordinal epistemic welfare/good principle: If we have no evidence that an unbiased super-set of options would differ, then of two options we are justified in believing that A represents more welfare/good than B if and only if we are justified in believing the number of evidenced arrangements in which individuals have less good than A minus the number in which they have more is greater than the number of evidenced arrangements in which individuals have less good than B minus the number in which they have more.[8]

What does the work here is unbiasedness, in that it rules out weighting individuals unequally – either directly, or indirectly by weighting certain scenarios/words unequally – unless we have a positive, evidence-based, reason for doing so.

HOW WOULD THIS WORK?

It's possible to illustrate how the ordinal epistemic principle works, and to personally test it out, by actually using it in a situation where we initially only have ranking information. Take, for instance, a class of students, whereby we get ten of them to write down the following: favourite author's surname, birth city, species of first pet, favourite singer's first name, last sport played, mother's maiden name and last holiday destination. Besides each they write a score that is how many letters the word has which represents their welfare in that situation (so you have an author-welfare, sport-welfare and so on). They then rank the scenarios by welfare and let the class know their ranking.

So: Orwell(6), Cambridge(9), Dog(3), Kylie(5), Snooker(7), Jones(5), Mykonos(7) would yield a ranking of:

City > Sport and Holiday > Author > Singer and Mother > Pet

Imagine we want to know which has more letters – the ten pet words all combined, or the ten author words all combined. Under the ordinal epistemic welfare/good principle what you would do is have each student's author and pet words given a score based on how many words are shorter minus how many words are longer. So with the example above the student's author word would score a 0 (3 words shorter, 3 words longer) and the pet word would score a -6.

For all ten students we simply then add these scores for each word (so add the pet scores to each other, add the author words to each other). This is your estimate of which set of words are longer. You can then ask the students how many letters their actual words have and check it.

Four very quick features to note:
(i) The closer the scores the less confident you should be.
(ii) As such, the fewer the students, or the fewer the options, the less confident you should expect to be.
(iii) The analogy is inexact as we do know lots of background things about author names and pets, so if you ask the students to guess before knowing the class rankings maybe they can do non-terribly.
(iv) The type of things that determined differences between particular students' various word lengths – their parents, birth-location, genetics and upbringing – seem to be the type of things that generate variance in welfare. The analogy is good is this regard.

You can also, rather than just comparing two options, compare all the options using the same method (give each word a score, add the respective scores up) to produce a class ranking, and then see how close it got to the actual ranking. (It's important not to conflate this particular result with the overall approach. The overall approach is a logic for how to make interpersonal comparisons given *any* set of evidence. This result is what that entails for a particular set of evidence, namely evidence of ordinal rankings, these and strictly these alone).

The mechanics of the actual solution are relatively straightforward (though some potential mis-uses are discussed subsequently). The justification of it however depends ultimately on the justification of unbiasedness.

Unbiasedness: Two sufficient types of justification

There are two, seemingly distinct, ways we might justify unbiasedness in the welfare case. The first is to see it as capturing a very general *methodological* principle. Here, for example, is Harsanyi setting out his 'principle of unwarranted differentiation':

If two objects of human beings show similar behaviour in all their relevant aspects open to observation, the assumption of some unobservable hidden difference between them must be regarded as a completely gratuitous hypothesis and one contrary to sound scientific method.[9]

This does seem to reflect a very core principle of empirical science in general, for when we think that gravity will hold next week, that Tyrannosaurus Rex bones weren't created and left in the ground by pixies, or that the earth will not be flat when we wake up next Christmas morning, we are using the fact that since we have no evidence for a hidden difference – such as that pixies exist and like to bury fake prehistoric T-Rex carcasses – that then to positively believe this is unwarranted.

Similarly, thinking more concretely about human variance, modern medicine simply could not function if we didn't adopt some sort of version of Harsanyi's principle. If all the evidence we have is that a drug is safe and effective at treating some illness, then that we cannot rule out the possibility that someone is allergic to it does not warrant that we believe this and deny him the drug. We form justified beliefs based on the evidence we have, and that requires not making beliefs contingent on factors that according to current evidence are not relevant.

The methodological principle – if you think it correct – is sufficient to justify unbiasedness. However, thinking about the welfare/good case, we might think instead that what is wrong with being biased is that the sort of treatment implied by biasedness is morally objectionable. That is, the alternative to the methodological route is to see unbiasedness as justified by an explicitly *ethical* principle.

When choosing policies, actions or institutions partly based on welfare estimates or estimates of the good we are impacting how we treat people. To give some people extra weight with no good reason for this is to violate the equal moral concern all are owed.

This is perhaps easiest to illustrate by considering how we could violate unbiasedness. Because the principle entails that evidence of welfare or the good, and this and this alone, should be used to produce overall beliefs, every violation of it has to, in effect, weight some factor other than welfare evidence or evidence of the good. In principle you could weight anything: give more weight to white people, or rich people, or people with certain types of rankings, or anyone called Bob. Doing so, of course, therefore means giving less relative weight to non-white people, non-rich people, people who don't have the favoured type of ranking, or anyone not called Bob. As an ethical principle unbiasedness rules this out because such people deserve to be treated with equal concern, that is for evidence of their interests, their good, to be given equal weight.

So which is correct? Personally, as subsequently briefly discussed here and more fully in the Epilogue, I believe the right way to think of these two defences of unbiasedness is as complimentary principles ultimately drawing upon the same idea, namely that arbitrary beliefs are incorrect beliefs. Under this approach, to reject unbiasedness is to make beliefs about overall welfare contingent on an arbitrary factor – someone's race, or whether they are called Bob and so on – and therefore to adopt unjustified beliefs about overall welfare.

In the context of this chapter, however, what centrally matters is that to reject unbiasedness sceptics have to demonstrate why it cannot be justified on *either* methodological or moral grounds, because either is sufficient.

Initial arguments against the analogy

Before going on to discuss what the epistemic approach entails for the meaningfulness of the overall good, and various issues it raises, it's worth considering three objections the sceptic could raise against the initial word-welfare illustrative analogy.

Firstly, they might simply object to argument-by-analogy, after all words and welfare are very different. This is true: every analogy has similarities and differences between the two things being compared. What matters, however, is whether the two things being compared are alike in the ways that are relevant to the task at hand. Viewed as an epistemic problem, the welfare and word analogy actually seems very tight: we by stipulation only know the ranking information, and we want to form justified beliefs about the underlying overall amounts.

Alternatively, the sceptic might claim that word variance and welfare variance are just driven by different things. Unfortunately for the sceptic, not only does this not invalidate the analogy – what matters is whether we know the same type of things – it also appears false. What drives variance in human welfare seems to be some combination of genes, parents, contingencies of birth, upbringing, culture, habit and chance. And these are exactly the sorts of things that drive variance in birth-location, sports played, mothers' names, favourite authors and first pets. If anything, the analogy is unnecessarily tight.

One final complaint about the word-welfare analogy would be that words are made of letters – that is discrete units – and welfare might not be. This is true, though scepticism wasn't supposed to depend on a particular hypothesis about the nature of our mental infrastructure.

Welfare variance might ultimately be driven by discrete properties – the ultimate mental facts it draws upon might be countably quantitative, such as based on the number of neurons or such like. But equally it might not, it might be based on the relative strength of certain clusters of connections and relationships. Even if the latter, this doesn't support scepticism.

Consider a different case where ten students go into a room and cut off a bit of string from each of five balls of string: a blue one, a red one, a green one, a yellow one and a black one. They then indicate (without showing us the string) how their relative strings compare. For instance someone might have red > yellow > blue > black > green. As we gain evidence of their rankings, can we form justified beliefs about which is longer overall, the red strings combined or the green strings combined?

Well, again, the answer here is straightforwardly yes, this is a tractable epistemic problem. As with the words we need to assess whether we have any non-ranking evidence that we should take account of, and we need a principle – like unbiasedness – to settle the question of how to comparatively weight people's ranking information, that is to decide if anything other than the ranking information is relevant. As long as we can do so this will allow us to form justified beliefs about the overall string lengths.

In this case, as with the words, we have used ranking information to form beliefs about the relative overall amounts of something even when we don't have direct knowledge of the absolute amounts. Here, however, the underlying amounts are not composed of discrete units – such as letters – but simply a continuous magnitude, the length of a bit of string. Hence why if individual welfare ultimately draws upon facts comprising discrete magnitudes then we can use the epistemic approach to form justified beliefs about overall welfare. Alternatively, if individual welfare ultimately draws upon facts comprising continuous magnitudes then we can use the epistemic approach to form justified beliefs about overall welfare.

The sceptic can't as such appeal to a particular empirical hypothesis about the nature of welfare facts (they being discrete or continuous) to demonstrate the epistemic approach inapplicable because you can use it whichever type of mental fact is ultimately correct.

What if we bundle (or split) the rankings?

Imagine if our class of students reveal their word rankings and we form justified beliefs about the overall word lengths. However, some student then notices that we could instead treat the pet and city words as one category – 'peticity' – rather than treating them separately. Couldn't the overall result change?

Well, yes: if we ignore some evidence – of how the words relate individually – then our overall beliefs might be different to a situation where we included it. But this is because we ignored the evidence, and that doing so is epistemically unjustified.

If we ignore all the evidence in favour of a round earth then certainly the evidence we are not ignoring should make us very nervous about sailing out into the Atlantic. But the problem here isn't the way we link included evidence to overall beliefs, it's that we ignore evidence.

This includes evidence concerning independent categories. After all, what separates the categories of individual-level information is not simply a theorist whim: under the epistemic approach our account of the individual variable structures and identifies the evidence. So, in the good case, it is our theory of the individual good that allows us to know what would comprise independent evidence (if you think welfare is determined by mental states, then it's evidence of distinct mental states, if you think it is about desires, it's evidence of distinct desires). What matters is whether we have evidence that justifies us believing the categories are independent – in the peticity case we have very good evidence that the category is not independent of the pet and city words as we've created it from them.

So what account of the good does this all depend upon?

Here are some prominent theories about what comprises the good of individuals (where this can vary between individuals due to their particular psychological states or mental make-up). People's good/welfare consists in:

- **(a)** Their revealed preferences;
- **(b)** What they value;
- **(c)** What they value when this isn't dependent of false beliefs;
- **(d)** Their happiness;
- **(e)** Their wellbeing;
- **(f)** Their preferences idealized to remove anti-social or irrational preferences;
- **(g)** Their satisfaction minus dissatisfaction;
- **(h)** Pleasure minus pain;
- **(i)** Something else …

The epistemic approach is perfectly consistent with any of these being true, in fact with any account of individual welfare (or the good). All it requires is that we can have evidence of the good of individuals. What it does is to then use this evidence to form justified overall beliefs. It is thoroughly agnostic as to which is the right account.

Furthermore, if we think of this evidentially, the differences between theories of the individual good might not actually be practically hugely important. If we have evidence someone values something more than something else, for instance, this will usually be reasonable evidence that it is of higher welfare for them, no matter what the account of welfare being used (mostly – obviously the above accounts do sometimes disagree).

Nonetheless, the key point for present purposes is that for interpersonal comparisons to be possible it simply needs to be the case that some account of individual welfare or the good is possible (sceptics presumably are not nihilists about individual welfare).

What about objective goods?

Many theories of the individual good, such as of individual wellbeing or individual welfare, hold that there are some goods that are objective. What this means is that their value is held to not depend on particular agents' subjective mental states.

Both Raz and Sen, for instance, while holding it is agents' subjective ends that matter – in Raz's terms their goals, in Sen's their 'functionings' – also hold that some ends are objectively good or bad, partly in Sen's case due to worries over the possibility of adaptive preferences.[10]

For the sake of argument, let us assume we are justified in accepting that such objective goods exist. How does this fit into the epistemic approach?

As it turns out, the answer is: very straightforwardly. Objective goods are analogous to the situation where we are justified in believing that everyone has the same length city words (or that everyone has the same length bit of green string). If so, in many ways this makes the task of forming beliefs about overall amounts even easier: we can partly index on such goods. It's true we need to modify the ordinal epistemic welfare/good principle, as this assumes we only have ordinal – that is ranking – evidence. But doing so is easy, as we now have a common denominator across individuals (if two people's city words are the same length, and one has a pet word longer than their city, the other a pet word shorter, we can know that the first has the longer pet word).

More generally, the cases discussed previously – with only ranking information – have been focused upon because these are the ones most sympathetic to scepticism. Under the epistemic approach, however, having further evidence than rankings is not a problem, it's a improvement: the more evidence we have the more confident we can be in our conclusions.

But how confident can we really be?

The epistemic approach gives us justified beliefs. One worry, however, is that even if so, sometimes we can't be that confident in our conclusions, even if they are justified over alternatives. Imagine, for instance, we have students cut bits of string from just two balls of string – red and blue perhaps – and that we only learn the ranking information from two individuals of a class of forty.

In this case we would indeed by very hesitant in saying much about the blue versus red strings of the class in general. This isn't a consideration against the epistemic approach however, its one in favour of it.

When we adopt an approach that uses evidence to justify overall beliefs, part of what we implicitly adopt is an account of second-order beliefs – beliefs about how reliable our conclusions can be given certain sets of evidence. Generally, the more evidence we have the more confident we can be, and the more the evidence favours one hypothesis over another, the more confident we can be.

This is because the confidence we have in the conclusions is affected by how we think the conclusions might change as we get more evidence. If we have hardly any evidence then future evidence could very easily change the conclusions. Similarly, if the evidence we have only slightly supports one hypothesis over another, then further evidence could easily 'tip the balance' so to speak, so our confidence is less.

This, however, is just a feature of forming justified beliefs based on evidence. The advantage of the epistemic approach is that it gives us a framework for thinking through these issues.

Very important interests and the too much evidence problem

Imagine we again have our class each cut off a piece of string from two balls of string: a blue one and a red one. And imagine that some student – Yusef – has a very, very long bit of blue string and a tiny red one. This is, by analogy, equivalent to the blue string representing a very, very important interest for Yusef: his 'amount' of welfare in the blue scenario is much, much more than the red, and if we end up believing that for the class the red strings are overall longer then Yusef, were this a policy, would have his very important interests not properly included. If the blue string represented torture or death, for instance, this seems to be a problem.

However, what is wrong with this example is that we have excluded a key feature underlying our judgement of something being a very important interest: namely the evidence that supports this conclusion.

The reason we believe that death or being tortured is very, very bad is that we can compare these options with a gigantic array of others: going for a walk, drinking tea, having an itchy leg, having a bad back, being tired, being drunk, watching a comedy, eating a delicious roast chicken lunch, gardening, paddling in the sea, working on a weekend, and so on, and on, and on ... What justifies our judgement of a very important interest is the judgement that it is very important compared to all the other thousands of permutations of interests that people can have. What is wrong with the two-string 'very important interest' case is not the epistemic approach, it's that it excludes the feature that allows us to justifiably believe that there is a very important interest at stake, namely how it compares to the gigantic number of other interests. This is clear as soon as we ask: how do you know some interest is very important? Well, obviously because we have a theory of the good or of welfare that tells us what evidence of this would comprise. But if so we can use that evidence to impact our overall beliefs.

The analogy is easily improved if we imagine Yusef taking string not just from red and blue balls but also from green, black, yellow, pink, magenta, ruby, orange, brown, white, turquoise, crimson, auburn, olive and grey balls (and possibly three hundred more). Here the fact that his blue string was longer than all the others is very good evidence that it is a very important interest: indeed the epistemic approach provides a way of thinking about evidence of very important interests, namely those that are ranked much more highly than other interests (or whose absence is ranked much lower than others).

More generally, if there is a practical challenge with the epistemic approach it isn't from objective goods or from very important interests, these are actually things the approach can handle very well, because evidence from these can be easily integrated.

The cases where things get practically more tricky, I think, is in those situations where in a sense we have too much evidence, so that integrating it all into a single framework is cognitively very demanding. If we think, for example, about the badness of slavery, we will have a huge amount of background understanding about human valuation and the patterning of our psychology. We can make really quite nuanced judgements of domination and subjugation, of the social bases of self-respect, of the undermining of autonomy, of vulnerability and economic dependence, of abuse and pain and suffering. With certain human practices or experiences any formal framework is going to be difficult to use because there is so much evidence we would have to factor in, because our brains are actually incredibly good at assessing and understanding a broad range of human experiences.

This is not, of course, an observation at all supportive of scepticism about interpersonal comparisons. It's simply a recognition that when thinking through how the overall good is impacted by our understanding of dignity, of exploitation, of autonomy, or of any rich, patterned cluster of interests and experiences, a formal framework is likely to be cumbersome and perhaps less reliable than some combination of empathy, sympathy and imagination. It is not that the formal framework is wrong, it's that sometimes it's easier to use human judgement. Learning to catch a ball is best done by experience; that doesn't mean calculating a ball's flight-path using Newtonian physics is in principle incorrect.

A formal framework of interpersonal comparisons using the epistemic approach is therefore going to find it relatively easy to capture certain types of interests: income, leisure, most assets, and most 'economic' choices for instance, particularly when affecting large numbers of people. With other phenomena, such as dignity, autonomy or oppression, we may practically be better off with imaginative empathy. As human beings we can value an incredibly wide range of things, and in quite diverse ways. This isn't an argument supporting scepticism about interpersonal comparisons; it's an argument for a certain amount of humility and careful thought when dealing with complicated clusters of human valuation.

The epistemic approach and the overall good

So how then does the epistemic approach relate to the overall good? Here this seems to depend on what we think about the nature of the underlying mental facts. Any account of welfare that encounters interpersonal comparisons as a problem will be premised on the idea that the welfare-producing facts in humans can vary. If everyone had exactly the same welfare rankings for exactly the same possibilities, and moreover did so because they had identical mental states and mental infrastructure then there would be no problem: not only could we use these rankings to produce an account that was valid for everybody, we could also know that the features of our brains that they draw upon are the same too, so there is no possibility of what Jevons dubbed the different 'susceptibility' between people.

Clearly, however, humans aren't like that, in that there is a certain amount of individual-level variance: people's rankings can differ. There are as such two possibilities here, and which you think is correct will potentially affect how you understand the overall good.

Firstly, the underlying mental facts that produce individual variance in human welfare could be absolutist: they have some feature that varies on a scale, either discrete or continuous, relating to single interests or options. This could be variance in the number or type of neural connections, or in the hormonal and chemical levels that influence mental activity, or in the way the neural connections are structured, strengthened, or processed, or in a combination of several or even all of these. Whichever ultimately will prove to be correct, the key thing here is that it is meaningful to think of these as ultimately being facts about amounts or levels.

Now if so, the string and word analogies work very well. Which analogy is closest will depend on whether these amounts are discrete, such as with the number of neural connections for instance, where the word analogy will be tightest, or whether these amounts are continuous, such as with the amount or strength of some neural chemical, where the string analogy will be tightest.

As such, whichever is correct, if absolutism about mental-welfare facts is true then the overall good is the sum or combination of these facts, and the epistemic approach gives you justified beliefs about these facts. Of course, these beliefs are not infallible, but the more evidence we have the more confident we can be, and perhaps some day our knowledge of neuro-biology will allow us gain more direct evidence. In this case there is nothing mysterious about the overall good: there are some mental facts that individual welfare supervenes upon and these facts can be added together as they capture an absolute magnitude.

Alternatively, however, it might be that the mental facts capture not an absolute magnitude but a comparative one, in that people's welfare varies because they vary in how much more or less welfare they have in one possibility *compared to another.*

If so, there are no absolute values to 'add up'. However, if so we can think of the overall good as a construct, one justified directly by unbiasedness. If unbiasedness can be justified morally then in constructing the good of all we should treat all with equal concern, and therefore that means giving equal weight to their combination of comparative mental facts. It's a bit like rather than asking all the students to take pieces of string we ask them to allocate percentages of their overall 'shmelfare' to three different colours – red, blue and green. 'Which combined colour does the class have more of?' is, as such, a question of what the sum of these percentages are for the relative colours. What we have done here is to allocate to each student an equal weighting, but there isn't a physical fact that we are trying to gain evidence about, there is a construction – the 'amount' of each colour if we were to create an object comprised of each student's overall combination with all students weighted equally.

Alternatively, we can think of the overall good as a methodologically justified construct. Since the justification here isn't by reference to an underlying object, the right way to think about it seems to be as a construct justified by certain properties of justified beliefs, notably that they be non-arbitrary. When we make beliefs about overall welfare contingent on something other than individual welfare we have constructed 'overall welfare' in a way that is arbitrary and therefore incorrect. To work, this argument needs of course to appropriately link up correctness with non-arbitrariness, and the Epilogue takes up this topic much more thoroughly.

However, for present purposes, whether justified morally or methodologically, or indeed both, what the overall-welfare as a construct approach indicates is that the possibility of mental facts being comparative doesn't entail that the concept of the overall good must be meaningless. To be meaningful all we need is a justification for the interpersonal weighting that allows us to produce the construct, in this case a justification for unbiasedness.

With the epistemic approach and the two empirical possibilities in mind – that the underlying mental-welfare facts might ultimately be absolute facts or comparative facts – we can return to scrutinize scepticism about interpersonal comparisons.

Revisiting the 'can't see the values' worry

The 'can't see the values' worry tried to justify overall-welfare scepticism by noting that it wasn't possible to get inside people's heads and thus that we cannot form justified beliefs about how much welfare they have in particular situations.

However, if we think of interpersonal comparisons as an epistemic problem then it becomes clear that the premise does not support the conclusion. There are lots of possible situations where even if we can't see the values that doesn't mean we can't gain evidence about the values and use this evidence to form justified beliefs.

When forming justified beliefs about words and string, for instance, we didn't know the values, but we did have some evidence – the individual rankings. If not-seeing-the-values is sufficient to justify scepticism, then the sceptic seems required on pains of consistency to deny that we can form justified beliefs in the empirical cases. This, however, would be bizarre – there's nothing particularly mysterious or problematic about word-lengths or bits of string. Scepticism about interpersonal comparisons isn't, presumably, meant to hinge upon general scepticism about using evidence to form justified beliefs.

What the 'we can't see the values' worry fundamentally gets wrong is that for the conclusion to be justified – for interpersonal comparisons to be impossible – it needs to be the case not only that we can't see the values, but that we can't gain any evidence about the values *at all*. That however is false: we do have evidence of something, namely how for individuals the different possibilities compare. This is true whether the underlying mental facts are absolute or comparative, and this is true simply by virtue of an account of individual welfare.

Revisiting the 'utility monster' worry

The nature of the 'utility monster' worry depends on whether individual welfare facts are comparative or absolutist. If they are absolutist then we are in the same sort of epistemic situation as with the word or string examples: we can gain evidence of the underlying relative amounts, but it is still possible, even with much evidence, that our conclusions could be wrong. The epistemic approach will give us justified beliefs, but ones both that further evidence could alter, and where there is some evidence that we can't currently have (evidence of direct measurements of the underlying phenomena, as neuro-biological science is not currently able to provide this, though under the absolute individual-welfare view it might be, one day).

What we have, however, will be justified beliefs. Which, when thinking about why we care about the overall problem, is actually great. Interpersonal comparisons matter because our actions, policies and institutions affect people differently, and sometimes we want our justified grounds for choosing to be based on the overall impact on all affected, that is on their good or welfare. This is exactly what the epistemic approach gives us. It also – via second-order beliefs – tells us how more or less confident we can be in the estimates.

Absolutism about individual amounts – that they comprise a certain number of units or a certain continuous magnitude – is not a problem for justified beliefs about overall amounts, because justified beliefs are possible in situations where the evidence does not deductively entail one hypothesis (which is almost every single case in all of empirical science and the social and historical sciences – it would be odd to believe the Second World War didn't happen because, strictly speaking, the evidence doesn't logically entail the belief that it did happen).

It's true that we need some sort of commitment either to unbiasedness as an ethical principle, something almost all (non-racist/sexist[11]) moral theories supply in one phrasing or another, or a commitment to unbiasedness as a methodological principle, which seems to be one manifestation of non-arbitrariness. But this, along with a general commitment to coherence in ones beliefs, is fully sufficient to provide justified beliefs. The problem for the sceptic is that both justifications for unbiasedness seem very compelling.

Ultimately, the 'utility monster' worry rests of the following faulty logical inference:

1. The evidence does not entail a unique hypothesis about overall welfare.
2. Therefore, we cannot justifiably choose between hypotheses about overall welfare.

Now, *even if*, premise one is correct, that is either welfare mental facts are absolute or alternatively that they are comparative and we only have partial evidence of them, premise two does not follow.

More widely, thinking about the sceptics' epistemic position as a general stance quickly indicates how mistaken it is. Clearly, evidence about evolution, or the earth being a rough sphere, or the movement of light, or the non-existence of fairies or witches – clearly, none of this evidence entails a unique hypothesis about the phenomena in question. It's perfectly possible there are witches and fairies or alternatively that the earth is flat and there has been a huge international pro-round-earth conspiracy (maybe even by witches and fairies). The logical possibility of beliefs being wrong does not refute the possibility of justified beliefs.

In general, statements supporting scepticism about interpersonal comparisons frequently gain their surface plausibility via a sort of verbal 'uncertainty trick' whereby it is stated that we 'don't know' that there are not utility monsters or we 'don't know' what the underlying values are, where 'don't know' here really means 'can't be certain'.

This, however, is not the key question, the key question is over what we can justifiably believe. This trick is frequently deployed too with general conspiracy theories or scepticism about science: we 'don't know for sure' that measles vaccines don't cause autism. True, definitely true. But we are not justified in believing they do (and we are justified in believing that not vaccinating children can cause widespread unnecessary suffering).

If welfare facts are, at root, absolute then the 'utility monster' worry can be seen as having the rough same status as any worry where we have evidence but not certainty. We will want to form second-order beliefs about how confident we can be, and we will want, where helpful, to try to gain more evidence, but ultimately justified beliefs about the overall good will be enough for us to be able to form justified beliefs about how different actions, policies and institutions compare in terms of the overall good.

This is similar to in the word and string cases. It's perfectly possible that someone is a word-monster: all her words are just much longer than those of most other people. And it's perfectly possible she is a word-waif: all her words are just much shorter than those of most other people. The more evidence we have – the more words we learn, the more people's words we find out – normally the more confident we can be that even if so our justified beliefs will not majorly change. But word-monsters are possible. However, what would the sceptic argue here: that justified beliefs are impossible? That we can't form beliefs about the overall numbers of letters? If welfare facts are, at root, absolutist then, as with the letters and string, 'monsters' are possible. But the task for the sceptic here seems to be to somehow justify a scepticism that also encompasses straightforward empirical situations.

By contrast, if welfare facts are, at root, comparative and overall welfare is simply a justified construct, then the 'utility monster' worry is fundamentally mistaken. There cannot be utility monsters if overall utility is a construct made from taking all knowable information about individual welfare and combining it in an unbiased (that is non-arbitrary) manner. All we have to worry about, if comparativism is true, is the fact that we might currently have only a small portion of the overall possible evidence, and our beliefs will be more hesitant as such. This, however, is a very familiar and manageable worry, one that accrues to any of the natural or human sciences: sometimes we have lots of evidence and can be confident, sometimes we don't and should be less so.

Sometimes, even, we will be awash in diverse evidence and cognitively struggle to integrate it all, a problem too for the understanding of contemporary political events where we have so much evidence – of human psychology, of culture, of economics, of recent history, of social change, of individuals and their motivations, of collective entities and social groups and on and on and on. In judging distant historical events we may have limited evidence and the challenge is to make the right inferences from it; in judging contemporary events simply managing to integrate most of the most important evidence is incredibly demanding. This can be the case too with epistemic interpersonal comparisons where the individual-level evidence is rich and diverse. But all of these approaches share an underlying methodological unity in that we use evidence to form justified beliefs.

That is, for the possibility of utility monsters to be a problem the sceptic needs to supply a general account of epistemic justification that is logically compatible with it being a problem. Overall-welfare scepticism, however, is not presumably meant to require a general scepticism about using evidence to form justified beliefs: worrying about interpersonal comparisons isn't meant to also require us to be complete sceptics about evolution or a round earth.

In summary: if comparativism about individual welfare facts is correct, there cannot be utility monsters. If absolutism about individual welfare facts is correct, we can never be justified in thinking some person or group of people to be utility monsters, and therefore the possibility poses no special threat to justified beliefs. Maybe some friend of yours, Sadiq, is actually being nefariously controlled by omnipotent discovery-averse witches, even though – cunning that they are – by stipulation it is impossible we could ever be justified in believing this. It's certainly possible, and the evidence doesn't rule it out, you can't know it's not true. That doesn't, however, mean you should worry about it, and it doesn't mean that when deciding whether or not to meet Sadiq for a coffee you should worry about it. You can have evidentially justified beliefs and proceed from there.

Revisiting the 'what is the overall good' worry

This worry, when made explicit, seemed to have three possible distinct variants.

Firstly, it might simply be a consequence of either the 'can't-see-the-values' worry or the 'utility monster' worry being correct. Since neither refutes the possibility of justified beliefs about the overall good or of the epistemic approach more generally, if this is the best version of the 'what is the overall good worry' then that worry can be met.

Alternatively, the worry might be that while individual welfare is based on an individual mind, social welfare would require a social mind, and this doesn't exist. However, as soon as you think about the overall good in an epistemic framework it becomes clear that we don't need a social mind for beliefs about social welfare to be justified. If the underlying mental facts are absolutist, these are beliefs about the overall sum of these facts. If the underlying mental facts are comparative, these are beliefs about the justified, that is unbiased, combination of these facts. In neither case do we need a social mind or any un-evidenced hypotheses about telepathy or group-thinking.

Finally, as discussed, even if there are no magnitudes to be summed, the overall good can be meaningful if we are justified in adopting unbiasedness in constructing it. If the underlying mental facts that create differences in welfare between individuals are comparative then this doesn't entail that justified beliefs about the overall good are impossible or meaningless. (It should be noted that this was, in any case, a very odd position for scepticism to take, as it apparently hinges upon a dispute over the empirical nature of certain mental facts, one about which we don't currently have a good enough understanding in neuro-biology to resolve. Sceptics don't seem to act as if their entire stance depends on a very uncertain empirical claim. But, in any case, what matters for present purposes is that, on examination, whether that claim is justified or not, either way it doesn't justify scepticism).

But didn't Arrow prove all this was impossible?

The overall epistemic approach to interpersonal comparisons is to ask: what evidence do we have about the welfare of different individuals, and how might this evidence be combined coherently and unbiasedly to form justified beliefs about overall welfare? As soon as you ask this question, the problem of interpersonal comparisons becomes, in a sense, a familiar epistemic one, and any issues that seem difficult – over objective goods, or utility monsters, or very-important interests – can be addressed by thinking through how these impact our evidence and therefore overall beliefs.

But, didn't Arrow prove, in some sense, that this was all impossible?[12]

The answer is straightforwardly no (and, as discussed below, it's not at all clear what, aside from a pretty formal result, Arrow really did prove, as his result seems to apply to no coherent well-motivated problem).

To see why we shouldn't worry about Arrow's Impossibility Theorem we can think about three students all of whom write down their birth city, species of first pet and favourite author's surname. We then learn some of their rankings and form a belief about how for all three students their sets of combined words – their cities, pets or authors – compare.

Now, one condition we might place on our beliefs is the following:

The Independence of Irrelevant Alternatives ('IIA'): Beliefs about whether A overall represents more or less of some quantity than B should solely be derived from evidence about the relative amount of the quantity in, or comparing, specific instances of A and B alone.

That is, that our overall beliefs about two categories – say how the cities compare to the pets – should only change based on information about how individuals' city and pet words relate. This seems somewhat intuitive perhaps, but epistemically it leaves you vulnerable to having incoherent beliefs and must be straightforwardly rejected.

To see why, imagine you start off with the belief that the overall words rank as follows: city > author > pets. You now learn that everyone has the same number of letters in their pets and cities, so you believe (on pain of incoherence) that the city and pet words of all three students combined contain the same number of letters. But under the IIA you should still believe that the author words combined contain less than the cities, *and* that the author words combined contain more than the pets. You have incoherent beliefs. What makes this happen is adopting the Independence of Irrelevant Alternatives (IIA).[13]

Surely the IIA really isn't that crazy as a condition on beliefs about welfare or the overall good? Actually, the answer is: yes. It really is. To justifiably accept it in this context you'd have to show why we should be justified in accepting logically incoherent beliefs. There is no reliance on intuitions here, no reliance on background assumptions of welfare being an absolutist rather than a comparativist magnitude (the problems arise in string-like situations too). And there's no reliance on unbiasedness, even biased initial beliefs are vulnerable to the difficulty.

Nor too do the problems only accrue if you have a non-equal initial ranking. Imagine you start with the belief that the city, pet and author words are combined all the same. You now learn that all students have city words longer than pet words. If you adopt the IIA again you have incoherent beliefs (you now believe the cities longer than pets, the pets the same as the authors, and the cities the same as the authors).

One way out of this would be to hold that it is impossible to have any justified beliefs unless you know all possible evidence, which seems both a very odd stance to take (in what other situations does this make epistemic sense?) and an utterly unnecessary stance to take – just reject the IIA and seek coherent justified beliefs.

An alternative impossibility-result-supporting position to take is to hold that the IIA wasn't intended to be applied to beliefs about overall welfare given information of individual welfare. Arrow's Impossibility Theorem, as such, simply has nothing to do with social welfare and was never intended or interpreted by most people to have anything to do with social welfare.

Now the first clause of the previous sentence is right: Arrow's Impossibility Theorem does tell us – literally nothing – about the problem social welfare, for those that reject incoherence in their beliefs at least. But it does seem as though people think it is somehow about social welfare, which is not surprising given the way Arrow presents it: the initial paper was after all called 'A Difficulty in the Concept of Social Welfare'. This is misnamed. It should be called 'No Difficulty in the Concept of Social Welfare if You Want Beliefs that are Not Incoherent' because one of the theorem's premises – the Independence of Irrelevant Alternatives – must be rejected, on pain of incoherent beliefs.

Arrow, of course, does provide some attempt at justifying the IIA, but he does so with reference to voting.[14] Specifically, he tries to justify the reasonableness of the IIA with three examples:

(i) an election system where a candidate dies
(ii) voting in a club to produce a rank-ordering
(iii) ranking teams in a contest

To state the obvious: forming justified beliefs about social welfare on the one hand, and deciding on rules for elections or for committee voting on the other hand, are not the same thing. The first is epistemic and methodological; the second is a question of institutional or procedural design.

That Arrow's famous theorem has somehow convinced several generations (of undergraduates at least) that a justified account of social welfare is impossible is perhaps one of the clearest cautionary examples of formalism fetishism: that the beauty or sophistication of an internal proof is taken as a near decisive consideration in favour of the externally implied conclusion.

The irrelevance of the IIA to the problem of social welfare and social choice is fairly obvious, however, as soon as we demand an explicit account of *exactly what problem faced by what agent or institution* it is meant to be representing. If it is the problem of 'adding up' welfare then clearly we must reject IIA (which is tellingly not even predominantly justified by Arrow in welfare terms).

If it is the problem of institutional choice then there seem to be two possibilities: that the institutions are justified instrumentally; or that the institutions are justified intrinsically by some account of collective or democratic legitimacy.

If the institutions are justified instrumentally then the problem, philosophically at least, collapses into the problem of how to form justified beliefs about welfare/the overall good (and we should reject IIA and the Theorem's relevance), and we additionally need to then pursue the important empirical question of how in practice institutions tend to work.

If the institutions are justified intrinsically then we need both to justify the desirability of legitimacy as a condition on political institutions (see Chapter 7 for scepticism on this front) and we need to explicitly defend each of the Theorem's conditions *in terms of political legitimacy*. It is very hard to see what even a rough coherent defence of the IIA in these terms would be like.

The ultimate worry here is that the plausibility of Arrow's Impossibility Theorem implicitly relies on its conditions being justified with reference to distinct tasks, and as such when these conditions are combined to produce the impossibility result we should be confident that there is no significant task that has been shown to be impossible. It is a bit like noting that to successfully cross the Atlantic a sea-craft for 500 people will need to weigh more than X; that to fly across the Atlantic an aircraft for 500 people will need to weigh less than X; and thus we have a nice 'Craft Impossibility Theorem': that no craft can cross the Atlantic with 500 people. Obviously this is wrong: we have taken two distinct conditions (weigh more than x; weigh less than x) that are justified by reference to distinct tasks and applied them to a vague amalgam of the two.

The slightly (though not very) plausible suggestion that Arrow's Independence of Irrelevant Alternatives should necessarily apply to candidates in an election tells us nothing about the task he implicitly employs it for, that of forming beliefs about overall welfare. We should simply reject the Theorem as telling us anything interesting about welfare, and indeed it is somewhat odd that it is so widely believed to have demonstrated the impossibility of social welfare.

The broader worry perhaps is that certain types of result are liable to systematically mislead, specifically if a theorem is (1) mathematically or formally expressed; (2) sufficiently difficult for some undergraduates to struggle with; (3) not impossible to learn for the more able undergraduates; (4) contains a vaguely plausible premise whose falsity entails the falsity of the main implied results; and (5) the premise is, on explicit reflection, clearly false (if empirical) or clearly unjustified in this context (if normative); then despite being false the conclusion will be widely accepted as having been 'proved'. Call this the 'bad-premise, pretty maths' problem. Condorcet's Jury Theorem is perhaps another likely example of this (see Chapter 7), with Nash Equilibria identifying what perfectly rational agents would do, Common Knowledge and Ordinary Least Squared Regressions being potential additions to this dubious category.

The theorem perhaps retains its influence because of the fundamental ambiguity of the whole notion of 'social choice' or 'social choice theory' as something separate to, but connected with, ethics and political philosophy. Institutions and policies can be justified instrumentally: as such we need an account of welfare or some similar concept (wellbeing, the good, justice and so on). Institutions might be justified intrinsically: as such we need an account of legitimacy and a very explicit justification of why we should base institutional evaluation on this. And in both cases institutions can adopt internal rules to govern their decision making.

Now, we can view these rules as 'social choice'. But why are these rules, not others, justified? Well, presumably by reference to the justification of the institutions. Any social choice theory that assumes certain features of voting, or assumes majoritarianism or the like – that is some internal rule – without reference to the institutional justification will likely find it easy to generate some impossibility results. But so what? If we face a coherently motivated task we can find a coherent solution. If we are presented with an incoherent solution – that is one that shows something is impossible – then we should find it easy to infer exactly where the problem starts: we have incoherently motivated premises. And this is exactly the case with the Arrow's Impossibility Theorem.

But do we really need interpersonal comparisons?

I've deliberately phrased the previous discussion stridently and provocatively because this debate does not take place in a real-world vacuum. There are various backdoor methods people use based on the assumption that these methods are somehow a viable alternative to interpersonal comparisons, such as willingness to pay (undifferentiated by income), or productive efficiency, or the alleged implications of models using pareto optimality.

These consistently have the straightforward morally repugnant effect of being interpersonal comparisons that weight as less important the interests of those with less income and less assets. Were we to explicitly do this based on race or ethnicity we would rightly be appalled. But somehow doing so based on wealth or income or willingness to pay has a faux air of neutrality and objectivity about it. Results that aid and abet this systemic harm should, at a minimum, be subject to some sustained intellectual scrutiny and should not gain deference because they manage to express their premises and conclusion in a formal framework. Any minimally coherent result can be put in a formal framework, but so what: that is not an argument for why we should accept the premises.

This obviously matters as, more generally, discussing policies in an implicit welfare-framework without interpersonal comparisons simply can't be done, partial conventional wisdom notwithstanding. One can see this with the modern discipline of economics, a discipline that if interpersonal comparisons were impossible would be an incoherent mess (it however isn't, because they aren't).

It's true that somehow, in the late nineteenth and then twentieth century, a view gained ground that held that interpersonal comparisons weren't needed because we could still use what are now called Pareto rankings: identify changes where someone was made better off and no one worse off.

The problem here, however, is that the existence of pareto-improving policies or changes is less empirically plausible than the claim the earth is flat: all policy changes always leave some people worse off. To produce exchange-models that use this concept you have to 'magic away' various features of human beings, typically requiring that (i) after exchanging a good we all immediately die and (ii) that there are no other human beings.

If I sell my car to you then plausibly I am right now made better off and you are right now made better off compared to my not selling it right now. But the other people I would have sold it to are worse off, as are the others you would have bought from or spent your money upon, as are your neighbours who now face more demand on parking, as are my colleagues who next week might have got a lift from me, as are your local shops who might have had more custom from you, as are some of the customers of various further-away shops who will now find you cluttering the aisles when they go, as is the person selling the car that you otherwise would have bought, as are thousands of other people who were impacted. And it might even have been the case that had I considered selling it later one of us would have been better off: so even the initial claim that we were both better off only securely holds if we ignore all consequences beyond the moment of exchange.

Even a trivial two-person exchange has marginal winners and losers: state policies always do, and usually not marginal ones. There has never been a pareto-improving policy or institutional change ever. In fact I have a long-standing bet to this effect, and no policy or change has withstood even a cursory amount of scrutiny. Furthermore, as a colleague Håkon Tretvoll pointed out, if such a change did exist I would lose the bet, making me presumably worse off, and preventing it from being a pareto-improvement. (The logic here is almost perfect but not quite: there could in theory be a policy change that was sufficiently good for me personally that it fully compensated me for losing the bet, though I can sadly report that this hasn't yet happened. One weird additional consequence of all this, however, is that if any pareto improvements had somehow historically occurred then they stopped being improvements the moment my friend and I made the bet. The potential history of human pareto-improvements was eliminated over a beer in New York City in 2006.)

That there are no pareto-improvements is not problematic, of course, if we have interpersonal comparisons. And, in reality, it's not that economics as a discipline ever practically gave up on interpersonal comparisons: it focuses upon recessions and depressions, upon measures and changes to wealth and real income, and none of these should be prioritized if interpersonal comparisons are meaningless. Similarly, every large scale economic model is a simplification, and without a coherent background idea – such as economic welfare – knowing what to simplify would be impossible, we'd be continuously arguing about why a certain model of recessions excludes a particular variable and over definitions of recessions and the like.

That economics as a discipline never actually abandoned implicit interpersonal comparisons is of course deeply reassuring, but does present a rather odd contrast with various practitioners who nonetheless formally maintain such things are impossible. (If so why think recessions and depressions are overall bad, or that a country stuck in poverty and low growth is bad? For there's always some people for whom such things are great. Or why think it meaningful to hold that competition or trade can be good for an economy? For someone is always made worse off.)

This, however, seems to be a weird quirk of the intellectual history of economics, fortunately one where even those who profess to think overall welfare meaningless clearly don't actually accept the logical implications of this view. Why be a macro-economist if you think there's no sense in which a devastating worldwide depression is worse than steady growth, less poverty and a sustainable environment? Because even in a world dominated by economic collapse and by widespread despair and suffering there will be some people who find comfort, others who find pleasure, and a few more who spy opportunity and the thrill of advancement.

The advantage here of interpersonal comparisons is thus that we can at least have a formal method of estimating economic welfare, and a sense of what its determinants are. We already do this implicitly – by looking at real income changes and various metrics of very bad outcomes (such as unemployment). The value of interpersonal comparisons lies in giving such judgements a certain rigor and giving us a grasp on when the variables are good and bad proxies for overall welfare.

In any case, however, the thought that making interpersonal comparisons puts one in conflict with the actual underlying logic of modern economics gets things directly backward: such economics has always made implicit interpersonal comparisons in selecting problems of importance and in simplifying the world by omitting various features. Making them explicit compliments this and, more importantly, allows us to do so in a justified manner, that is based on unbiasedness, not on the morally repugnant willingness-to-pay and its various efficiency-proxies. It also frees us from delusions of inhabiting an absurd fantasy world where pareto optimality has any practical use. We need interpersonal comparisons.

Conclusions

Aside from the central importance to economics, there is obviously also a need for interpersonal comparisons for the feasibility of a wide range of moral theories.

The possibility and meaningfulness of interpersonal comparisons clearly matters greatly for a theory that uses the overall good to make moral evaluations – such as with motivation ethics or utilitarianism. However, the set of moral theories that sometimes use interpersonal comparisons is much larger: a very coherent deontological position, for instance, is that often the right thing to do is to bring about the most good, it's just that this policy can't be pursued when it involves violating various side-constraints or rights.

Similarly, accounts that hold that justice consists in giving a certain extra weight to the worse-off – usually called 'prioritarianism' – are obviously predicated on it being possible and meaningful for us to produce judgements of a base-line weighting that the prioritization then acts upon. In other words, they require interpersonal comparisons.

As such, for a wide range of well-established theories, and for some less established ones like motivation ethics, interpersonal comparisons are important. And they seem essential for coherently motivating and structuring economics as a discipline, if it is to even vaguely resemble how we now think of it.

This is a very positive thing. It matters greatly what happens to people, and justified interpersonal comparisons give us an extremely useful and wide-ranging tool for assessing this. Why anyone would actively want scepticism to succeed is a mystery, but fortunately, in any case, it doesn't. Viewed in an epistemic framework interpersonal comparisons of the good/welfare are possible and meaningful.

Conclusions

Here is the argument so far. People's lives can go better or worse, that is their good can be promoted or harmed. And one historically prominent approach is to link moral action evaluations to the good of some or all affected by what an agent might do. That is, we might think actions right if they best promote the interests of the agent (egoism), if they protect some part of the good of to whom one acts (a harm-based deontology), or if they promote the good of all (consequentialism). Yet if we do so we need to then determine how to evaluate agents. This is surprisingly difficult if we want to meet three criteria:

(i) Invulnerability to amoralism
(ii) Evaluative coherence between an agent and her actions
(iii) Non-arbitrary agent evaluations

The difficulty arises because the action evaluations do not appropriately reflect motivational content or ease, that is they do not reflect the motivations favouring and opposing the undertaking of one action rather than another. Because of this, if we make agent evaluations roughly track action evaluations – that morally good agents tend to act rightly, morally bad ones do not – then the agent evaluations will not be determined by features of the agents (hence identical agents could be evaluated contradictorily, and the comparative evaluation of two agents be reversed while their features remain the same). This is the moral agent problem.

To avoid it we need to base moral evaluations on features of the agents and then derive action evaluations from what we would expect of agents with (and without) such features. Now the most prima facie justified conception of the good upon which moral evaluations should be based is simply the good of all, thus motivation ethics holds that agents are morally better the more motivated they are to promote the overall good.

If we do so we still retain the claim that moral concern is impartial in that it is equal concern for all, but by focusing on a moral motivation this diverges from a focus directly on actions in three prominent cases in particular: (a) where promoting the overall good is incredibly demanding; (b) where agents typically have strong motivations aimed at the interests of particular individuals due to some relationship with them; (c) where institutions transform the ease or difficulty of a range of other-affecting acts. Thus Chapters 4 to 6 examined some of the difficulties action moralities had in these cases, specifically, how to conceive of agent evaluations if acting rightly is potentially very demanding; how to evaluate special relationships and the apparent conflict with universal moral concern; and how to reconcile actions that benefit co-nationals and the apparent moral irrelevance of borders.

Each chapter, though discussing a distinct problem, was in effect responding to the observation that if we are to evaluate agents then a range of factors that affect whether agents will do some action or not – the demandingness of the action, the personal relationships promoted or harmed by it, and the state-created incentives for doing it – should change our evaluation of what agents do and do not do. Chapter 6 concluded by considering what motivation ethics entails for institutional evaluation: that institutions are morally better the better they promote the good.

Chapters 7 and 8 then considered two possible counter-responses: that there is a separate realm of normative evaluation – 'legitimacy' – that has been left out of the picture and might alter our theory of institutional evaluation, notably in the political sphere, or that an account of the overall good was not possible, determinate or meaningful. It was argued that it was hard, however, to establish the desirability of legitimacy as a separate realm of evaluation, and that viewing the good as an epistemic problem could overcome the sceptical worries.

Thus part of the case made here for motivation ethics has been a critique of the action morality approach in two parts. Firstly, that consequentialism encounters the moral agent problem and motivation ethics overcomes it while retaining consequentialism's determinant of evaluation. Secondly, that prominent problems in the literature – demandingness, special relationships, global duties and the state – arise from the assumption of action primacy, and we can overcome them by rejecting this assumption as motivation ethics does.[1]

The problems have principally been with the assumption that actions are the primary object of moral evaluation, as this created the moral agent problem when then linking actions to the good (of the agent, of to whom one acts, or of all affected).

However, motivation ethics is not the only way to overcome the moral agent problem, for as discussed previously one could hold that there are certain virtues the possession of which will enable an individual to lead a good life (a virtue ethics theory[2]), or that there is a particular good will, the possessor of which will respect certain side-constraints on how to treat to whom we act (a will-based deontology).

That is, from the options discussed earlier:

		Primary object of evaluation	
		Actions	Agents
Determinant of evaluation	own good	egoism	virtue ethics
	good of to whom done	harm-based deontology	will-based deontology
	good of all	consequentialism	motivation ethics

Now in a sense *any* proposal for there being certain agential features that comprise an agent's moral evaluation would overcome the moral agent problem, so why should the three suggested structures of 'agent-morality' theories be privileged? The reason, I think, it is right to focus on these three is that each overcomes the moral agent problem and aims to respond to a *different* further particular condition we might wish to meet. That is, motivation ethics is the structure that most obviously meets the following four desiderata:

(i) invulnerability to amoralism
(ii) evaluative coherence between an agent and her actions
(iii) non-arbitrary agent evaluations
(iv) evaluations based on the good of all

The latter represents one very important way of thinking about morality as being universal or impartial in that the interests of everyone count and count equally (a point made repeatedly by consequentialists). Alternatively, however, we might instead want to retain the first three conditions, but conceive of ethical evaluations as identifying what a good life might be. That is:

(i) invulnerability to amoralism
(ii) evaluative coherence between an agent and her actions
(iii) non-arbitrary agent evaluations
(iv) good agents expected to lead a good life

The structure that meets this most obviously is a virtue ethics theory whereby (i) the virtuous individual has certain character features ('the virtues'); and (ii) the possession of the virtues enables one to lead, or constitutes, a good life (or at least, a better life than the non-virtuous person). Such a theory might be able to show that a certain amount of benevolence would be undertaken by a virtuous agent but it would only have this at a level that did not conflict with the agent leading a good life.

To see the contrast with motivation ethics think perhaps of someone utterly motivated by the good of others so that everything she does is done with this goal in mind, to the extent she is ever truthful, or keeps promises, or has a friendship or close relationships, then this in done for entirely instrumental reasons, that doing so helps her promote the overall good. Her entire life is devoted to this goal, and she will quite possibly die alone and very poor. For a virtue ethics theory she will at best have only cultivated one virtue – that of benevolence – though to such an excess that it crowds out room for all the others, and she lacks the virtues to lead a good life. For motivation ethics this may be true, but as a result she is morally heroic, she has sacrificed her own good for that of others to an extent that is exceptional.

Thirdly, we might alternatively retain the first three conditions but additionally then hold that reasoning about what to do can itself only correctly entail that we can will certain acts and not others, and thus that agent evaluations of moral worth should be based on whether one possesses such a good will (and action evaluations be based on what an agent with it would or would not do). A will-based deontology is the most prominent theory to attempt to argue that rational willing leads to certain things being a duty or forbidden, and if the argument could be shown to be correct this would indicate that the other theories, motivation ethics among them, evaluate agents as morally good who are in fact irrational or making some error of practical reason.

As such, all three theories, though potentially overcoming the moral agent problem, do so by additionally aiming to meet differing further requirements: evaluations based on the good of all (motivation ethics); evaluations based on the living of a good life (virtue ethics); evaluations determined by practical reason (will-based deontology).

This book has not, however, said very much about the choice between these three theories, aside from scepticism about intuition-based defences of alternatives to motivation ethics. The main focus has been on the difficulties of theories with action-primacy and how motivation ethics overcomes these problems while retaining the claim that moral evaluations should be based on the good of all. A detailed comparison of the three agent moralities is as such not attempted here, but the overall shape of such a comparison arises from the theories' different fourth condition. What then, in outline, is the broader case for and against the other two agent-moralities?

The motivation ethics case against a will-based deontology is importantly contingent. It is not that such a theory is necessarily incorrect, rather that its key feature is prima facie unjustified and (currently) insufficiently justified. A will-based deontology holds that the good of to whom we act matters morally in a way that the good of all affected does not. Since the relative 'goods' in these cases may well be identical this seems straightforwardly arbitrary.

Potentially it might not be however if its justification stems from the nature of willing or of self-legislating or of some similar formulation of practical reason and we can show that the particular formulation does not smuggle-in some arbitrary concern or unjustified distinction. If such an answer could be given it would indicate why one could not – justifiably – will that the good of all be promoted, and as such why agents motivated to promote the good of all, and acting partly on this motive, were making some sort of mistake or exhibiting some sort of failure.

The burden here is clearly on the will-based deontology, because it involves an apparent restriction of moral concern, which it seeks to show, however, is not a restriction of moral concern but a consequence of correct reasoning.

Now to the sceptic a will-based deontologist is simply engaged in moral alchemy: the component parts and the desired end-product are the wrong type of thing, and the search for such moral gold is futile. To someone sympathetic the better analogy might be with cold-fusion: we have some grounds for thinking this might be possible, the outlines of what such an account might be like, and given the potential importance of the result a serious reason to endeavour to make progress.

Whichever attitude it is ultimately better to hold, the case for motivation ethics here is one of default: there is nothing mysterious about the concept of the good of all, thus motivation ethics enjoys a presumptive advantage over a will-based deontology because the ambitions of the latter are so much greater (for the same reason, the success of the latter would be in many ways so much more impressive).

The core motivation ethics disagreement with virtue ethics arises instead over the latter's scope and justification. Virtue ethics – at least as set out here – provides an answer to the question of 'why be moral/just?' in that it seeks to show that there are various character traits, 'the virtues', whose possession is in the interests of the agent, contributing to their Eudaimonia, happiness, flourishing, psychological unity or whatever the specific associated account of the good of agent.[3] There is admittedly the question of whether any such account would deliver the sort of character-virtues that have typically been cited, but it does not seem empirically implausible. If an agent is primarily or significantly motivated by a concern for his own interest then the theory can supply an answer to the question of 'why be just?', in principle at least.

But imagine we then take the search for a justification back one stage and ask: why should a theory give such weight to the agent's own interests? Well, we could appeal to some idea of human nature: we just are motivated by our own interests, and the question of 'why be just?' is as such inevitably going to be asked. Yet, not only is this not a justification, it may present the psychology as overly deterministic: for we do have some influence over our future motivational sets, and the question of what is a better or worse motivational set thus can arise.

That is, imagine an agent wondering what it is to live an objectively better life. Well, one way to understand this and give it concrete content is to ask what ultimately will make that agent's own life personally better and derive evaluations from that. But imagine the agent then asks: why are my interests objectively more important than those of others? They clearly aren't. They might, depending on the agent's psychology, be more important to her. But this is a description of her psychology, what she is seeking is to evaluate it based on some objective measure (that is, a measure that isn't simply contingent on the desires she happens to have).

This motivation ethics critique of virtue ethics is specifically a critique of the latter's scope, not its content. Even if, for example, motivation ethics is completely correct, then virtue ethics as a body of thought will still potentially represent our best extant account of how to think about living a good life, that is a life that is good for the agent, and how this is structured by our human nature, capabilities and the types of collective lives we lead.

Under motivation ethics this is going to remain a question of central importance to moral agents, and the theory does not of itself entail a particular answer. It is just that, if motivation ethics is broadly correct, then moral agents are going to have to think about a further set of questions than those surrounding the good life, namely how they might throughout their lives and by how they live come to promote the good of others. This may sometimes conflict with the pursuit of the good life for them personally, and part of what makes them moral is that the good of others remains something they are nonetheless significantly motivated to pursue.

The overall case for motivation ethics as such is two-fold: that action moralities cannot supply coherent and non-arbitrary agent evaluations, and that the other two agent moralities – a will-based deontology and virtue ethics – seem to make moral/ethical evaluations contingent on an arbitrary distinction between identical objective goods (respectively: between that of to whom we act and all affected; between that of the agent herself and all affected).[4] These critiques, put most ambitiously, amount to the claim that the imposition on moral beliefs of the conditions of coherence and non-arbitrariness supports motivation ethics.

Now this seems specifically implausible when thinking of motivation ethics' multiple components: that of moral goodness, moral progress, moral duties, quasi-moral duties, comparativism and so on. For coherence and non-arbitrariness appear likely to give us a very clean and straightforward theory, not one so heavily patterned and with so many components. Yet, the core motivation ethics claim, put abstractly, is in fact extremely simple: it is that agents are objectively better qua agents the more motivated they are to promote what is objectively better. In more familiar words, that agents are morally better the more motivated they are to promote the good of all. The various components of the theory simply represent the combination of this with specific *empirical* facts.

Thus the account of moral goodness arises from the core claim combined with the fact of human motivational variance, namely that we can be more or less motivated in particular ways. Moral progress in motivation combines the core claim with the possibility of motivational change, that through effort or outside influence we might change the motivation sets of our future selves. Moral progress in understanding arises from the core claim combined with the observation that our normative beliefs can change, we can for instance improve our beliefs about what interests and whose interests matter morally. Moral progress via efficiency arises from the core claim and the fact that empirical beliefs can be better or worse, and as agents we can be more or less effective at bringing about certain results. 'The good of others' re-formulation occurs due to the combination of the core claim and the empirical observation of typically strong egoistic human motivational patterning. The account of moral duties takes the core claim and abstracts from it to reflect co-variance in human psychology. The idea of moral comparativism arises from the combination of the core claim and the observation that human motivations are scalar in strength, thus qualitative evaluands must ultimately be reducible to comparative ones.

None of these introduces a new normative claim aside from the core one, that agents are objectively better qua agents the more motivated they are to promote what is objectively better. As such the texturing and different components of the theory may perhaps disguise its underlying simplicity.

*

It matters what happens to people. And thus as agents we can be more or less motivated to promote the good. In particular, we can think about how we live our lives and think about what impact we might have on the good of others, how we might use our abilities and assets to make things better, and how we might integrate this goal into our future decisions. We can have this aim as one of the main things that motivate us in what we do and live morally decent lives. Or we can strive to go beyond this, to have it as one of the central influences in our major decisions and in what we do with our lives.

This will often be difficult; it will often be in tension with a reflexive self-concern or the myriad of pulls, temptations and weaknesses that structure and pattern our human nature. That, after all, is the point: to be highly or even exceptionally motivated by the good of others is demanding, it's why doing so is morally exemplary and sometimes even heroic.

If we focus purely on actions these concerns are at best submerged, at worst lost. If instead we focus on agents, on the potential and constraints of our motivations, then we might at least begin to understand the trade-offs, pitfalls and possibilities of living morally better lives, of better promoting the good of others. This is the motivation ethics approach.

EPILOGUE

On the scope of reason

Previous sections of this book have all been two-pronged: although arguing for a particular substantive positive position they have first tried to show what's wrong with the obvious alternatives, and why rectifying that specific wrong led to the proposed view.

So although Chapter 2 argued for using the good of all to ground an agent-morality, the previous chapter had tried to show the problems of using the good of all to ground an action-morality. Chapters on demandingness, special relationships and global duties first set out what was wrong with the common action-centric approach before offering the motivation ethics alternative. Theories of the value of political legitimacy and of overall-welfare scepticism were actively argued against.

This chapter is different, and for that reason is explicitly put as an epilogue. What I want to sketch here is, in the main, just the positive view, its promise, and the type of challenges it would face. No attempt will be made to exhaustively survey all the possible alternatives and to show why we shouldn't accept them.

Then why include it at all? Well, because at key junctures throughout this book the argument has relied on coherence and above all else non-arbitrariness as conditions on beliefs to show why we should reject some position or argument. Now perhaps, for most people, this is enough. But relying on these principles does raise questions of why them, why not others, what non-arbitrariness is, and why it indicates correctness. This chapter explores one possible answer.

To be very clear: none of this book's substantive arguments require accepting the expansive theory of ethical and empirical non-arbitrariness outlined here. On their own a simple account of non-arbitrariness and of coherence in moral evaluations are enough for most of the book's key arguments (a correct moral theory being invulnerable to amoralism is also required for some). But since it would be one way of justifying these, it is sketched below. However, it's perfectly coherent to think of the rest of this book as substantively correct and yet hold an alternative meta-methodological account to that of this chapter.

1. A case to begin with

Consider the following theory:

Green-eyed weighting
Overall welfare is determined by the preferences of all affected, and the preferences of green-eyed individuals should be given double the weight of blue-eyed individuals in overall welfare.

We should probably call this 'green-eyed weighting' rather than 'pro green-eyed discrimination' or 'anti blue-eyed prejudice' as we want to find a phrasing that itself is neutral. To call something prejudiced or discriminatory is to already imply a strong disapproval – which is justified – but the question we are going to be asking is exactly why. If we verbally stack the deck against a position then our case against the position may be weaker than it appears. In what follows, let a 'green-eyed theorist' be someone who advocates or supports green-eyed weighting. The question is: what mistake does the green-eyed theorist make or what is wrong with this view or views of this type?

The argument below is going to be that the problem is that the theory is arbitrary, and therefore incorrect, and furthermore that non-arbitrariness should be a condition on justified evaluative and empirical beliefs *for the same reason*. But before trying to give an account of what's wrong with green-eyed weighting in terms of arbitrariness, we should ask why this is really necessary. Can't we use intuitions – green-eyed weighting is, after all, a bizarre view – coherence, or some general moral principle such as that everyone is owed equal respect or 'each counts for one and only one'?

Intuitions

Most of us would immediately find green-eyed weighting both bizarre and morally rather repugnant, presumably because we recognize its structural similarities with racial prejudice and that directed against other minorities (and, sometimes, majorities, such as under colonialism or apartheid). As such can't a commitment to a reflective equilibrium simply identify what is wrong here if, for present purposes, we ignore the Intuition Regress Problem?

The difficulty is that while green-eyed weighting does indeed seem bizarre and would almost certainly not survive a reflective equilibrium of contemporary thoughtful people, many views that are similar to green-eyed weighting have, to a large majority of people in a great many societies, been very, very intuitive.

It used to be commonplace, for instance, to accept that different races should have different roles, or that because of their 'superior' ethnic background some were born with a natural aptitude to rule, or that the lives and interests of certain races should be treated with much greater concern. It's not the case that the historic race-based practices we now find repugnant were at the time widely viewed as odious but somehow tolerated; it's that they were often endorsed, woven into the culture, and seen as part of common-sense morality itself. And it wasn't just racial or ethnic cleavages that were used for implicit 'weighting'. For almost all of the twentieth century in every developed democracy on earth the idea that certain key interests of gays and lesbians should count for less was so widespread and deeply entrenched that any actual reflective equilibrium would have supported such a view, and this still holds for probably a majority of people alive today. The idea that women's interests should count for the same as men's is still implicitly resisted across the board, often without any self-awareness that this is happening, and even in supposedly egalitarian societies: children being bought up with differential expectations of attitudes, emotions and roles (try visiting a large toy store even now, they're places where egalitarian optimism goes to quietly die[1]). Norms of appropriate male/female workplace behaviour still dominate, the division of domestic and family labour is still stacked against women, and the cultural celebration of exemplars and the exceptional still reinforces the character traits and roles that are considered gender-appropriate irrespective of actual aptitude, inclination or ability.

Green-eyed weighting seems intuitively wrong because we don't live in a society where blue-eyedness versus green-eyedness has come to activate the very strong cultural and social group-norms that can predominate and ground people's intuitive judgements, even after scrutiny.

We can, however, easily imagine such a society. This would be one where green-eyed weighting was the norm and as such school teaching, political discourse and cultural mores would reflect that those with green-eyes were more deserving, or contribute more, or are more hard-working, or are wealth-creators, or can be expected to excel.

This might well be a society with immense social stability, especially if blue-eyed individuals weren't too numerous, or if they were that green-eyed weighting was preserved by abstract-sounding principles, such that long-term assets should not be taxed (it 'just happens' that these are overwhelmingly controlled by those with green-eyes). The society might have the rule of law and a vibrant economy. If so, arguing about green-eyed weighting using people's intuitions or even the intuitions of some selected elite sub-group would likely lead us to endorse the position of the green-eyed theorist. The problem isn't that general intuitions, common-sense morality or a reflective equilibrium can't be relied upon to decisively reject green-eyed weighting, it's that if such weighting was a dominant social practice and feature of social relations they might actually lead us to strongly endorse it.

Of course, if we had independent, non-intuition-based, grounds for rejecting the green-eyed theorist's positions then a reflective equilibrium might be able to keep these intuitions in check. But that is exactly the point: when evaluating widespread socially-endorsed practices, relying on intuitions is going to be extremely vulnerable to proposing the marginal modification of the status quo or of what is conventional. If green-eyed weighting should be universally judged wrong then our intuitions will likely only deliver this result if we happen to live in a society where it is already significantly rejected by most, or at least by culturally or politically highly influential groups.

Coherence

Instead of relying on intuitions, perhaps we can rely on the need for coherence. Coherence in one's beliefs is often held to be an epistemic virtue and, on simple realist accounts, necessary (if there is a world of things that exist, and we have beliefs about them, then it seems that with incoherent beliefs we can know we are wrong).

The difficulty here, however, is not that coherence is incorrect or incapable of justification, it's that it's insufficient. This is because logical coherence is ultimately a very, very weak principle and, as such, it does not seem to have the resources to capture what is wrong with green-eyed weighting.

It's true that the following would indeed seem to violate coherence:

1 Overall welfare is determined by facts about the content of people's preferences, with identical preferences weighted equally.
2 The content of the preferences of green-eyed people contributes double to overall welfare than the content of the preferences of blue-eyed people.

This might indeed violate a coherence requirement once these premises were suitably spelled-out. But the green-eyed theorist could just preserve their view by amending premise one:

1 Overall welfare is determined by facts about the content of people's preferences.
2 The content of the preferences of green-eyed people contributes double to overall welfare than the content of the preferences of blue-eyed people.

There is nothing, at all, incoherent here. The overall difficulty is this: we can use coherence to reject green-eyed weighting *if we have already adopted a separate premise that entails eye-colour cannot affect overall welfare*. But the green-eyed theorist can do the same with a separate premise of their own, that eye-colour should affect overall welfare, and they can then use coherence to reject the alternative views, namely those that don't make moral evaluations dependent on eye-colour. Important though it is, coherence is not enough.

Equal respect for all

Surely this whole debate is a bit redundant? The reason we can reject green-eyed weighting is that it violates the equal respect that is owed to everyone. Different theorists might want to put this idea in alternate ways, thus here are some variations, all of which seem to allow us to refute green-eyed weighting:

1   All humans are worthy of equal respect for their interests.
2   A correct moral principle should not be reasonably reject-able.
3   Eye-colour based discrimination is ipso facto morally wrong.

Any of us that accept any of these seem to have grounds for rejecting green-eyed weighting. The difficulty, however, is that the green-eyed theorist could in principle also endorse all of these, doing so by maintaining that in each case we are smuggling in a bias against green-eyed people by implicitly weighting their interests the same as blue-eyed people.

According to the green-eyed theorist, equal respect means equally respecting the appropriate combination of people's preferences and eye-colour status. Obviously, if you only respect their preferences then green-eyed weighting can be rejected, but we have simply smuggled in the assumption that differential eye-status should not be something we respect.

Furthermore, the green-eyed theorist could enthusiastically endorse the idea that moral principles should not be reasonably reject-able, maintaining that a system that failed to appropriately weight the interests of green-eyed people could and should be rejected by them. Blue-eyed people could not reasonably reject green-eyed weighting because it would be unreasonable to treat people with very different eye-colours as though they were identical.

Similarly, the green-eyed theorist would undoubtedly think that eye-colour based discrimination was morally wrong, for them the test of such discrimination would be failing to weight the interests of green-eyed people appropriately. Giving equal weight to the identical preferences of green and blue-eyed people would be straightforwardly to discriminate against the green-eyed people. Indeed, the green-eyed theorist not only could endorse anti-discrimination, they also have a remarkably clear and coherent theory of what such discrimination entails:

1   To give the preferences of green-eyed people less than double the weight of those of blue-eyed people is to discriminate against the green-eyed.
2   To give the preferences of blue-eyed people less than half the

weight of those of green-eyed people is to discriminate against the blue-eyed.

Presumably they could come up with various tests of public policy, enshrine these in the law, and make anti-discrimination a requirement of all civic and public bodies.

Someone might protest that all this is not what equality means or involves, specifically not how we understand that ideal. But, as noted, this is potentially because green-eyed weighting is not a dominant organising principle of current society. If it was, it might well be an integral part of how we understand the ideal of equality.

We could instead argue that all the previous moral principles at the very least entail that we should treat identical people identically. But the green-eyed theorist has a straightforward response: 'What, you think people with green-eyes and blue-eyes are identical? They're not: they have different eye-colours!' And, furthermore, in a society with green-eyed weighting, people with green-eyes and those with blue-eyes would be expected to display very different characteristics, these being products of education, cultural background, expectations and self-image. The green-eyed theorist's critique – 'You're wrongly assuming green-eyed and blue-eyed people are exactly the same!' – would presumably resonate with many in such a society.

The core difficulty with all of the above principles is that they require us to fill-in the content, and the green-eyed theorist will argue that the content should be filled-in to appropriately respect green-eyed weighting. The principles themselves don't seem to determine this without assuming that green-eyed weighting is unjustified. *It's not that these principles are wrong or bad at all*. Indeed, these principles are, I believe, very important statements of a conclusion we should all accept, and they should powerfully shape our attitudes and the way we approach moral and political philosophy. The problem being discussed here is not their falsity. It's that we need a further principle to translate them into concrete content.

But what if a commitment to the equal numerical weighting of all individuals implicitly unites these egalitarian principles, some version of the old utilitarian refrain that 'everyone counts for one and only for one'? We could simply argue that equal respect, or treating people with equal worth, simply means weighting them each with a value of one (or just any identical numerical value).

This seems abstractly right, but to implement it we need to specify exactly what is weighted with value one, *for you don't weight people, you weight certain facts about them*. What most of us want to do here is to weight facts about people's welfare with a joint value of one (and this is what 'unbiasedness' did in Chapter 8, allowing us to produce interpersonal comparisons). But the green-eyed theorist could hold that once again we have smuggled in a bias. The correct thing to be weighted is a 'welfare-eye-colour' function. This function takes an individual's implied relative welfare, multiplies it by two if they are green-eyed, *and then weights this final sum equally across all individuals*. This, the theorist will argue, is what equal respect entails: that we weight everyone's 'welfare-eye-colour' function equally.

2. Non-arbitrariness in outline

So if intuitions are unreliable, coherence too weak, and moral-equality-principles not specific enough in that they require a further principle to flesh them out, what resources does 'non-arbitrariness' have to make progress?

The previously used, and perhaps the most straightforward, test of evaluative arbitrariness – 'non-feature arbitrariness' – seems to be where a theory is arbitrary if the evaluation of an object is not determined by features of the object and the evaluation is exclusionary. By 'exclusionary' is meant that if it is correct to evaluate an object as 'P' then it is not also correct to evaluate it as 'not-P'.

This, note, does not entail only intrinsic evaluations can be non-arbitrary. Take, for instance, the earlier discussed laissez-faire instrumentalism, where an instrumental evaluation can be correct in reference to a particular situation but no situation is privileged above others.[2] In other words, it can be perfectly correct that a large wooden hammer is both a good hammer (if hitting a wooden joist) and a bad hammer (if hitting a narrow steel nail). This type of instrumentalism rejects the exclusionary clause when it comes to the evaluation 'good hammerness' and thus is not necessarily arbitrary. The key requirement – that to be non-arbitrary the evaluation of an object be determined by features of the object – should only as such apply to evaluations that are held to be exclusionary. Such an evaluation can of course be at root qualitative or quantitative depending on the content (as discussed in Chapter 4).

This type of testing for arbitrariness can take us a surprisingly long way, and it did the argumentative work at key junctures in this book. The difficulty, however, is that it does not rule out all of the ways we can smuggle in an arbitrary premise.

The cunning of green-eyed weighting is that although it does make the evaluation dependent on something seemingly irrelevant (the individuals' eye colour), it picks an irrelevant feature that is nonetheless arguably part of the object of the evaluation (the individuals and how their lives go). 'Non-feature arbitrariness', though very powerful, doesn't obviously rule out green-eyed weighting.[3]

The right way, I think, to begin to pin down the arbitrariness of green-eyed weighting is to view it as two clauses, the second of which qualifies the scope or application of the first. That is:

Green-eyed weighting
(1) Overall welfare is determined by the preferences of all affected; and (2) the preferences of green-eyed individuals should be given double the weight of blue-eyed individuals in overall welfare.

What potentially creates the arbitrariness here is that the justification of the first clause (why preferences matter, not desires or happiness for instance) is not dependent on the feature that according to the second clause the evaluation is dependent upon (green-eyed versus blue-eyed status). Having green-eyes is neither necessary nor sufficient to have preferences, nor does it necessarily affect the content of those preferences.

This is perhaps clearer if we compare the following two theories:

Green-eyed weighting
(1) Overall welfare is determined by the preferences of all affected; and (2) the preferences of green-eyed individuals should be given double the weight of blue-eyed individuals in overall welfare.

Blue-eyed weighting
(1) Overall welfare is determined by the preferences of all affected; and (2) the preferences of blue-eyed individuals should be given double the weight of green-eyed individuals in overall welfare.

To justify green-eyed weighting we would have to justify why blue-eyed weighting should be rejected. But we can see that nothing in the justification of the first premise speaks to the greater value of green vs blue eyes, and as such making our beliefs about overall welfare contingent on our beliefs about green-vs-blue eye-colour is arbitrary.

Before discussing this idea in more detail, here is one immediate worry: isn't this the wrong type of answer? The badness of green-eyed weighting, and in particular various racist, sexist, homophobic or colonialist analogies, seems to be much more forceful than mere arbitrariness: it's morally odious, a violation of equal respect and dignity. This is true, but as a criticism of non-arbitrariness is mis-premised. Non-arbitrariness speaks to the question of what are justified beliefs, not of how we should respond to entrenched norms celebrating and spreading unjustified ones.

The normal right response to the casual sexism that predominates in most workplaces, for example, is almost certainly to challenge it, perhaps by being reasonably confrontational and even unkind. Joking about the inferiority of the supporters of a rival sports team, in most contexts, is a very different matter. Both sets of implied beliefs – over superior supporters or appropriate gender roles – may hinge on the alleged importance of an arbitrary distinction. But the social contexts of both are very different. Even if non-arbitrariness is the right way to identify why certain distinctions should be not relevant to evaluative claims, this doesn't settle the question of how we should respond to such divisions in the social and cultural contexts we find ourselves in. Non-arbitrariness is primarily about justified beliefs; how we respond to social practices that encode and promote unjustified beliefs will bring in a whole host of further considerations.

Even if we do accept that non-arbitrariness should be a condition on justified beliefs, one obvious question concerns what would be the best version of such a condition (and section 4 sets this idea out using the two-clause approach somewhat more formally and clearly). However, a second larger issue concerns the scope of such a principle: when and why we should adopt it. Why, in essence, are we unjustified in thinking that moral evaluations can be arbitrary? And should this answer only apply to moral evaluations?

3. The expansive view: Non-arbitrariness as a general condition

Consider the following two theories:

'Welfare-2040'
The welfare of individuals is determined by their preferences, unless it's the year 2040.

'Gravity-2040'
All bodies with mass attract each other, unless it's the year 2040.[4]

One refers to a moral evaluation, the other to an empirical theory about the universe. Assume, for arguments' sake, that we are currently justified in believing the first clause of each in reference to present day (that is, the bit in each up until 'unless …'). What then is wrong with these theories?

Well, it's possible to provide very different types of accounts of what is wrong with each. With regard to the rejection of Welfare-2040 we might cite the fact that it clashes with our moral intuitions or common sense morality, or that it would not survive a reflective equilibrium, or that it does not reflect an equal respect for everyone or everyone's equal moral worth. As noted, there are difficulties with these responses, but perhaps some of them could be overcome. In each case, however, what is wrong with Welfare-2040 is inextricably linked to the fact that it is an evaluative/ethical theory.

The second theory, 'Gravity-2040', is much harder to provide a clear and justified argument against. All the evidence that we have supports the theory (so far). Similarly, the most prominent formal epistemic framework, that of Bayesian epistemology, would have the theory confirmed: $P(H/E)>P(H)$ where E is any observation of two bodies with mass attracting each other before the year 2040 (as $P(E/H)=1$). As would a likelihood framework. And furthermore, the theory could have been falsified numerous times and hasn't been. This, of course, is simply one part of the problem of the justification and content of induction.

But what if what is wrong with Welfare-2040 and Gravity-2040 is exactly the same thing: namely the inclusion in both of an arbitrary premise? As such any justified account of induction whose key principles each can only apply to empirical theories, or any account of ethical justification that can only apply to normative theories, will not be able to capture that both theories are wrong for the same reason. Of course, this does not entail that any such principle of non-arbitrariness will exhaust the content of an inductive framework or an account of normative justification. But if it really is true that what is wrong with both theories is the same type of thing (and not two independent things that just happen to superficially look the same), then we may be able to make progress in trying to pin down and articulate this principle, and to think through what the justification of it might be.

Before going any further, let me just prevent one serious bit of sceptical over-reach: aren't we making some fallacy here in deriving an 'ought' from an 'is'? Well, no. We are discussing what conditions there should be upon beliefs for them to be justified, whether there are conditions that should hold for both empirical and normative beliefs, whether non-arbitrariness should be one such condition, and what it might concretely involve. By analogy: you can think that justified empirical beliefs must be coherent and that justified moral beliefs must also be coherent and do so in both cases for the same reason without thinking you can derive an ought from an is.

The larger challenge therefore is to give an account of arbitrariness that handles both sorts of cases, and to provide an account of why we should adopt this, again in both cases.

4. What might a general condition of non-arbitrariness look like?

A full defence of a non-arbitrariness condition spanning empirical and normative beliefs would need to address a huge number of issues, both in general and in each realm. A complete account would need to set out what was precisely the best version of the principle and why it was preferable to all alternatives, a book-length project at the very least. However, for present purposes, a rough outline may be sufficient to illustrate the potential and also the very real challenges.

The core of such a condition is possibly hinted at in the previous discussion of how the justifications of a theory's different clauses relate. That is, with regard to Gravity-2040 and Welfare-2040, it seems that the key problem with both theories is that the justification of our believing the first clause is not dependent on the justification of the conditional of the second clause, even though the theory makes the application of the first cause dependent via the second.

So here is Gravity-2040 as two clauses:

1   All bodies with mass attract each other;
2   Clause (1) holds unless it's the year 2040.

The claim that this is arbitrary would be roughly justified by something like the following: that the evidence we have for believing the first clause – say we drop an apple and see it fall to the ground – is not dependent on our believing it before 2040. Imagine you drop the apple, see it fall, and then wonder if perhaps you've had a super-sleep and it's 2040. You still have evidence that objects with mass attract each other. In other words, if you were uncertain as to whether it was 2040 or not, the other evidence you have would still support the first clause.

Now, it's true that we do believe it to be before 2040, and do observe apples falling. But these are evidentially independent. On the one hand you look at your calendar and have various beliefs about time-travel, long-naps and date-errors, on the other hand you see the apple move towards the earth (and vice versa). As such, scepticism about one would not necessarily entail scepticism about the other. Thus a theory that makes a generalization of one dependent on the other introduces an arbitrary condition.

Similarly, in the welfare case, we can write this as two clauses, with the second qualifying the first.

Welfare-2040:

1   Overall welfare is determined by the preferences of those affected;
2   Clause (1) holds unless it is 2040.

Again, while we do need a realm-specific account of justification – why we are justified in believing (1), and this seems different to the empirical case where this was evidence-based – the arbitrariness arises because the justification of (1) is independent of the justification for believing the conditional in (2) is met. Knowing it is 2040 or not is not necessary to an argument for why preferences (not desires say) matter to welfare.

There are, of course, various ways of verbally roughly capturing this and most of us can probably spot glaring arbitrariness fairly easily. The challenge, however, is to provide an account that is sufficiently clear that it can handle both sets of cases – empirical and evaluative – and can be explicitly justified.

One example of the type of principle being cautiously approached here is something like the following:

Epistemic arbitrariness condition
If a theory entails 'P iff Q' (but not 'P and Q') then to be non-arbitrary the theory-independent justification for our believing P has to be dependent on the theory-independent justification for our believing Q, or vice versa, if we are justified in believing P and Q.

That is, if the grounds we have for believing Q are not also a necessary part of the grounds we have for believing P, then the theory 'P iff Q', or one entailing this, makes P unjustifiably dependent on something, and such a restriction is arbitrary (unless P iff Q is justified via a reformulation such as Q iff P).

The general approach here is to convert a theory's contingent logical claims – such as 'P iff Q' – into epistemic claims about premise-justification, such as 'we are justified in believing P if and only if we are justified in believing Q' and then to see if the latter in fact holds independent of accepting the theory.

So here, for instance is one thing Gravity-2040 entails:

'An apple will always fall to the ground'[5] iff 'it is not 2040.'

We might as such have evidence justifying the clause 'An apple will always fall to the ground.' And we might have evidence justifying 'it is not 2040'. But, crucially, if the currently sufficient and necessary evidence justifying the second is not necessary to the first then holding the overall hypothesis evidentially supported is currently arbitrary.

Similarly, with Welfare-2040, if the justification for believing that preferences are what matter for overall welfare is not dependent on the justification for believing it is before 2040 then the theory is arbitrary, even if we are justified in thinking preferences matter for welfare and in believing it is before 2040.

The suggestion is that one potential way of making non-arbitrariness concrete is to take a logical clause with a contingency, such as of the type 'P iff Q' for instance, and see how the justifications for believing different component premises, such as for believing P and for believing Q, relate. We can be justified in believing P, and justified in believing Q, and yet the theory 'P iff Q' can still be arbitrary, even if everything we believe is perfectly coherent.

Now this view faces a series of immediate local challenges of clarification: why phrase arbitrariness in terms of beliefs? Why relativize to an agent? Why 'currently' arbitrary – is it possible to think a currently arbitrary theory could subsequently not be arbitrary?

The right way therefore to think about the above 'Epistemic Arbitrariness Condition' – for present purposes – is as an example of the type of form a condition of non-arbitrariness in our beliefs might take, one that potentially covers *both* empirical beliefs and evaluative beliefs. Non-arbitrariness is also one condition on beliefs: it does not necessarily exhaust the justification of such beliefs.

However, if the best version of this condition should ultimately be one covering the logical relations between the justifications of different beliefs, we should in principle be able to set it out formally and fully, not simply sketch the idea as above. In the first instance, this challenge is best, I think, attempted in the empirical case. In the ethical case we don't currently have a formal framework of ethical logic, nor do we even have agreement on the type of form ethical descriptors should take, and as such in trying to set these out the worry will always be that we have somehow smuggled in the desired conclusion. In the empirical case, by contrast, we have both propositional and predicate logic as long-standing tools, plus a very good understanding of the myriad challenges such an account would have to overcome (see, on that, section 6).

The overall 'project' would therefore involve doing the following:

1. Provide an account of non-arbitrariness that covers both empirical and normative beliefs.
2. Provide a justification for thinking correct beliefs are non-arbitrary.
3. Show why the justification in (2) supports the principle in (1) rather than some other principle.

Section 6 discusses some general sceptical worries such a project would have to overcome. Before doing so, however, here is one view that might have the resources to meet (2) and (3).

5. What's wrong with believing that the (empirical or normative) universe might be arbitrary? The epistemic realist answer

What if the universe is sometimes arbitrary? Or what if correct moral evaluations can sometimes be both correct and arbitrary (it *just is* that the preferences of green-eyed individuals contribute more to overall welfare)?

On a very simple realist account, this is perfectly possible, and if one adopts non-arbitrariness as a key condition on justified beliefs then whether justified beliefs approach true beliefs will depend on the degree to which the universe is arbitrary.

An alternative, however, is to hold that the relationship should be thought of as the other way around: correct beliefs are those that non-arbitrary beliefs approach as our epistemic situation improves. This is not, note, some variant of solipsism, where what exists is what one believes exists, or is currently justified in believing exists. The idea is something like the following:

Epistemic realism
The universe comprises of that which we would be justified in believing were we in what we are justified in believing would be the best epistemic situation possible available to us.

On the surface this just looks somewhat like regular realism (where the best epistemic situation is the one where we would have true beliefs). However, it really isn't. To illustrate the difference via the empirical case, imagine that there are entities – 'mysterons' – that travel through the galaxy and do not interact with anything with which we can directly or indirectly interact. Mysterons do not shift the positions of objects with mass, they do not change the amount of energy or its distribution, they have no impact on entropy, or any variables about which we can gain evidence. In fact the framing of them 'moving through' the galaxy almost certainly needs qualifying, as it implies they do interact with space-time, thus perhaps we should have them just existing and doing whatever it is that mysterons do, so long as it's not interacting with anything with which we can interact. What they do is a mystery, and will always be a mystery.

Specifically, for the thought experiment to correctly capture the regular-realist vs epistemic-realist distinction what is crucial is that we stipulate that we are not currently justified in believing there are mysterons – based on our current evidence – and there is no possible future evidence that would justify us believing in them.

Under a simple realist account, in this case we have and will always have justified but false beliefs. And indeed, this is certainly how many of us would intuitively understand the case as described. Under Epistemic Realism, however, mysterons do not exist as part of the universe. The universe consists of that which we would be justified in believing exists were we in what we are justified in believing would be the best epistemic situation possible. If we assume that the best epistemic situation is one where we believe all possible evidence, and reasoning correctly from such evidence we cannot be justified in believing in mysterons, then under epistemic realism mysterons do not exist as part of the universe. Now the final clause seems somewhat nit-picky: mysterons do exist but don't exist as part of the universe, which just suggests that we've defined the universe in some restricted manner. This is true, up to a point. But the disagreement is substantive, for it is about what type of claim can be truth-apt. For Epistemic Realism, if we could not in principle be justified in believing P then P cannot be truth apt. For simple realism, whether claims can be true or not is simply a feature of whether it is in principle possible for the claim to be correct: anything bar a logical contradiction can be truth apt.

This example of mysterons both existing and not existing as part of the universe will, admittedly, probably seem intuitively odd. But that may just be that our minds are not very good at thinking of something that both exists and cannot interact with anything without smuggling in the assumption that these things have mass or travel through space-time and so on.

In the evaluative case this perhaps seems less crazy as we're more used to the idea of correct evaluative objects potentially being a construct whose correctness depends on certain conditions of justification. Hence it appears less counter-intuitive to hold that overall welfare – as a measure of how well multiple individuals' lives go – simply cannot be justifiably constructed by giving double the weight to those with green-eyes as this is arbitrary, and correct beliefs are non-arbitrary. Epistemic realism entails however that this approach applies to correct evaluative beliefs and true empirical beliefs. It's an interesting but admittedly somewhat odd view. The reason for introducing it here specifically, though, is that it is the sort of view that can appropriately link correctness and non-arbitrariness.

Under Epistemic Realism, theories are both claims about the world we can experience and simultaneously claims about what we should be justified in believing about the world we can experience either currently or as our epistemic situation improves.

A theory that claims 'P iff Q' thus is interpreted as claiming not only that in our universe P iff Q, but also that in an ideal epistemic situation we would be justified in believing P iff we would be justified in believing Q. As such, the overall theory is supported not only by our believing P and Q but by the justification of our believing Q being necessary in justifying why we believe P, that is holding a non-arbitrary belief according to the Epistemic Arbitrariness Condition. Epistemic Realism entails that, in an ideal epistemic situation, the theory 'P iff Q' is correct if we are justified in believing P *because we are justified in believing Q*. Even if we do believe P and do believe Q, if counter-factual scepticism about P turns out to be perfectly compatible with non-scepticism about Q, and vice versa, then the theory is arbitrary.

Epistemic Realism thus provides one type of justification for non-arbitrariness as a guide to correctness. If correct beliefs are those that we can be justified in believing in the best epistemic position, and if in such a position having justified beliefs requires having non-arbitrary beliefs, then non-arbitrary beliefs are going to approach correct ones as our epistemic situation improves.

The greatest difficulty here admittedly lies not in providing a potential meta-epistemic account that appropriately links non-arbitrariness with correctness: that's something quite a few accounts could do, I personally suspect Epistemic Realism might be a promising way to do it but it's easy to imagine non-arbitrariness as a general principle being supported by a wide range of theorists for fairly diverse reasons. The real difficulty is in showing that there even exists a principle of non-arbitrariness that can overcome a series of challenges to its use in justifying empirical and normative beliefs.

6. Challenges and scepticism

Challenges to the empirical prong: 'This is just logical empiricism. Yeah, we tried that ...'

Basing empirical justification on a logic of non-arbitrariness is a form of logical empiricism, a view that very much fell out of favour during the twentieth century, and so we should expect a large degree of scepticism about its potential.

The previous sentence, however, significantly understates the difficulties of a non-arbitrariness based logic that applies to the empirical (as well as ethical) universe. For the problem is not only one of a clash with current conventional wisdom – that logical empiricism is almost universally viewed as flawed, and in fact as literally unworkable – it's that some of the problems that were so devastating for logical empiricism, notably the 'paradoxes of induction', appear *especially* problematic for a non-arbitrariness based resolution.

To illustrate: take the two most famous and most important paradoxes, that of the ravens and of grue. Under the ravens' paradox if an instance confirms a generalization – so 'All F are G' is confirmed by an F that is G – and if what confirms one statement also confirms all statements logically equivalent to it, then it can easily be shown that a white shoe confirms 'All ravens are black' ('All ravens are black' is logically equivalent to 'All non-black things are non-ravens' which is confirmed by a non-black non-raven, such as a white shoe).[6] This has widely been taken to be a problematic result, and the difficulty for a non-arbitrariness view is that it seems almost inescapably committed to endorsing it. That an instance confirms a generalization seems completely non-arbitrary, and that logically equivalent sentences are treated equivalently seems a constitutive commitment of non-arbitrariness.

Now, some have tried to argue that the paradoxical result can be explained away (one prominent attempt argues that if you observe the shoe's whiteness first, then its shoeness, it could have been a white raven, so the theory has in a sense been tested). So perhaps the force of this problem can be muted, though I personally think this is the wrong solution. The second problem, however, appears even worse.

Under Goodman's New Riddle of Induction, often called the grue paradox, something is defined as grue if it is green before time t (some future time) or blue after t. The statement 'There exists a green emerald before time t' turns out to have all the same logical relations in predicate logic to 'All emeralds are green' as it does to 'All emeralds are grue'.[7] This is because 'There exists a green emerald before time t' is logically equivalent to 'There exists a grue emerald before time t'. Attempts to rule out 'All emeralds are grue' because it asserts the possibility of a predicate change – from green to blue – don't work because there is only a predicate change if we assume that the basic predicates are green and blue as opposed to grue and bleen (something is bleen if blue before time t or green after). Nothing in predicate logic or the evidential sentence justifies this.

Why bring up this very well-known paradox? Well, because 'All emeralds are grue' appears to be an almost perfect exemplar of a hypothesis with an arbitrary clause compared to 'All emeralds are green'. If we can't identify why 'All emeralds are grue' shouldn't be confirmed by a green/grue emerald before t, and can't set this out in some sort of formal logic, then the prospects seem dim for a non-arbitrariness principle spanning the empirical and normative realms. The paradox has, of course, been around for a very long time and resisted such a type of resolution, so this really is a significant challenge.

Furthermore, as noted, any attempt to provide an account of logical arbitrariness would surely be a form of logical empiricism. Since most professional philosophers of science judge this approach doomed to failure (there's even a discussion in the literature over whether its most prominent variant is literally 'hopeless'[8]), scepticism about its prospects seems warranted.

Indeed, many introductions to the philosophy of science begin with logical empiricism as a way of demonstrating why a pure logic-based approach simply cannot work, and as a way of introducing the theories that came after and why they rejected the approach in different ways.[9]

This isn't alas a case of textbooks underselling a newly flourishing view. I recently went to an excellent philosophy of science conference in Helsinki where among many, many sessions they had one on logical empiricism. The chair introduced it by noting that while no one these days thought the approach at all feasible it was still important to have a session on it because of its historical importance. I think she pretty accurately reflected the consensus view. Obviously, a well-established consensus in a discipline can be wrong, but in any given case you'd be brave to bet on it being so.

In sum, the odds seem very low for a non-arbitrariness based logic that can even overcome the paradoxes of induction, let alone fulfil most of the tasks of providing a broad account of the justification of empirical beliefs.

Challenges to the ethical prong: 'This is the wrong type of answer'

The prospects for the ethical prong perhaps seem better than for the empirical one, yet to make non-arbitrariness the really fundamental evaluative condition would still strike many as just mistaken as to the nature of ethics.

The worry would presumably be that the phenomenology is all wrong: ethics isn't about some dry analytic condition, it's about what it's like as human beings to be engaging with each other, living in a shared community or exploring how we might do better or worse, how we might come to understand and care for others. Now, motivation ethics, by example, may at least partly meet this demand, to the extent that it relied on non-arbitrariness for its justification at key junctures, and yet it still supplies rich evaluations shaped by the empirical patterning of human psychology.

This is, however, unlikely to persuade those who simply start with a very different view of how to engage in ethical reflection, and indeed if the Intuition Regress Problem can be overcome then some sort of reflective equilibrium should probably restrict the role of non-arbitrariness.

The ethical prong looks incompatible with various constitutive views of what normative philosophy involves, and the empirical prong looks crippled by paradox and the normally reliable judgement of widespread professional consensus. Only a fool would think non-arbitrariness can ground an account of justified beliefs spanning the normative and empirical universes.

The project does, admittedly, look doomed.

And yet. And yet. In a sense it has to be doable. If we can have justified beliefs we simply have to be able to rule out arbitrariness. And as such, the belief that the knowable universe is arbitrary in some area can never be justified (why that area and in that way? If we can justify that, then the arbitrariness is simultaneously removed. It just defeats itself, has to defeat itself.)

Furthermore, the potential upside is huge. A very common complaint about analytic philosophy is that it simply amounts to trying to get one's beliefs coherent, but either has no resources to get such beliefs right, or has to collapse into getting one's intuitions coherent and leaving it at that. Non-arbitrariness promises more: it holds out the possibility that we can choose between two different perfectly coherent sets of beliefs.

This book has taken non-arbitrariness and explored how it can help us choose between different structures of moral theory. The principle took the argument surprisingly far. Whether it can go much further, providing a unified strong condition on normative and empirical beliefs is ultimately a question of the scope of reason.

I've tried above, in sketching the overall project, to simultaneously air the sceptical case as openly and hopefully as fairly as possible, for it does look strong, indeed very strong. Yet, for what it's worth, my suspicion is that, in the end, reason will prove far more powerful and far-reaching than we now credit it, and that these challenges can in fact be met.

Placing one's faith in 'the scope of reason' is of course open to easy misrepresentation. It isn't a hope for some Platonic wise guardians to use reason to decide our fate, we are clearly much better off trying to devise political and economic institutions that can avoid terrible outcomes and sometimes do marginally well, a difficult goal, one frequently not met and one still poorly understood. Nor is it the arrogant assumption that, if in principle reason can guide us towards fully justified beliefs, that this in any way supports us thinking that we have in practice personally travelled such distance. Anyone with even a vague understanding of the many ways we can fail as human thinkers should be sceptical that most of the beliefs we find ourselves with, even after much reflection, will survive the scrutiny of time and of other minds.

No, the hope is that, if we can use non-arbitrariness to choose between sets of beliefs then, if we are lucky, we can make cautious, sometimes reversed, but slow and perhaps steady progress in better understanding what it is to live in a universe where beings can value, and where they can experience. Such a project's scope and challenges should, probably, leave us very sceptical. But the upside should also leave us striving.

NOTES

Introduction

1   In principle, it's possible even to combine all three. See, for instance, Griffin, whose conception includes 'enjoyment, accomplishing something with one's life, deep personal relations, certain sorts of understanding, and the elements of a characteristically human existence (autonomy, liberty)'. James Griffin (1992), 'The Human Good and the Ambitions of Consequentialism'. *Social Philosophy & Policy* 9 (2): 118–32 at p. 118, and also James Griffin (1986), *Well-Being*. Oxford: Oxford University Press.

2   This example will not do justice to the richness of modern consequentialist thought, where often we should not only look to the near consequences, such as how many die, but also the long-term and generalized effects. Sometimes cultivating motives, virtues or adopting rules against killing may have better expected outcomes.

3   Indeed this 'equal consideration of interests' is sometimes held to be a central justification of consequentialism, with the additional notable implication that non-human animal suffering should be included in assessing the overall good of outcomes (non-human animals after all have interests, indeed some of these appear in type similar to a range of human interests). See Peter Singer (1993), *Practical Ethics*. Cambridge: Cambridge University Press.

4   Perhaps most famously in those of 'trolley cases', where we could for example push a fat man to his death to save five workers threatened by a runaway trolley, and 'transplant cases', where we could secretly cut up an innocent patient to provide organs to save five others. See for instance on the former Judith Jarvis Thompson (1985), 'The Trolley Problem'. *The Yale Law Journal* 94 (6).

5   Thomas Nagel (1979), *Mortal Questions*. Cambridge: Cambridge University Press.

6   Gautthier takes, for instance, this to be a requirement of rationality. David Gautthier (1986), *Morals By Agreement*. Oxford: Oxford University Press.

7   John Rawls (1999), *A Theory of Justice*. Harvard University Press: Cambridge, MA, p. 21.

8   See notably Robert Nozick (1974), *Anarchy, State and Utopia*, New York: Basic and on the problems with this, in principle, Samuel Scheffler (1982), *The Rejection of Consequentialism*. Oxford: Oxford University Press.

9 Warren Quinn (1989) 'Actions, Intentions, and Consequences: The Doctrine of Doing and Allowing'. *The Philosophical Review* 98 (3): 287–312, and Warren Quinn (1989), 'Actions, Intentions, and Consequences: The Doctrine of Double Effect'. *Philosophy and Public Affairs* 18 (4): 334–51.

10 The problem does not depend on any commitment to agent evaluations being the most important task of a moral theory. Nor does it have anything to do with a desire to 'blame people' (we can always, for instance, be interested in the question of agent evaluations because we want to know what a morally good or exception life for someone like us might be like).

Chapter one

1 Jeremy Bentham (1988), *The Principles of Morals and Legislation*. Buffalo, NY: Prometheus; John Stuart Mill (1998 [1871]), *Utilitarianism*. Oxford: Oxford University Press; Henry Sidgwick (1981), *The Methods of Ethics*. Indianapolis, IN: Hackett.

2 Brad Hooker (1990), 'Rule-Consequentialism'. *Mind* 99: 67–77; Brad Hooker (2000), *Ideal Code, Real World: A Rule-Consequentialist Theory of Morality*. Oxford: Oxford University Press.

3 Dale Jamieson (2007), 'When Utilitarians Should be Virtue Theorists'. *Utilitas* 19: 160–83.

4 Robert Adams (1976), 'Motive Utilitarianism'. *The Journal of Philosophy* 73: 467–81.

5 Philip Pettit and Michael Smith (2000), 'Global Consequentialism' in Brad Hooker, Elinor Mason and Dale Miller (eds), *Morality, Rules, and Consequences: A Critical Reader*. Edinburgh: Edinburgh University Press, pp. 121–33.

6 The term 'direct consequentialism' is sometimes used more narrowly to refer only to act-consequentialism, but here it includes act, rule, motive, virtue and global consequentialism where the right act / rule / motive / virtue / combination is that which brings about the best consequences.

7 It is important to distinguish this 'evaluative coherence', (that between an agent and her actions) with what Jennie Louise calls 'evaluative conflict' ([2006], 'Right Motive, Wrong Action: Direct Consequentialism and Evaluative Conflict. *Ethical Theory and Moral Practice* 9 65–85 or Derek Parfit calls 'blameless wrongdoing' ([1984], *Reasons and Persons*. Oxford: Oxford University Press, pp. 31–7). These latter two terms refer to the fact that for direct consequentialism the actions arising from a rule, motive or virtue that is right may individually be wrong if considered singly. The concern here is orthogonal to this: it is the conflict or coherence between the evaluation of an agent and her actions (whether singularly or as a set arising from a rule, motive or virtue).

8 Any plausible account of the agent's constitutive features is intended to be included – beliefs, emotions, attachments, values, will, virtues, inclinations, dispositions, aspirations etc.

9 'Identical agents' refers here and throughout to the agents being identical in terms of their constitutive features, whatever a theory wishes to regard these as. Two agents are not, however, presumably identical in their temporal-spatial location, thus not all accounts are included: there is a very minimal notion of constitutive features underpinning the identical agent problem.

10 As Jamieson has perceptively observed, 'Utilitarianism is a universal emulator: it implies that we should lie, cheat, steal, even appropriate Aristotle, when that is what brings about the best consequences.' The question raised in this chapter concerns what criteria consequentialism should use to evaluate someone who does lie, cheat or steal and as such always acts rightly and someone who does not and as such acts wrongly. Jamieson, 'When Utilitarians Should be Virtue Theorists', p. 160.

11 Philippa Foot (1967), 'The Problem of Abortion and the Doctrine of Double Effect'. *Oxford Review* 5: 28–41; Francis Kamm (1989), 'Harming Some to Save Others". *Philosophical Studies* 57 (3): 227–60; Judith Jarvis Thompson (1976), 'Killing, Letting Die, and the Trolley Problem'. *The Monist* 59: 205–17.

12 Bernard Williams (1973), 'A Critique of Utilitarianism' in J. J. C. Smart and B. Williams, *Utilitarianism: For and Against*. Cambridge: Cambridge University Press, pp. 77–150; Bernard Williams (1981), 'Persons, Character, and Morality' in Bernard Williams, *Moral Luck*. Cambridge: Cambridge University Press, pp. 1–19.

13 G. E. M. Anscombe (1958), 'Modern Moral Philosophy'. *Philosophy* 33: (124).

14 Shelly Kagan (1984), 'Does Consequentialism Demand too Much? Recent Work on the Limits of Obligation'. *Philosophy and Public Affairs* 13: 239–54; Shelly Kagan (1989), *The Limits of Morality*. Oxford: Clarendon Press.

15 Matthew Tedesco (2011), 'Intuitions and the Demands of Consequentialism'. *Utilitas* 23: 94–104.

16 Thomas Nagel (1993), 'Moral Luck' in D. Statman, ed., *Moral Luck*. New York: State University of New York Press, pp. 57–71.:

17 Bernard Mandeville (1988), *The Fable of the Bees*. Indianapolis, IN: Liberty Fund.

18 This is similar to the observation that if institutions are evaluated over the long term, not merely in particular cases, then consequentialism may be much more intuitively plausible than otherwise. See notably John Stuart Mill (1998 [1871]), *Utilitarianism*. Oxford: Oxford University Press and John Rawls (1955), 'Two Concepts of Rules.' *Philosophical Review*; 64: 3–32. As discussed, this very important observation cannot, however, by itself ground a compelling answer to the moral agent question.

19 Adam Smith (1976). An *Inquiry into the Nature and Causes of the Wealth of Nations*. Indianapolis, IN: Liberty Fund.

20 A recent discussion of the logic and challenges for such a move is Brad Hooker (2000), *Ideal Code, Real World: A Rule-Consequentialist Theory of Morality*. Oxford: Oxford University Press.

21 Or at least, if such a claim only seems plausible of some societies and less so of others, then consider someone in a society where the empirical claim is plausible. It would be bizarre to hold such an empirical claim impossible.

22 Rawls, *A Theory of Justice*, p. 45.

23 Or one could determine evaluations by reference to a single agent, where the first part of the clause here would be 'An agent is morally good if he/she would generally bring about the best consequences was he/she to face situations represented by ...'.

24 This shares partial similarities with Hurka's 'intrinsic consequentialism'. See for instance his (2001) *Virtue, Vice, and Value*. Oxford: Oxford University Press.

Chapter two

1 Consequentialist disagree, of course, as to what is right – whether it is single actions or those as a set arising from a rule, motive or virtue – and as to whether it is actual or expected consequences that count, and as to how to understand the good (and its promotion). Despite this variety the theory has a remarkably coherent structure.

2 At the risk of becoming tiresomeley repetitive: this framing is not meant to exclude rule, motive, vitue or combination variants of consequentialism. For such theories, the term 'actions' in these generic desciptions refers to *the set of actions* actually or expectedly arising from the stipulated features, i.e. the rules, motives or virtues.

3 My own opinion is that the exclusion of non-human animals from the overall good cannot be non-arbitrarily justified. Since, however, this question does not bear on motivation ethics specifically, it is not taken up properly here. The basic case, however, perhaps most succinctly yet very clearly put, is in Peter Singer (1993), *Practical Ethics*. Cambridge: Cambridge University Press. See also Peter Singer (ed.) (1985), *In Defense of Animals: The Second Wave*. Oxford: Blackwell.

4 See Nagel, 'Moral Luck', pp. 61–2. Since such luck does not undercut the agent evaluations, it poses no special problems for the theory.

5 Williams, *Moral Luck*, pp. 101–13.

6 Evaluative coherence is a general relationship, not necessarily about isolated cases. Yet the feature that produces this case – false empirical beliefs – could well be systematic across cases, thus this observation doesn't address the worry.

7 Adams, 'Motive Utilitarianism', p. 470.

8 This question will obviously also depend on one's wealth and income due to the diminishing marginal personal welfare of income.

9 Excepting the rare situations where this isn't a reliable expected means to better promote the good of others, on this see the subsequent section on motive fetishism.

10 Where it doesn't make a difference to how we would have lived otherwise is one of those rare but important situations where promoting the good of others does not track promoting the good (imagine a hermit on an uninhabited animal-free desert island). As noted before, technically the correct formulation here of the moral goal is to promote 'the good'; the 'good of others' reflects the fact that normally being more motivated to promote the good is to be more motivated to promote the good of others. Yet this is not necessarily always the case.

11 I'm grateful to Simon Beard for this delightful illustrative example.

12 Samuel Scheffler (1982), *The Rejection of Consequentialism*. Oxford: Oxford University Press, p. 14.

13 This is also similar to the idea that right actions might not be those that are consequentially optimal but rather 'good enough' or 'sufficient' somehow. These will suffer analogous problems as Scheffler's suggestion.

14 There is a range close to zero, both positive and negative, where these judgements are functionally equivalent as neither morally bad nor good.

15 These numbers are selected for expositional clarity and to not give the illusion of more certainty than is warranted (one can always re-base the scale to 100 or to whatever one likes, but as such the difference between a 25 and a 28 may mislead as to how confident we can be in such small increments).

16 Aristotle, *Nichomachean Ethics*, Terence Irwin, trans. Indianapolis, IN: Hackett, see especially Book I. A modern account grounded in flourishing or living well, and its application to a specific problem, is Rosalind Hursthouse (1991), 'Virtue Theory and Abortion'. *Philosophy and Public Affairs* 20 (3): 223–46.

17 Alasdair MacIntyre (2007), *After Virtue*. Notre Dame, IN: Notre Dame University Press. MacIntyre has a rich conception of a practice, additionally holding that the virtues necessary for obtaining the goods internal to a practice also contribute to a good life that itself makes sense within an ongoing social tradition.

18 MacIntyre argues that virtues can be partially divided into those appropriate to a role (such as the Homeric virtues), those allowing the achievement of a human goal (such as of Aristotle), and those useful in achieving success (such as of Franklin).

19 All of these conditions can actually arguably be found in Aristotle (a role-specific virtue might lie in the practical wisdom appropriate to rulers, for instance), although contemporary theories disagree as to which offers the primary, or best, account. For a very clear survey of the sheer range of theories self-classifying as virtue ethics see Daniel Statman's introduction to (1997) *Virtue Ethics: A Critical Reader*. Washington, DC: Georgetown University Press, pp. 1–41.

20 See for instance Harold Alderman (1982), 'By Virtue of a Virtue'. *The Review of Metaphysics* 36: 127–53.

21 Plato (2004), *The Republic*, C. D. C. Reeve, trans. Indianapolis, IN: Hackett.

22 Michael Slote (2001), *Morals from Motives*. Oxford: Oxford University Press.

23 Ibid., p. 180.

24 See for instance the discussion in Singer, *Practical Ethics*, notably pp. 8–15. For Singer, 'The universal aspect of ethics, I suggest, does provide a persuasive though not conclusive, reason for taking a broadly utilitarian position.' This, I think, is not quite right: what he is arguing for is that the good of all be the determinant of evaluation, where the interests of all are taken into account equally. But this does not at all entail that the primary object of evaluation be actions, as the proposal of motivation ethics makes clear.

Chapter three

1   To repeat: consequentialism is an action morality even for those variants that focus on rules, motives, virtues or combinations thereof, as for all of these it is the set of actions (with their consequences) that ultimately determine the moral evaluation.
2   Thomas Nagel (1979) *Mortal Questions*. Cambridge: Cambridge University Press.
3   Jarvis Thompson (1985), 'The Trolley Problem', p. 1409.
4   Bernard Williams in Smart and Williams, *Utilitarianism*, pp. 97–9. Williams is not arguing for deontology here, though the force of the example is recognizably deontological.
5   Thomas Nagel (1986), *The View From Nowhere*. Oxford: Oxford University Press, p. 176.
6   The discussion of harm-based deontology here follows that of Kagan. See in particular pp. 70–105 of Shelly Kagan (1998), *Normative Ethics*. Boulder, CO: Westview Press.
7   Rawls makes this point more strongly: 'It should be noted that deontological theories are defined as non-teleological ones, not as views that characterise the rightness of institutions and acts independently from their consequences. All ethical doctrines worth our attention take consequences into account in judging rightness. One which did not would simply be irrational, crazy.' Rawls, *A Theory of Justice* p. 26.
8   Consequentialism might well agree with deontology on some of these cases, but the reason it would agree would be very different. For consequentialism it would be that not harming the person leads to the best overall consequences. For deontology it would be that harming them is forbidden *even if* it might lead to the best consequences.
9   The rights-based approach may seek to ground relatively stringent constraints on the state in particular; see for instance Robert Nozick (1974), *Anarchy, State and Utopia*. New York: Basic.
10 On the Doctrine of Doing and Allowing, see Quinn 'Actions, Intentions, and Consequences: The Doctrine of Doing and Allowing', pp. 287–312 and the contrast with the distinction between an act and its unwelcome but unavoidable side effects in Quinn, 'Actions, Intentions, and Consequences: The Doctrine of Double Effect', pp. 334–51.

11 That is, it doesn't first give an account of a morally good agent and then identify as right (or wrong) what such an agent would always do (or avoid).
12 Or instead of a motivation to do her duty, it could be a motivation not personally to harm others etc.
13 We could of course reject evaluative coherence such that doing what is morally forbidden would still be morally good (ie expected of a morally good agent), but if so the problems discussed in Chapter 1 would apply.
14 Specifically, that reason supplies us with our duties and at the same time supplies our motive for doing them (that they are not done from 'inclination'). This twin idea is stated somewhat differently depending on which formulation of the categorical imperative is being discussed, but the idea is consistent. That, for instance, 'where the proper worth of an absolutely good will – a worth raised above all price – consists just in the principle of the action being free from all influences of contingent grounds, which only experience can furnish" – Immanuel Kant (1997), *Groundwork of the Metaphysics of Morals*, Mary Gregor, (ed.) Cambridge: Cambridge University Press, p. 35 – or that 'We have also shown how neither fear nor inclination but simply respect for the law is that incentive which can give actions a moral worth', ibid., p. 46. The common distinction here is the difference between acting in conformity with duty (i.e. doing what is right), and of acting from duty. Only the latter has moral worth (see for instance the statement at ibid., p. 19).
15 I personally cannot see how precisely the argument for side constraints from the nature of a good will could be justified. It is very easy to re-describe side constraints in will-like terms, such as treating people as an ends not a means, or respecting their separateness as persons, or legislating that certain acts are forbidden. But these just push the justification back one stage: if respecting the separateness of persons could cause more overall harm than not doing so, what justifies this etc.? However, these problems – of the precise justification of a deontological will-based theory – are not specific to the moral agent question, and might just reflect a lack of insight or understanding on the part of those of us who cannot see how this argument is precisely supposed to work. And furthermore if the argument could work it would be breathtakingly brilliant. For these reasons this book's main focus is thus on the problems of moral agent evaluation, problems a will-based deontology in principle has the resources to overcome.
16 Such a theory would obviously need to stipulate what 'doing' harm to others involved, presumably with the same sort of distinction as with a harm-based deontology, such as for instance that allowing something was not doing it.
17 Scheffler, *The Rejection of Consequentialism*.
18 This is not, note, the same as weakness of will. One's will aims at an action. One's motivations are potentially plural and aim at features of outcomes (in other words, one wills that one do X; one's motivation is that Y obtains).
19 These cases are somewhat hard to intuit based on common experience as such a will seems remarkably rare, as Kant himself noted (Kant, *Groundwork of the Metaphysics of Morals*, p. 20):

> And then nothing can protect us against falling away completely from our ideas of duty and can preserve in our soul a well-grounded respect for its law other than the clear conviction that, even if there never have been actions arising from such pure sources, what is at issue here is not whether this or that happened; that, instead, reason by itself and independently of all appearances commands what ought to happen; that, accordingly, actions of which the world has perhaps so far given no example, and whose very practicability might be very much doubted by one who bases everything on experience, are still inflexibly commanded by reason.

The potential rarity of people acting morally is not a problem given Kant's project of deriving duties from our nature as rational beings. It is only if one adopts the goal of providing comparative human evaluations that difficulties arise – see Chapter 4 for a discussion of this choice.

20 Strictly speaking, a will-based deontology need not have the good of to whom we act as the determinant of evaluation – the good will could cause us to protect something else. In practice, however, all such theories do (no theory holds, for instance, that the rights people have are things that are bad for them, or that it is always impermissible to relieve someone's suffering). Still, if the will-based deontology could not show that the good will leads us to protect aspects of the good of to whom we act then the classification should be revised (and this would presumably be a big problem for such a theory, for it either would cease to be recognizably deontological or would seem perverse – such as if harming people was a duty).

21 Steven Severdlik, for instance, has argued at length that action evaluations do seem intuitively to *sometimes* depend on the motivations involved and that a range of arguments for why motives never make a difference to the deontic status of actions should be rejected. See Steven Sverdlik (1996), 'Motive and Rightness'. *Ethics* 106: 327–49 and Steven Sverdlik (2011), *Motive and Rightness*. Oxford: Oxford University Press. Sverdlik's focus, however, does not really support motivation ethics, as his is more a permissive argument: motives can make a difference sometimes. This is very different to one of the main claims of motivation ethics: that motives are central to agent and action evaluation in general.

22 My own opinion is 'perhaps yes'. If true, Rawls' key move in his 'Two Concepts of Rules', pp. 3–32, does not in fact address the underlying philosophical worry.

23 Peter Singer (2005), 'Ethics and Intuitions'. *Journal of Ethics* 9: 348.

24 Mathew Tadesco (2011), 'Intuitions and the Demands of Consequentialism'. *Utilitas* 23 (1): 102.

25 Rawls, *A Theory of Justice*, p. 20.

26 Or more precisely perhaps a small set of conclusions.

27 Russell Hardin (1988), *Morality Within the Limits of Reason*. Chicago, IL: Chicago University Press, p. 189.

28 Infinitism is possibly the least well known of these positions, and by far the most recent to receive prominence. See notably Peter Klein (1999), 'Human Knowledge and the Infinite Regress of Reasons'. *Nous* 33: 297–325.

Chapter four

1. Kagan's initial formulation includes the clause 'of those acts not otherwise forbidden', but for clarity the more simple definition is used here (and nothing is meant to hang on this simplification): Kagan, *The Limits of Morality*, p. 1. His important substantive point, however, is that if a deontological theory also holds that one has a duty to promote the good, save for when acts are forbidden, then it too may be incredibly demanding.
2. Ibid., p. 21.
3. For the positive case, see perhaps most famously Peter Singer (1972), 'Famine, Affluence and Morality'. *Philosophy and Public Affairs* 1: 229–43. Integrating both strategic and psychological considerations may somewhat reduce the demandingness even of standard variants of consequentialism, see Hardin, *Morality Within the Limits of Reason*. Influential suggestions for how to reform the theory to make it less so include, via agent permissions, the revised edition of Samuel Scheffler (1994), *The Rejection of Consequentialism*. Oxford: Clarendon Press. Via indirect rule variants, Hooker, *Ideal Code, Real World*, or via some form of satisficing, see Michael Slote (1984), 'Satisficing Consequentialism'. *Proceedings of the Aristotelian Society* 58: 139–63 and the discussion in Philip Pettit (1984), 'Satisficing Consequentialism'. *Proceedings of the Aristotelian Society* 58: 165–76.
4. An argument for the potential demandingness – in addition to consequentialism – of our post-scrutiny basic moral values is Peter Unger (1996), *Living High and Letting Die*. New York: Oxford University Press.
5. Kagan, 'Does Consequentialism Demand Too Much?', p. 254.
6. The central premise of Kagan's book is that the intermediate position between the minimalist and the extremist is impossible to simultaneously defend against both extremes.
7. Perhaps most influentially, Williams, 'A Critique of Utilitarianism', pp. 77–150; Williams, 'Persons, Character, and Morality'. There are a range of suggestions for how precisely to understand the point Williams is making. Chapell, for instance, has argued that William's integrity objection depends on acceptance of the internal reasons thesis and suggested the key component is best thought of a type of autonomy. Timothy Chappell (2007), 'Integrity and Demandingness'. *Ethical Theory and Moral Practice* 10 (3). For present purposes, so long as the relevant understanding of integrity imposes some constraints on what can be morally required to be compromised or violated the Sacrifice Condition would still require the rejection of extremism.
8. There are additionally a series of further more general problems for a moral theory that rejects evaluative coherence, see the arguments of section 1.2 for instance. However, since rejecting the principle removes in large part the specific problem of extremism (because fulfilling the demands of morality or doing what is morally required is not what one needs to do to live a morally good life or be a morally good agent: that is something much less demanding), this chapter leaves discussion of these issues mostly to one side.

9   The term 'absolutism' is sometimes used to refer to deontological theories where the side-constraints are inviolable no matter what the overall level of harm produced, throughout this chapter however it refers to non-comparativist evaluations, that is those that do not implicitly or explicitly reference a distribution.

10 See also the discussion of section 3.4.

11 Indeed, the notion of being a 'mild' misanthrope may already implicitly concede compartivism on this criterion at least, as we are implicitly comparing their loathing for others to some general human variance.

12 On all three see the account of moral progress and failure of section 2.4.

13 One can, of course, try to create such a formula, see Chapter 2, but this may come with a loss of nuance and richness.

14 A related discussion with regard to special relationships is in Chapter 5.

15 John Mackie (1977), *Ethics: Inventing Right and Wrong*. London: Pelican, p. 38. Comparativism, I think, may perhaps help with both his concerns, that of the metaphysical status of moral entities, and the epistemological question of how we can know about them.

16 This worry only applies if the relevant metric is scalar rather than a single property (such as having a 'good will').

17 Extremism is a much broader position than consequentialism (as Kagan notes, it may include a range of deontological views too), but it shares consequentialism's 'action morality' structure, and that is what creates all the agent evaluation difficulties.

Chapter five

1   Not all special relationships are positive: they may be abusive or fuelled by a particular loathing and hatred of some other person. Such relationships seem less problematic, however, as we view them negatively and if an impartial morality does so too then there is no apparent normative conflict. Thus this chapter focuses on positive instances.

2   If the particular person were easily substitutable for others then the subsequent worries might be lessened; for why a shared history potentially prevents this see, Niko Kolodny (2003), 'Love as Valuing a Relationship'. *The Philosophical Review* 112 (2).

3   By motivates us 'to Z' I mean here very roughly that it becomes either more probable that we will Z, or more easy for us to Z (and sometimes harder for us to not Z) than if we lacked that motivation. Relationships that do not motivate us to promote the other person's interests are not considered as they do not appear to create the problems canvassed (we may have a cordial relationship with someone but not be motivated to show them partiality in what we do: if so the conflict with equal concern is not evident).

4   The notion of impartiality can be decidedly ambiguous. The claim, for example, that 'it is morally permissible to show greater concern towards

white people' is clearly not impartial, but the claim that 'it is morally permissible to show greater concern towards one's own race' is impartial in a sense – in that it is not in principle biased towards any one race or set of people – but is not impartial in the morally relevant way, as is clear by its conflict with a principle of equal moral concern for all. The formulation of being justifiable based on 'an equal concern for all', which is meant to convey the same basic idea as impartiality, is used in contexts where it is more clear or less liable to ambiguous interpretation.

5 This is, I think, best seen as an instance of the more general demandingness worry of Chapter 4.
6 Wolf's characterization of such relationships as 'among the greatest goods in life' does not seem wildly implausible: Susan Wolf (1992), 'Morality and Partiality'. *Philosophical Perspectives* 6, Ethics: 243–59, 243.
7 This is Railton's core argument concerning alienation, see Peter Railton (1984), 'Alienation, Consequentialism, and the Demands of Morality'. *Philosophy and Public Affairs*, 13 (2). Yet, as noted subsequently, even though our special relationships might – given the right empirics – turn out to be justified impartially based on the interests of all, this is a decidedly contingent possibility, and seems furthermore, in the current world, empirically unlikely.
8 Both claims are made by Sidgwick and Mill, see for instance Sidgwick's claim that 'generally speaking, each man is better able to provide for his own happiness than that of other persons, from his more intimate knowledge of his own desires and needs, and his greater opportunities for gratifying them'. Sidgwick, *The Methods of Ethics*, p. 431 and his discussion of pp. 430–6, and for instance Mill's judgement that 'the occasions on which any person (except one in a thousand) has it in his power to do this on an extended scale, in other words to be a public benefactor, are but exceptional … in every other case, private utility, the interest or happiness of some few persons, is all he has to attend to'. Mill, *Utilitarianism*, p. 66. Yet both are importantly contingent, and seem false in a very large set of cases.
9 Jack appears to have better motivations on an indirect consequentialist account too: if everyone in developed countries gave money to charity to spite their children then a great, great many lives would likely be saved.
10 Let us assume those in each boats are of similar age and other demographic fundamentals.
11 Williams famously uses the example of a man who sees his wife drowning to highlight that it is the man acting out of partiality and simply motivated by a concern for his wife that seems appropriate, 'it might be hoped by some (for instance, by his wife) that his motivating thought, fully spelled out, would be the thought that it was his wife, not that it was his wife and that in situations of this kind it is permissible to save one's wife'. Williams, 'Persons, Character, and Morality', p. 18.
12 The structural identity between the argument made here and that of Chapter 1 is hopefully relatively clear.
13 Note that sometimes agents can change their features based on the situations

they tend to or expect to face. For simplicity I illustrate with an agent who is unchanging, though the basic point does not depend on this restriction.

14 See also the earlier worries with this type of response, for instance sections 1.2 and 3.5.

15 As subsequently discussed, motivation ethics does provide a framework for thinking about non-moral motivations that nonetheless have concern for some particular individual as the focus. However, for those persuaded by the Intuition Regress Problem of Chapter 3, this is best seen as a side-effect of the theory, one whose degree of intuitive plausibility should not count for or against the theory's acceptance.

16 By way of contrast, for an attempt to link love for a particular individual to a more general recognition of their (bare Kantian) moral worth, see David Velleman (1999), 'Love as a Moral Emotion'. *Ethics* 109 (2).

17 I am indebted here to Kolodny's discussion of valuing the particular via a relationship and shared past. See Kolodny, 'Love as Valuing a Relationship'.

Chapter six

1 A famous classic statement is in Singer, 'Famine, Affluence and Morality'. pp. 229–43.

2 Loren Lomasky, 'Toward a Liberal Theory of National Boundaries' in David Miller and Sohail H. Hashmi, eds. (2001), *'Boundaries and Justice: Diverse Ethical Perspectives*. Princeton, NJ: Princeton University Press, pp. 55–78.

3 See Ronald Dworkin (1986), *Law's Empire*. Cambridge, MA: Harvard University Press. The group here is grounded in a similar concept of association as that commonly attributed to families and to friends.

4 John Rawls (1999), *The Law of Peoples*. Cambridge, MA: Harvard University Press), in particular pp. 23–30.

5 Thomas Nagel (2005), 'The Problem of Global Justice'. *Philosophy and Public Affairs* 33: 113–47.

6 Michael Blake (2001), 'Distributive Justice, State Coercion, and Autonomy'. *Philosophy & Public Affairs* 30: 257–96.

7 For some scepticism about their success at such tasks see for instance A. J. Julius (2006), 'Nagel's Atlas'. *Philosophy and Public Affairs* 34: 176–92 and Joshua Cohen and Charles Sabel (2006), 'Extra Rempublicam Nulla Justia?' *Philosophy and Public Affairs* 34: 147–75 both on Nagel, 'The Problem of Global Justice', or Arash Abizadeh (2007), 'Cooperation, Pervasive Impact, and Coercion: On the Scope (not Site) of Distributive Justice'. *Philosophy and Public Affairs* 35: 318–58, on Blake, 'Distributive Justice, State Coercion, and Autonomy'.

8 An extended discussion is David Heyd (1982), *Supererogation: Its Status in Ethical Theory*. Cambridge: Cambridge University Press. For some theories this category may be empty, and nothing in what follows is meant to hang on whether or not it is assumed to be or not.

9   In general the illustrative examples will draw on the left-cosmopolitan assumption of some basic welfare duties, but the argument can be re-run with right-cosmopolitan duties, and this important view is not meant to be sidelined. The left cosmopolitan position does appear, however, to be much more widely avocated in the literature.

10 I assume here such duties are to provide benefits to those in greatest need, or those who can be helped most easily. The examples can however easily be altered to other conceptions.

11 That is, for instance, that two identical agents (identical motivations, beliefs, inclinations, values, emotions, goals, etc.) should not be overall evaluated contradictorily based solely on where they live.

12 See in this vein, among a large literature, Larry Bartels (2008), *Unequal Democracy: The Political Economy of the New Guilded Age*. Princeton, NJ: Princeton University Press.

13 Those in democratic societies with most influence over the institutions are possibly, in order of sway, the politicians in power, then the political class in general (and those with large private resources), then the media and commentariat, then those regularly involved in politics in the widest sense, and then the electorate. To morally evaluate a nation's institutions and behavior is thus to evaluate to different extents such individuals, and those who could assume these positions.

Chapter seven

1   Parts of this chapter are adapted from my (2011) 'On the Value of Political Legitimacy' published in *Politics, Philosophy and Economics* 10 (4), doi: 10.1177/1470594X10387272. I'm grateful to the editors for allowing the inclusion of the sections here.

2   Scepticism about such theories often worries that the stipulated conditions are in fact never met, or met in ways that invalidate the overall claim. Perhaps the earliest example of such a critique is David Hume (1985), 'Of the Original Contract' in *David Hume: Essays Moral, Political and Literary*, (ed.) E. F. Miller. Indianapolis, IN: Liberty Classics.

3   A coherent anarchist position is that legitimate government is not necessarily undesirable but rather, in modern states, simply unachievable in that it could only ever be grounded on actual explicit freely given consent. This seems compatible with the central arguments of both Simmons and Green in their scepticism about whether we have ever (and plausibly, for most people, will ever) meaningfully consent to a state in a way that would correctly obligate one. See A. John Simmons (2001), *Justification and Legitimacy: Essays on Rights and Obligations*. Cambridge: Cambridge University Press and Leslie Green (1989), *The Authority of the State*. Oxford: Oxford University Press.

4   A. John Simmons (1999), 'Justification and Legitimacy'. *Ethics* 109: 739–71, p. 746.

5   David Estlund (2008), *Democratic Authority: A Philosophical Framework*. Princeton, NJ: Princeton University Press, p. 2.

6   These consequences could be due to the particular instance of the punishment, or more generally due to the set of instances falling under the punishment rule as an institutional policy: see Rawls, 'Two Concepts of Rules', pp. 3–32.

7   The problem doesn't require acceptance of these particular examples: it arises for any desert or consequence based theory of punishment irrespective of the specific content.

8   'Those affected' may include giving extra consideration to the agent's own prudential concerns: the argument is not meant to assume a strong impartiality where the interests of the agent are only given the same weight as those of all others in assessing what should be done. It is thus intended to be perfectly compatible with what Scheffler has called an agent-centered prerogative or indeed with a mixed-motive moral agent (on both see Chapter 2). Scheffler, *The Rejection of Consequentialism*.

9   Robert Paul Wolff (1970), *In Defense of Anarchism*. New York: Harper & Row.

10 An extremely cogent modern account is A. J. Simmons (1979), *Moral Principles and Political Obligations*. Princeton, NJ: Princeton University Press. Such scepticism seems, however, to be faced with repeated challenges: witness for example consent re-emerging in Gilbert's account of obligation as joint commitment. Margaret Gilbert (2006), *A Theory of Political Obligation: Membership, Commitment, and the Bonds of Society*. Oxford: Oxford University Press.

11 This, I think it is fair to say, is both the most widespread current assumption about legitimate government, and true of arguably the most impressive recent accounts in the literature. An illuminating comparison of two is Thomas Christiano (2009), 'Debate: Estlund on Democratic Authority'. *The Journal of Political Philosophy* 17: 228–40 and David Estlund (2009), 'Debate: On Christiano's 'The Constitution of Equality'. *The Journal of Political Philosophy* 17: 241–52.

12 A Fridocracy would seem to be illegitimate for Christiano, for instance, as such a state explicitly does not treat citizens publicly equally, affirming the unequal political status of its non-Friday-born citizens. See Thomas Christiano (2008), *The Constitution of Equality: Democratic Authority and Its Limits*. Oxford: Oxford University Press. A Fridocracy might also be illegitimate for Rawls: subjects not born on a Friday seem to be able to reasonably reject a constitutional order affording them no voting rights nor political influence. See John Rawls (1993), *Political Liberalism*. New York: Columbia University Press.

13 Though arguably eclipsed in the recent literature by proceduralists, legitimacy as consent has both a long and extremely influential lineage capturing two very powerful ideas. The first, drawing on Locke, is that we have some pre-political rights that we must consent for government to violate (which government typically will): John Locke (1988), *Two Treatise of Government*,

(ed.) P. Laslett. Cambridge: Cambridge University Press. The second, drawing on Rousseau, holds that legitimate governance requires a certain type of participation, as this is the only way to enjoy the value of freedom as self-rule: Jean-Jacques Rousseau (1988), *On The Social Contract*, (ed.) D. Cress. Indianapolis, IN: Hackett.

14 I am very grateful to the first anonymous reviewer for my *Politics, Philosophy and Economics* article 'On the Value of Political Legitimacy' for suggesting that this response may be at the back of many readers' minds.

15 I think this is the central thrust of Senor's response to Simmons when he worries that political duties may be more extensive than basic moral duties, although his account is not explicit on whether one would only have these duties under legitimate government (if they hold under all governments then they have no implications for legitimacy per se, thus for the sake of argument let us assume some duties that go beyond our basic moral ones do indeed depend upon legitimate government to be required). See Thomas Senor (1987), 'What if there are no Political Obligations? A Reply to A. J Simmons'. *Philosophy and Public Affairs* 16: 260–8.

16 Estlund, *Democratic Authority*, p. 8.

17 Ibid., p. 7.

18 Joseph Raz (1986), *The Morality of Freedom*. Oxford: Oxford University Press, pp. 70–1.

19 Assuming the expected errors are correlated. If not, one should take an appropriately weighted mixture of them.

20 See Keith Baker (1976), *Condorcet: Selected Writings*. Indianapolis, IN: Bobbs-Merill, pp. 33–70.

21 There are a range of ways of relaxing these conditions, for instance by requiring the *average* probability of being right to be over a half. See for instance Bernard Grofman, Guillermo Owen and Scott Feld (1983), 'Thirteen Theorems in Search of the Truth'. *Theory and Decision* 15: 261–78.

22 For relaxing the binary question assumption see Christian List and Robert Goodin, 'Epistemic Democracy: Generalizing the Condorcet Jury Theorem'. *Journal of Political Philosophy* 9 (3): 277–306.

23 If, as a jurisdiction approaches a million voters, the probability a majority will be correct approaches one, then the probability that two jurisdictions each of well over a million voters will disagree should be close to zero. To illustrate the obvious potential problem with this: Texas and California are large jurisdictions; they frequently disagree (over president and a range of policies). If the CJT were true and established the very high probability of majorities being correct then their disagreement should be spectacularly rare. In fact it is common.

24 For an excellent survey of the recent main US data see, for instance, Andrew Gelman (2008), *Red State, Blue State, Rich State, Poor State: Why Americans Vote the Way They Do*. Princeton, NJ: Princeton University Press.

25 Bernard Manin (1997), *The Principles of Representative Government*. Princeton, NJ: Princeton University Press, p. 86.

Chapter eight

1. The logic of this chapter builds upon my *Utilitas* article 'Interpersonal Comparisons of the Good: Epistemic not Impossible'. *Utilitas* 28 (3): 288–313, and readers furthermore looking for formal proofs of the subsequent ordinal epistemic principle and the claims relating to Arrow's Impossibility Theorem can also find them there.
2. Sometimes these debates are framed in terms of 'welfare', sometimes 'utility', sometimes as with previously in this book 'the good'. In this chapter, whichever best fits the context will be used, and nothing is meant to hang on this.
3. Lionel Robbins (1962), *An Essay on the Nature and Significance of Economic Science*. London: Macmillan, p. 140. And see Chapter 6 for the general discussion.
4. Stanley Jevons (1871), *Theory of Political Economy*. Macmillan: London, p. 21.
5. Nozick, *Anarchy, State and Utopia*, p. 41.
6. Kenneth Arrow (1963), *Social Choice and Individual Values*. New York: John Wiley & Sons: p. 9.
7. Ibid., p. 11.
8. This can be proved in either an expected value or a credence framework, for such a demonstration of the former see my 'Interpersonal Comparisons of the Good: Epistemic not Impossible'. *Utilitas* 28 (3): 288–313.
9. John Harsanyi (1955), 'Cardinal Welfare, Individualistic Ethics, and Interpersonal Comparisons of Utility'. *The Journal of Political Economy* 63 (4): 309–21, p. 317.
10. See Raz, *The Morality of Freedom* and Amartya Sen (1999), *Development as Freedom*. Oxford: Oxford University Press.
11. Obviously, there exist theories that take various traditional beliefs – such as over the superiority of certain races – and try to systemize them into a moral theory. However, as soon as one demands why that particular distinction is justified, such theories quickly collapse into assertion or evasion.
12. At one point I didn't plan to include this section, as it seemed so obvious that Arrow's Theorem was irrelevant to social welfare and interpersonal comparisons. However, when presenting an early version of the argument to a group of mainly social choice theorists the very first question was 'You know this is all impossible right?' Most people in the room seemed to agree. Thus there is perhaps some value in explicitly setting out why this isn't impossible, and why it matters that the premises of formal results are coherently motivated.
13. For a formal proof of this in a credence framework see my *Utilitas* paper, 'Interpersonal Comparisons of the Good'.
14. See Arrow, *Social Choice and Individual Values*, with the key section at pp. 26–8 and Kenneth Arrow (1950), 'A Difficulty in the Concept of Social

Welfare'. *Journal of Political Economy* 58 (4): 328–46, where the IIA is presented as non-crazy by appeal to intuitions about election candidates, with no justification based on welfare at all, at p. 337.

Conclusions

1. The case both against legitimacy as a separate realm of evaluation and for the meaningfulness of the overall good were necessary to support motivation ethics, but in principle permissive of other options too.
2. Again, it is important to state that these descriptions refer to the structural option, not all theories that so self-describe. While a theory that holds that certain character virtues allow their possessor to lead a good life is a virtue ethics theory (at least in the Platonic, Aristotelian, Epicurean and Stoic traditions), this is not necessarily true of every possible theory self-described as a virtue ethics theory.
3. A second distinct possible strand of justification instead seeks to systemize our ethical intuitions. A critique of this was in Chapter 3.
4. The word 'seem' in this sentence is important: for a will-based deontology aims to show that the restriction isn't arbitrary as it isn't based purely on the good in question but on practical reason / rational willing / self-legislating etc. Thus, as noted, the ME case against such a theory is one of default and in principle could be fully addressed.

Epilogue

1. Or watch the adverts on children's TV.
2. The problem for consequentialism with endorsing the laissez-faire instrumentalism option, as such, was not that the evaluations were arbitrary, but that the option entailed everyone could be a morally good agent, even if always doing what is morally wrong, creating a whole series of prescriptive and other problems.
3. One option would be to define how individuals' lives go as the relevant object and to exclude eye-colour as a possible feature. Perhaps this might work with the particular example if it could meet the worry that we have simply defined things in a way to produce the desired result. Even if this could deal with green-eyed weighting, however, it does not address the underlying problem: we could still 'over-weight' some feature that was included.
4. The first clause is, of course, both a simplification of Newton's law of gravity, and not a good description under relativity. It is included for expositional simplicity. Nothing substantive in this chapter's argument hangs on this.
5. Because Gravity-2040 is phrased somewhat vaguely, this entailment leaves out some detail. The first clause should actually stipulate that the mass of the Earth and the apple divided by the square of the distance between them is

greater than that of other object-combinations pulling the Earth or the apple in alternative directions (and modified depending on the angle of the other directions). The overall idea is, however, hopefully clear.

6   Carl Hempel (1945), 'Studies in the Logic of Confirmation'. *Mind* 54 (1–26): pp. 97–121.
7   See Nelson Goodman (1946), 'A Query on Confirmation'. *Journal of Philosophy*: 43; and Nelson Goodman (1955), *Fact, Fiction and Forecast*. Cambridge: Cambridge University Press.
8   See, for instance, the debate as captured by (and indeed continuing after) Clark Glymour (1980), 'Hypothetico-Deductivism is Hopeless'. *Philosophy of Science* 47 (2).
9   An extremely clear and cogent example is Peter Godfrey-Smith (2003), *Theory and Reality*. Chicago, IL: Chicago University Press.

BIBLIOGRAPHY

Abizadeh, Arash. 2007. 'Cooperation, Pervasive Impact, and Coercion: On the Scope (not Site) of Distributive Justice'. *Philosophy and Public Affairs* 35: 318–58

Adams, Robert. 1976. 'Motive Utilitarianism'. *The Journal of Philosophy* 73: 467–81

Alderman, Harold. 1982. 'By Virtue of a Virtue'. *The Review of Metaphysics* 36: 127–53

Anscombe, G. E. M. 1958. 'Modern Moral Philosophy'. *Philosophy* 33 (124)

Aristotle. 1999. *Nichomachean Ethics*, trans. Terence Irwin. Indianapolis, IN: Hackett

Arrow, Kenneth. 1950. 'A Difficulty in the Concept of Social Welfare'. *Journal of Political Economy* 58 (4): 328–46

Arrow, Kenneth. 1963. *Social Choice and Individual Values*. New York: John Wiley & Sons

Baker, Keith. 1976. *Condorcet: Selected Writings*. Indianapolis, IN: Bobbs-Merill

Bartels, Larry. 2008. *Unequal Democracy: The Political Economy of the New Guilded Age*. Princeton, NJ: Princeton University Press

Bentham, Jeremy. 1988. *The Principles of Morals and Legislation*. Buffalo, NY: Prometheus

Blake, Michael. 2001. 'Distributive Justice, State Coercion, and Autonomy'. *Philosophy and Public Affairs* 30: 257–96.

Chappell, Timothy. 2007. 'Integrity and Demandingness'. *Ethical Theory and Moral Practice* 10 (3)

Christiano, Thomas. 2008. *The Constitution of Equality: Democratic Authority and Its Limits*. Oxford: Oxford University Press

Christiano, Thomas. 2009. 'Debate: Estlund on Democratic Authority'. *The Journal of Political Philosophy* 17: 228–40

Coakley, Mathew. 2011. 'On the Value of Political Legitimacy'. *Politics, Philosophy & Economics* 10: 345–69

Coakley, Mathew. 2016. 'Interpersonal Comparisons of the Good: Epistemic not Impossible'. *Utilitas* 28 (3): 288–313

Cohen, Joshua and Sabel, Charles. 2006. 'Extra Republican Nulla Justia?' *Philosophy and Public Affairs* 34: 147–75

Dworkin, Ronald. 1986. *Law's Empire*. Cambridge, MA: Harvard University Press

Estlund, David. 2008. *Democratic Authority: A Philosophical Framework*. Princeton, NJ: Princeton University Press

Estlund, David. 2009. 'Debate: On Christiano's *The Constitution of Equality*'. *The Journal of Political Philosophy* 17: 241–52

Foot, Philippa. 1967. 'The Problem of Abortion and the Doctrine of Double Effect'. *Oxford Review* 5
Gautthier, David. 1986. *Morals By Agreement*. Oxford: Oxford University Press
Gelman, Andrew. 2008. *Red State, Blue State, Rich State, Poor State: Why Americans Vote the Way They Do*. Princeton, NJ: Princeton University Press
Gilbert, Margaret. 2006. *A Theory of Political Obligation: Membership, Commitment, and the Bonds of Society*. Oxford: Oxford University Press
Godfrey-Smith, Peter. 2003. *Theory and Reality*. Chicago: Chicago University Press
Goodman, Nelson. 1946. 'A Query on Confirmation'. *Journal of Philosophy* 43
Goodman, Nelson. 1955. *Fact, Fiction and Forecast*. Cambridge: Cambridge University Press
Glymour, Clark. 1980. 'Hypothetico-Deductivism is Hopeless'. *Philosophy of Science* 47 (2)
Green, Leslie. 1989. *The Authority of the State*. Oxford: Oxford University Press
Griffin, James. 1986. *Well-Being*. Oxford: Oxford University Press
Griffin, James. 1992. 'The Human Good and the Ambitions of Consequentialism'. *Social Philosophy & Policy* 9 (2): 118–32
Grofman, Bernard, Owen, Guillermo and Feld, Scott. 1983. 'Thirteen Theorems in Search of the Truth'. *Theory and Decision* 15: 261–78
Hardin, Russell. 1988. *Morality Within the Limits of Reason*. Chicago: University of Chicago Press
Harsanyi, John. 1955. 'Cardinal Welfare, Individualistic Ethics, and Interpersonal Comparisons of Utility'. *The Journal of Political Economy* 63 (4): 309–21
Hempel, Carl. 1945. 'Studies in the Logic of Confirmation'. *Mind* 54 (1–26) 97–121
Heyd, David. 1982. *Supererogation: Its Status in Ethical Theory*. Cambridge: Cambridge University Press
Hooker, Brad. 1990. *Rule-Consequentialism*. Mind 99: 67–77
Hooker, Brad. 2000. *Ideal Code, Real World: A Rule-Consequentialist Theory of Morality*. Oxford: Oxford University Press
Hume, David. 1985. 'Of the Original Contract'. In *David Hume: Essays Moral, Political and Literary*, ed. E. F. Miller. Indianapolis, IN: Liberty Classics
Hurka, Thomas. 2001. *Virtue, Vice, and Value*. Oxford: Oxford University Press
Hursthouse, Rosalind. 1991. 'Virtue Theory and Abortion'. *Philosophy and Public Affairs* 20 (3): 223–46
Jamieson, Dale. 2007. 'When Utilitarians Should be Virtue Theorists'. *Utilitas* 19: 160–83
Jarvis Thompson, Judith. 1976. 'Killing, Letting Die, and the Trolley Problem'. *The Monist* 59
Jarvis Thompson, Judith. 1985. 'The Trolley Problem'. *The Yale Law Journal* 94 (6)
Jevons, Stanley. 1871. *Theory of Political Economy*. London: Macmillan
Julius, A. J. 2006. 'Nagel's Atlas'. *Philosophy and Public Affairs* 34: 176–92
Kagan, Shelly. 1984. 'Does Consequentialism Demand Too Much? Recent Work on the Limits of Obligation'. *Philosophy and Public Affairs* 13: 239–54
Kagan, Shelly. 1989. *The Limits of Morality*. Oxford: Clarendon Press
Kagan, Shelly. 1998. *Normative Ethics*. Boulder, CO: Westview Press
Kamm, Francis. 1989. 'Harming Some to Save Others'. *Philosophical Studies* 57 (3)

Kant, Immanuel. 1997. *Groundwork of the Metaphysics of Morals*, trans. Mary Gregor. Cambridge: Cambridge University Press
Klein, Peter. 1999. 'Human Knowledge and the Infinite Regress of Reasons'. *Nous* 33
Kolodny, Niko. 2003. 'Love as Valuing a Relationship'.*The Philosophical Review* 112 (2)
List, Christian and Goodin, Robert. 2001. 'Epistemic Democracy: Generalizing the Condorcet Jury Theorem'. *Journal of Political Philosophy* 9 (3): 277–306
Locke, John. 1988. *Two Treatise of Government*, ed. P. Laslett. Cambridge: Cambridge University Press
Lomasky, Loren. 2001. 'Toward a Liberal Theory of National Boundaries' in David Miller and Sohail H. Hashmi, eds. *Boundaries and Justice: Diverse Ethical Perspective*. Princeton, NJ: Princeton University Press, pp. 55–78
Louise, Jennie. 2006. 'Right Motive, Wrong Action: Direct Consequentialism and Evaluative Conflict'. *Ethical Theory and Moral Practice*, 9: 65–85
MacIntyre, Alasdair. 2007. *After Virtue*. Notre Dame, IN: University of Notre Dame Press
Mackie, John. 1977. *Ethics: Inventing Right and Wrong*. London: Pelican
Mandeville, Bernard. 1988. *The Fable of the Bees*. Indianapolis IN: Liberty Fund
Manin, Bernard. 1997. *The Principles of Representative Government*. Cambridge: Cambridge University Press
Mill, John Stuart. 1998 [1871]. *Utilitarianism*. Oxford: Oxford University Press
Nagel, Thomas. 1979. *Mortal Questions*. Cambridge: Cambridge University Press
Nagel, Thomas. 1986. *The View From Nowhere*. Oxford: Oxford University Press
Nagel, Thomas. 1993. 'Moral Luck' in D. Statman, ed. *Moral Luck*. New York: State University of New York Press, pp. 57–71
Nagel, Thomas. 2005. 'The Problem of Global Justice'. *Philosophy and Public Affairs* 33: 113–47
Nozick, Robert. 1974. *Anarchy, State and Utopia*. New York: Basic
Parfit, Derek. 1984. *Reasons and Persons*. Oxford: Oxford University Press
Pettit, Philip. 1984. 'Satisficing Consequentialism'. Proceedings of the Aristotelian Society 58: 165–76
Pettit, Philip and Smith, Michael. 2000. 'Global Consequentialism' in Brad Hooker, Elinor Mason and Dale Miller, eds. *Morality, Rules, and Consequences: A Critical Reader*. Edinburgh: Edinburgh University Press, pp. 121–33
Plato. 2004. *The Republic*, trans. C. D. C. Reeve. Hackett: Indianapolis IN
Quinn, Warren. 1989. 'Actions, Intentions, and Consequences: The Doctrine of Doing and Allowing'. *The Philosophical Review* 98 (3): 287–312
Quinn, Warren. 1989. 'Actions, Intentions, and Consequences: The Doctrine of Double Effect'. *Philosophy and Public Affairs* 18 (4): 334–51
Railton, Peter. 1984. 'Alienation, Consequentialism, and the Demands of Morality'. *Philosophy and Public Affairs* 13 (2)
Rawls, John. 1955. 'Two Concepts of Rules'. *Philosophical Review* 64: 3–32
Rawls, John. 1993. *Political Liberalism*. New York: Columbia University Press
Rawls, John. 1999. *The Law of Peoples*. Cambridge: Harvard University Press, MA
Rawls, John. 1999. *A Theory of Justice*. Cambridge, MA: Harvard University Press

Raz, Joseph. 1986. *The Morality of Freedom*. Oxford: Oxford University Press
Robbins, Lionel. 1962. *An Essay on the Nature and Significance of Economic Science*. London: Macmillan
Rousseau, Jean-Jacques. 1988. *On the Social Contract*, D. Cress ed. Indianapolis, IN: Hackett
Scheffler, Samuel. 1982. *The Rejection of Consequentialism*. Oxford: Oxford University Press
Scheffler, Samuel. 1994. *The Rejection of Consequentialism*, revised ed. Oxford: Clarendon Press
Senor, Thomas. 1987. 'What If There Are No Political Obligations? A Reply to A. J. Simmons'. *Philosophy and Public Affairs* 16: 260–8
Sidgwick, Henry. 1981. *The Methods of Ethics*. Indianapolis, IN: Hackett
Singer, Peter. 1972. 'Famine, Affluence and Morality'. *Philosophy and Public Affairs*, 1: 229–43
Singer, Peter. 1985. *In Defense of Animals: The Second Wave*. Oxford: Blackwell
Singer, Peter. 1993. *Practical Ethics*. Cambridge: Cambridge University Press
Singer, Peter. 2005. 'Ethics and Intuitions'. *Journal of Ethics 9*
Simmons, A. John. 1979. *Moral Principles and Political Obligation*. Princeton, NJ: Princeton University Press
Simmons, A. John. 1999. 'Justification and Legitimacy'. *Ethics* 109: 739–71
Simmons, A. John. 2001. *Justification and Legitimacy: Essays on Rights and Obligations*. Cambridge: Cambridge University Press
Slote, Michael. 1984. 'Satisficing Consequentialism'. *Proceedings of the Aristotelian Society*, 58: 139–63
Slote, Michael. 2001. *Morals from Motives*. Oxford: University Press Oxford
Smart, J. C. and Williams, Bernard. 1973. *Utilitarianism: For and Against*. Cambridge: Cambridge University Press
Smith, Adam. 1976. *An Inquiry into the Nature and Causes of the Wealth of Nations*. Indianapolis, IN: Liberty Fund
Statman, Daniel, ed. 1993. *Moral Luck*. New York: State University of New York Press
Statman, Daniel, ed. 1997. *Virtue Ethics. A Critical Reader*. Washington, DC: Georgetown University Press
Sverdlik, Steven. 1996. 'Motive and Rightness'. *Ethics*, 106: 327–49
Sverdlik, Steven. 2011. *Motive and Rightness*. Oxford: Oxford University Press
Tadesco, Matthew. 2011. 'Intuitions and the Demands of Consequentialism', *Utilitas* 23 (1): 94–104
Unger, Peter. 1996. *Living High and Letting Die*. New York: Oxford University Press
Velleman, David. 1999. 'Love as a Moral Emotion'. *Ethics* 109 (2)
Williams, Bernard. 1973. 'A Critique of Utilitarianism' in J. J. C. Smart and B. Williams, *Utilitarianism: For and Against*. Cambridge: Cambridge University Press, pp. 77–150.
Williams, Bernard. 1981. *Moral Luck*. Cambridge University Press: .Cambridge
Williams, Bernard. 1981. 'Persons, Character, and Morality' in Bernard Williams, *Moral Luck*. Cambridge: Cambridge University Press, pp. 1–19.
Wolf, Susan. 1992. 'Morality and Partiality'. *Philosophical Perspectives* 6, Ethics: 243–59
Wolff, Robert Paul. 1970. *In Defense of Anarchism*. New York: Harper & Row

INDEX

action vs agent primacy
  in moral evaluations 2–3, 4–6, 18–19, 59–61, 130–1, 141–2, 154–5
  psychological reactions to 104–5
agent-centred prerogative 79–80
alienation 134, 147–8
Arrow, Kenneth
  the Independence of Irrelevant Alternatives 200–3
  interpersonal comparisons scepticism 182
authority, epistemic 173–7

bi-conditional testing 226–7
Bob, the Agnostic 20

charity
  demandingness of 115–16
  and motivation ethics 68, 84
  state-based incentives for 156–7
comparativism
  arbitrariness worries 127–8
  distributions 120–1
  and indeterminacy 126–7
  outline of 117–19
  and realism 129
  and the status quo 123–4
Condorcet, Jury Theorem 176–7
consequentialism
  bestness 28–31
  and the egoist 19–20
  fundamentalist and the agnostic 20
  hybrid versions 55–6
  ideal agents 41
  indirect variants 34–6
  and instrumentalism 48–52
  long term actions 32–3
  subjective evaluations 33–4
cosmpolitanism
  duties 150–2
  left and right variants 149

deontology
  cases 92–3
  harm-based 93–6
  structural choices 92–3
  will-based 96–8
desert, counterfactual worries about 163–4
Difficulty Condition 115
Double Punishment 172

economics and interpersonal comparisons 204–6
egoistan 155–6
epistemic arbitrariness condition 226
epistemic interpersonal comparisons
  confidence in 191–2
  examples of 185–6
  need for 203–6
  principle 185
  string example 188–9
  word example 183–5
epistemic realism
  and arbitrariness 228–9
  outline of 227
evaluative coherence
  mirror theories 32
  options 26
  prescriptive ambiguity 25
  rightness line 27
  special relationships 140–1
extremism 113–14

Fridocracy 165–7

good, diversity of accounts of 190
Goodman, Nelson, and the New Riddle of Induction 230–1
green-eyed weighting
  coherence 218–19
  outline of 216
  non-arbitrariness 221–3

Harsanyi, John, and principle of unwarranted differentiation 186–7
hypothetical choice sets 38–9

Independence of Irrelevant Alternatives 200–3
Intuition Regress Problem 106–8
intuitions
    arbitrariness 43–6
    green-eyed weighting 216
    localized scepticism 102–6
    origin of 102–3
    and motivation ethics 101–2
    psychological object of 104–5

legitimacy
    conditions of 161–2
    counterfactual problem 163–5
    institutional improvement 177–8
    reasonable disagreement 169–71
    value of 162–3
Lottocracy 165–7

Mandeville, Bernard and moral agent problems 23
methodology, outline 13–15
moral agent question, outline 13–15
moral failure and progress
    in efficiency 72–4
    in motivation 69–71
    in understanding 71–2
moralistan 155–7
motivation ethics
    duties 67–8
    harm-based 96–8
    moral goodness 61–6
    and states 155–9
    and virtue ethics 86–9
motive fetishism 76–9
Mysterons 228–9

Nationalstan 153–4
Non-arbitrariness
    in "gravity-2040" 223, 236
    in empirical justification 223–4
    in ethics 223–4
    logical empiricism 230–1
    and the universe 227–9
    in "welfare-2040" 223, 225
Normal Justification Thesis 174–7
Not-Thursday Act-Consequentialism 44

obedience, to the law 162, 164, 170–1
objective goods and interpersonal comparisons 191

pareto optimality,
    end of 205
    impotence of 204–6
persuasion 15–16
Political Associationism 149, 153–4
poor-cosmostan 153–4
practical reasoning critique 81–6
principles
    against intuitions 16
    as intuitions 111–12

quasi-moral duties 144–5

Ravens' paradox 230
reflective equilibrium 103–4
rich-cosmostan 153–4
rights
    pre-political 168–9
    to rule 167–8

Sacrifice Condition 115
Sally, the Fundamentalist 20
Slotean motive-based ethics 88–9
special relationships
    and agent evaluations 138–40
    and motivation ethics 142–4
    the problem of 133–6

unbiasedness
    methodological principle 186–7
    moral principle 187
    as non-arbitrariness 187–8
utility monsters 182, 196–9

virtue ethics, justification 209–12

will-based deontology, justification 210–12

www.ingramcontent.com/pod-product-compliance
Lightning Source LLC
Chambersburg PA
CBHW051806230426
43672CB00012B/2652